CONFLICT AND AMITY IN EAST ASIA

Ian Nish
Professor of International History
London School of Economics

Conflict and Amity in East Asia

Essays in Honour of Ian Nish

Edited by

T.G. Fraser
Head of the History Department and Professor of History
University of Ulster

and

Peter Lowe
Reader in History
University of Manchester

M

First published 1992

Published by
MACMILLAN ACADEMIC AND PROFESSIONAL LTD
Houndmills, Basingstoke, Hampshire RG21 2XS
and London
Companies and representatives
throughout the world

Printed in Great Britain by Billing & Sons Ltd, Worcester

ISBN 0–333–54539–7

A catalogue record for this book is
available from the British Library

Contents

Preface

Ian Nish has made distinguished contributions in many spheres – in research, innovation and direction within the discipline of International History, within the broad field of Japanese Studies in the United Kingdom, the United States and Europe, and within the University of London. He has retained a relatively youthful appearance down the years which has led many to express surprise that he has reached the normal age of retirement in a British university. The aim of this volume is to honour his career by examining central themes in the history of East Asia in the late-nineteenth and twentieth centuries with particular reference to the role of Japan, thus complementing his pioneering contributions, notably in his works examining the antecedents and evolution of the Anglo-Japanese Alliance and his study of the origins of the Russo–Japanese War. The contributors are a mixture of Ian's colleagues and former students, each of whom knows him well and has gained from his incisive scholarship and warm friendship. Our subjects range from the aftermath of the Sino–Japanese conflict of 1894–5 to the nature of the relationship between Britain and Japan in the 1980s. The principal theme is the astonishing development of Japan from the first serious expansion in the 1890s to the catastrophe of the Pacific War, and then to the meteoric rise of the Japanese economy to the point where Japan is on the verge of becoming the strongest economy in the world. The authors examine Japan's domestic record and the contributions made by Great Britain, the United States, China and New Zealand to international relations in East Asia. In the broad span conflict is more discernible than amity but it is appropriate to emphasise the latter as a more peaceful era materialises in the period after the Vietnam War, notwithstanding the difficulties resulting from friction in trade involving Japan and the savage intolerance displayed by the Chinese leadership in Peking.

Ian Nish's work has centred around the Department of International History at the London School of Economics which he joined in 1963 and from which he has retired as Professor. As Stevenson Professor, W. N. Medlicott had worked hard to raise the status of International History and to expand its geographical base. Ian was a natural choice to assist him in this. Military service in the later stages of World War II and in the Allied occupation of Japan had stimulated his interest in the country and its history. After studying History at Edinburgh University, he embarked on postgraduate work at the School of Oriental and African Studies under the direction of W. G. Beasley, graduating with an MA in Japanese History and a PhD on the Anglo–Japanese Alliance. Five years at the University of Sydney broadened his understanding of the Pacific region. He was well prepared to play a full part in the expansion of higher education in this country which, coincidentally with his appointment in London, was signalled with the publication of the Robbins Report. An exciting, if sadly brief, period began for British universities. The Robbins Report did not simply expand student numbers, for in doing so it enabled new thinking to come forward in university teaching. This was particularly important for History, where teaching in most universities remained in an Anglo-, or at best Euro-, centric rut. International History was largely confined to the Concert of Europe, the so-called Eastern Question, and the causes of war in 1914. Of Japanese History there was next to nothing: Japan was little more than the far-away country with which Britain had chosen to end her isolation. This now began to change, a process made easier by the announcement in 1966 that the old fifty-year rule for access to British archives would be progressively reduced to thirty years. A whole new era in the study of International History now beckoned and it was entered with enthusiasm by many of those who were beginning postgraduate work in the wake of the Robbins expansion. Many of them would find in Ian their ideal mentor, an historian with the essential combination of deep scholarship, fine attention to detail, and broad understanding.

With the increased demand for International History, there was much work to be done. Ian was never a narrow specialist; his undergraduate teaching included 'Political History, 1763–1939', 'British–American–Russian Relations, 1815–1914', and 'International History since 1815'. He had a sound knowledge of India and in 1969–70 spent a year in the United States as Visiting Professor at Yale, itself a recognition of his international stature. But, of course, his real area of expertise was Japan, which he soon began teaching in a course on 'The Manchurian Crisis, 1931–33'. The seal on his reputation as a scholar of Japan came with the publication in 1966 of *The Anglo–Japanese Alliance: the diplomacy of two island empires, 1894–1907*. This has stood for a quarter of a century as the definitive study and it was followed in 1972 by *Alliance in Decline: a study in Anglo-Japanese relations, 1908–1923*. Other major volumes have been *Japanese Foreign Policy, 1869–1942: Kasumigaseki to Miyakezaka* (1977), *Anglo–Japanese Alienation, 1919–1952* (1982), and *Origins of the Russo-Japanese War* (1985). A full appreciation of his contribution to scholarship can be seen in the list of publications included in this volume.

As interest in Japan and its international role grew, so did his specialist teaching. Inevitably, however, he also came under increasing demand as a university administrator, for he was respected at all levels of the LSE and he was to serve it well in a number of responsible positions over a long period. He was a Convener of his Department, Chairman of the Centre of International Studies, Chairman of the Publications Committee, Chairman of the Senior Common Room and active on the Editorial Board of the new journal *L. S. E. Quarterly*. He was also Dean of the university's Faculty of Economics and Political Science. He was reliable, unfailingly courteous and in the view of a senior colleague who worked closely with him he was 'a clear-headed, unfussy and above all human administrator'. With all his administrative gifts and scholarly achievements, he never forgot that he was a university teacher. Relationships were formed which lasted long after the formalities of graduation.

Japan has been the lodestone of Ian's career. Within the LSE he was closely associated with the development of the International Centre for Economics and Related Disciplines (ICERD) since its inception in 1978 and served as a member of its Planning and Steering Committee. He regularly organised symposia covering numerous topics and through his strenuous efforts attracted a loyal audience reward with tea or white wine at suitable points in the proceedings. The symposia are noted for the speed with which papers have emerged hot from the ICERD press enclosed within the characteristic orange (or occasionally green) covers with the ICERD/ LSE logo. These papers have been extensively cited in monographs and journals and have done much to enhance knowledge of ICERD's role in fostering graduate studies within the LSE.

It was natural that he should be one of the founders of the British Association for Japanese Studies (BAJS), established in 1974 in order to bring together those concerned with improving understanding of Japan with the aim of making representations, where appropriate, to relevant bodies. He was the Association's first honorary secretary from 1974 to 1977 and then served as president in 1978–9. His qualities of intense industry pursued in an unassuming manner allied with tact, patience and diplomacy were deployed to good effect. His service as secretary and president encompassed the inauguration of annual conferences, assembling in March or April, and the publication of the constituent academic sections. Ian did as much, if not more, than any other individual to ensure that the BAJS evolved into the successful organisation functioning today.

During the 1970s and 1980s, Ian became deeply involved in the European Association for Japanese Studies (EAJS). This was set up with similar aims to BAJS, applied to the whole of Europe: from the outset EAJS endeavoured to bridge the divide between western and eastern Europe during a period when it was far more difficult to achieve this objective than it has since become and it was encouraging that at least some colleagues from central and eastern Europe attended EAJS conferences. Because of the problems inherent in organising a European body it was not feasible to meet with the frequency shown in BAJS: instead EAJS conferences meet every three years gathering in a different city on each occasion. Ian acted as the British representative for purposes of collecting annual subscriptions before going on to serve as president of EAJS between 1985 and 1988: his term of office culminated in the holding of the sixth triennial conference which met in the University of Durham in September 1988. He contributed enormously to the planning and direction of the conference and it proved to be a highly successful and enjoyable occasion. Ian played a major part in assisting with the publication of two volumes of EAJS proceedings, a considerable task keeping in mind the number of disciplines and individuals contributing.

Ian's single most important contribution to the encouragement of Japanese Studies in Britain arose from his chairmanship of the Japan Foundation Endowment Committee (JFEC), an office he occupied between 1983 and 1990; the chairman was appointed by the University Grants Committee, now the Universities Funding Council. The JFEC was created in 1974 to determine the expenditure of the sums of money donated by the Japanese government, to stimulate the growth of Japanese Studies in the United Kingdom and to discuss general issues regarding the development of Japanese Studies. The office of chairman is onerous and involves appreciable correspondence and consultation of a broader nature beyond the formal meetings of the JFEC. Ian's term of office covered a period of much anxiety which was then followed by far more optimistic developments. The swingeing reductions in spending on higher education implemented during the 1980s caused deep concern over the future of Japanese Studies. The familiar pattern of early retirements, frozen posts and inability to recruit young academics unfolded. Despite the success of the University of Oxford and of the LSE in attracting significant sums from Japanese sources, the prospects were gloomy. Belatedly the realisation grew within certain government departments that continuation of the existing policy would prove disastrous for the strengthening of the economy and for the wider political, social and cultural aims of British policy. Ian influenced official thinking not only as chairman of JFEC but through his membership of the Economic and Social Research Committee panel on Government and Industry with special reference to the relationship between Japanese government and industry; in addition, he served as a member of the Department of Trade and Industry Advisory Committee on increasing the teaching of the Japanese language. The government decided in 1988 to allocate funds for the creation of new posts in Japanese Studies and a more buoyant atmosphere surrounded the subject than had obtained for most of the 1980s. This was further strengthened by the generosity of the Japanese government in making further sums available and by the work of the Daiwa Foundation which developed its role in Britain in 1989–90 with the particular intention of fostering the teaching of the language.

Ian's invaluable contribution to this transformation was given well-merited official recognition in Her Majesty the Queen's Birthday Honours List in June 1990 with the announcement that the CBE (Commander of the British Empire) would be conferred upon him in November. One of the contributors to this volume remarked to the editors that Ian had become the doyen of Japanese Studies in the United Kingdom and the award of the CBE constitutes a fitting recognition of his hard work and inspiration over a prolonged period. A further important honour was bestowed upon Ian by the Japanese government in April 1991 with the award of the Order of the Rising Sun, Gold Rays with Neck Ribbon, in recognition of his outstanding contribution to Japanology and to fostering friendship between the United Kingdom and Japan.

No account of Ian's work would be complete without consideration of the part played so effectively by his wife, Rona. Rona has participated in social and cultural activities involving the Japanese community in London. At the time of writing, she is about to assume office as chairman of the *Nichi-ei Otomodachikai:* this is an association for women with social and cultural aims. With Rona playing the piano, her delight and expertise in classical music has promoted Anglo–Japanese cooperation in tangible form. She and Ian have been extremely magnanimous in entertaining numerous guests at their home. Anglo–Japanese (and Anglo–Chinese and Anglo–Korean) relations have been advanced over many years via the splendid evenings when visitors to London have been entertained with great warmth in Oxshott. It is perhaps trite but is no less valid to state that Ian could not have accomplished all that he has done without Rona's love and support. Their daughters, Fiona and Alison, have often joined in entertaining guests in Oxshott and have kept Japan in mind in their own careers.

While the publication of this volume marks the occasion of Ian's formal retirement from university teaching and administration, we know that he will continue to take an active interest in the study of International History and in the evolution of Japanese Studies. We look forward to reading his assessment of the Japanese role in the Manchurian crisis of 1931–3 and to further analyses of international relations in East Asia and in the Pacific region in the late-nineteenth and twentieth centuries. We thank Ian most warmly for his many activities and extend our best wishes for a happy and productive retirement.

TGF PL

Acknowledgements

The editors wish to thank a number of individuals who have helped with the preparation of this volume: all those who gave information and comment about Ian Nish's career, especially Professor W. G. Beasley and Professor James Joll; Mr Tim Farmiloe and the staff of Macmillan for their unfailing courtesy; and Miss Joanne Taggart of the University of Ulster without whose patience and skill the final text could not have appeared.

Notes on the Contributors

Louis Allen is a former Reader in French Studies at the University of Durham. He is the author of *Burma: the Longest War, 1941–45*.

W.G. Beasley is Professor Emeritus in the History of the Far East, School of Oriental and African Studies, University of London. He is the author of *Japanese Imperialism, 1894–1945*.

Roger Buckley is Associate Professor of Political Science, College of Liberal Arts, International Christian University, Tokyo. He is the author of *Occupation Diplomacy: Britain, the United States and Japan, 1945–1952*.

Sir Hugh Cortazzi was HM Ambassador in Tokyo, 1980–4, and is a Director of Hill Samuel Ltd. He is the author of *The Japanese Achievement*.

T.G. Fraser is Head of the History Department, and Professor of History, University of Ulster. He is the author of *The USA and the Middle East since World War 2* (Macmillan, 1989).

Hosoya Chihiro is Professor of International History, International University of Japan, Niigata. He is the author of *San Furanshisuko Kōwa e no Michi* (The Road to the San Francisco Peace).

Janet Hunter is Saji Research Senior Lecturer in Japanese Economic and Social History, London School of Economics. She is the author of *The Emergence of Modern Japan*.

Ikeda Kiyoshi is Professor of Modern History, School of International Politics and Economics, Aoyama Gakuin University, Tokyo. He is the author of *Nihon no Kaigun* (The Japanese Navy), 2 vols.

Akira Iriye is Professor of History, Harvard University. He is the author of *The Origins of the Second World War in Asia and the Pacific*.

Peter Lowe is Reader in History, University of Manchester. He is the author of *The Origins of the Korean War*.

Ann Trotter is Associate Professor of History, University of Otago, New Zealand. She is the author of *New Zealand and Japan, 1945–1952*.

1 The Sino-Japanese Commercial Treaty of 1896

W. G. Beasley

The Treaty of Shimonoseki, ending the war between China and Japan in April 1895, gave Japan political and territorial advantages which were to play a major part in the international relations of the region in the next fifty years: a new power base from which to deal with Korea; the acquisition of Taiwan as a colony; and initially the cession of Liaotung, including Port Arthur, though this had for the time being to be abandoned as a result of the Triple Intervention. Less often remarked upon are the commercial provisions, for all that these were the starting-point for an equally significant change in Japan's position in East Asia. The treaty gave Japan economic and legal privileges in China equivalent to those already possessed by 'European Powers'. Since the latter's rights were exceedingly complex – and had been subject to a constant process of interpretation and amendment since being embodied in the Treaty of Tientsin in 1858 – they were not set out at length at Shimonoseki. Instead, it was agreed that a full commercial treaty was to be concluded subsequently. The task proved a difficult one, taking until October 1896 to complete.

Central to the treaty port system, as it operated in East Asia, was the most-favoured-nation clause. This gave countries which had treaties with China not only the same privileges as had already been secured by others, but also the right to claim those which others obtained at any future time. At Shimonoseki Japan won most-favoured-nation status (Article VI). She also acquired certain specific advantages which by virtue of the most-favoured-nation concept would be extended to all other treaty powers. These, it was stated, would later be incorporated in the commercial treaty.[1]

The first was the addition of further treaty ports to be opened to foreign trade, a 'reward' which all the powers had claimed whenever they had won victory in disputes with China. Japan had originally wanted seven such ports, including Peking, but in face of Chinese objections the list had been reduced to four: Shashi, Chungking, Soochow, Hangchow. The result was substantially to increase foreign access to the Yangtze valley.

1

Closely related was the second gain, an extension of navigation rights on China's river system. As finally agreed this covered the routes from Ichang up the Yangtze to Chungking, and from Shanghai via the Woosung to Hangchow and Soochow. Initial demands for steamer navigation on the Tungting lake in the central Yangtze valley, and in southern China on the West River between Canton and Wuchow, were dropped in the course of the negotiations. The West River, at least, was more a British than a Japanese interest.

The third item concerned bonded warehouses. There had long been disagreement between China and the West about the tax treatment of imported goods which were intended for destinations in the interior. At its simplest, foreign merchants sought the establishment in the treaty ports of warehouses at which goods could be stored, pending trans-shipment, without payment of duty. This was a point on which Japan successfully insisted at Shimonoseki. More contentious was another matter which had also been raised in Japan's demands there, namely, the charges (especially those known as *likin*) levied by local Chinese officials in the interior on foreign trade goods in transit through their areas. Given the nature of the Chinese revenue system, which for the most part left provincial governors to find their own sources of funds for locally-incurred expenses, foreign complaints about such levies had met with little sympathy or effective action from the central government. Nor did Japan succeed in making more headway than Britain and other powers had done in earlier years. The Japanese peace terms handed to Li Hung-chang on 1 April 1895 included a provision that Japanese goods destined for the interior should pay a composition tax of two per cent *ad valorem* in addition to customs dues, which would free them from any further payment inland. There was to be no levy on exports or other Chinese goods when they were shipped by Japanese between different treaty ports. Neither proposal met with Li Hung-chang's approval and both items were omitted from the treaty. The whole question was to be raised again during the commercial negotiations.

The fourth issue, which in the end proved the most difficult of all, was that of manufacturing in the Chinese treaty ports. The immediate occasion for raising the question arose from a plan put forward in the spring of 1893 (against a background of longstanding disagreements on the subject between China and the powers over the interpretation of existing treaties), by which Japan hoped to expand her interests in China by setting up cotton-ginning plants in the treaty ports, where they could operate under favourable conditions of tax and labour costs. In May 1893 the Japanese Consul General in Shanghai was authorised to protest against a Chinese ban on imports of

Japanese textile machinery for use in this connection. The matter was then taken up by the Japanese legation in Peking, supported by the diplomatic body as a whole, which condemned China's decision – described as limiting imports of steam-powered machinery for cotton-ginning to 'cotton mills which are under official management' – as a form of trade monopoly contrary to treaty. Citing the permission given to foreigners to conduct both trade and industry in China, as stated in several treaties between 1858 and 1869, the diplomats claimed the right for the citizens of their countries 'to import steam machinery and use it at the open ports in converting crude native products into manufactured articles'.[2] Their stand was supported by some industrial interests in Britain on the grounds that it was important to defend a right which might in time prove valuable; but in reporting this to Tokyo in November 1893, the Japanese Consul General in London, Ōkoshi Narinori, had sounded a warning. In the first place, he noted, if the démarche were successful, the privilege would not automatically be extended to Japan, since she did not at that stage possess most-favoured-nation rights. Secondly, the development of a foreign-owned cotton-spinning industry in China, using imported machinery and Chinese labour, would not necessarily be to the benefit of Japan's own textile firms. They would not find it easy to compete with Americans and Europeans under these conditions.[3]

Ōkoshi was transferred soon after to be Consul General in Shanghai. From there he reported in March 1894 that the Chinese government had announced regulations for the import of machinery into China which left decisions very much to the discretion of Chinese officials on the spot. His understanding was that this discretion was likely to be exercised in such a way as best to defend the economic interests of Chinese subjects. In other words, Japanese machinery was not likely to be admitted. He did not, however, regard this as altogether to the bad:

> Japanese trade with China has taken an important step forward in recent years, there having been a great increase in the demand for our manufactured goods in that country. . . . However, if foreign merchants in China are given permission to import machinery and establish factories, it is likely that they will set up factories with European and American capital and produce goods at low prices, so competing not only with Europe's products, but also with those of Japan. . . . In fact, believing that Japan's interests differ somewhat from those of other countries in this matter, I question whether we should join them wholeheartedly in it.[4]

In April Mutsu Munemitsu, the Foreign Minister, passed these comments to Komura Jutarō, minister in Peking, but the rapid deterioration in Japanese relations with China immediately afterwards meant that this issue dropped temporarily out of sight. It was revived in the demands presented to Li Hung-chang in April 1895. These required China to permit Japanese subjects freely to engage in manufacturing in China and to import all kinds of machinery for this purpose on payment of the regular import dues. Goods manufactured by Japanese in China were to be treated as imports and enjoy the same exemptions from tax. Li Hung-chang promptly rejected the demand, the matter, he said, having 'been much discussed with the diplomatic corps in Peking and . . . settled against the privileges asked for in this clause'. To grant it 'would tend to destroy the livelihood of the Chinese and work a serious injury to native industries which it is the duty of the Government to protect'.[5] A note in English in the Foreign Ministry files in Tokyo,[6] undated and unsigned, but apparently a comment on this statement, first challenged Li's implied belief that the powers had accepted this state of affairs, then observed that Japan was not in any case claiming the right under existing treaties, as others had done, but was making a new and independent demand. Whether or not as a result of this comment, the item was retained in the revised draft of Japanese peace terms dated 10 April; and despite Li Hung-chang's assertion that this and the other commercial provisions were 'unreasonable . . . and highly derogatory to the sovereignty of an independent nation',[7] it found its way almost unchanged into the final text of the treaty. Like the other matters raised in Article VI, it therefore fell to be included in the envisaged commercial agreement.

By the time negotiations for this began in the late summer of 1895 the bargaining position of the two countries concerned had changed a good deal. The Triple Intervention, by which Russia, France and Germany had forced Japan to renounce her claim to Liaotung, had done much to revive China's self-confidence.[8] Moreover, the circumstances in which the commercial talks were held differed widely from those obtaining in the spring. Whereas the peace terms had been discussed by senior statesmen, to whom points of detail were subordinate to larger aims – the Japanese Foreign Ministry in Tokyo, for example, was kept regularly informed by telegram of what was happening at Shimonoseki, but not in a manner to suggest that it was being consulted – the later discussions were conducted by professionals, much concerned with precedents and matters of wording. And they were held in Peking, where it was clearly recognised that what was at stake were arrangements applicable to all the treaty powers, not just Japan. As a result, the standard techniques of Chinese diplomacy, finely honed by several decades of practice, were brought into play to limit China's losses. Even Western diplomats had a part in the process, especially those who represented Britain.

A Japanese draft for a commercial treaty was approved by the cabinet in Tokyo on 21 August 1895 and forwarded to Hayashi Tadasu, minister plenipotentiary in Peking, on the following day.[9] The draft was in forty articles, most of which were based on the provisions of various European treaties with China (identified severally in Foreign Ministry annotations). The effect was to grant to Japanese the same privileges with respect to the conduct of trade, extra-territoriality and residence in China as were already enjoyed by the majority of Western citizens there. In a few cases, where disputes had occurred from time to time, Japan attempted to define established foreign rights with more precision. With respect to interpretation of the text she accepted the customary Western provision that in the event of disagreement the English translation of the treaty was to be taken as the master copy.

There were nevertheless a number of features of the draft which were new, or had a particular application to Japan. An annexe setting out a number of revisions to customs duties significantly reduced those on Japanese tea and edible seaweed exported to China. It also removed duties on silk and cotton thread exported from China to Japan, a benefit, Hayashi was told, to which he must give some priority, since it was of major importance to the future of Japanese industry. Article VIII provided that regardless of the specific rates set out in the annexe on customs dues, Japanese goods were not at any time to be taxed more heavily than those of any other country.

On trade more generally the crucial articles were those numbered 14 and 15, partly new, partly a restatement of matters with which the powers had expressed dissatisfaction in the past. The first laid it down that Japanese imports into China, or goods manufactured by Japanese in the treaty port settlements, were not to be subject to any kind of levy while they were held in a settlement or were in transit between two foreign settlements. Article 15, going a step farther, tackled the difficult subject of transit dues payable in other situations. The best the powers had been able to secure by earlier agreements was a formula, never fully put into practice, by which foreign goods for sale inland were to be provided with a pass, exempting them from all further dues while en route to a stated destination, subject to payment of a fifty per cent surcharge on the relevant import tariff. Japan now proposed to extend this system to cover trans-shipment to any part of China, regardless of the nationality of the carrier, in return for an increase in the surcharge to sixty per cent of import dues, or three per cent *ad valorem* on goods manufactured by Japanese in China (which, it was assumed, under the terms of the Shimonoseki treaty would not be taxed as imports). Since imports were taxed at a notional five per cent, these two rates were in fact comparable.

On the question of transit dues Japan sought the cooperation of China's foremost trading partner, Britain. In Tokyo the Foreign Ministry sent a copy of the proposals to the British minister, Ernest Satow. In China Hayashi, having been given formal permission to do so, showed the draft to O'Conor, Satow's opposite number in Peking. O'Conor had already some weeks previously written to London expressing the view that while the Sino–Japanese treaty might 'to some extent enlarge and ameliorate the conditions under which foreign trade is at present conducted', he had some doubts about whether China's leaders would take it as an opportunity 'to meet the financial difficulties of the country . . . by developing new sources of revenue'.[10] So he welcomed Hayashi's approach, when it came, chiefly as an opportunity to inject into the negotiations some consideration of matters of particular concern to Britain, such as navigation of the West River above Canton (which, as we have seen, had been included in Japan's original demands at Shimonoseki, but had later been omitted from the treaty).

This was not a good omen for the Japanese initiative. Nor did John Jordan, O'Conor's principal expert on trade relations, show much more enthusiasm. As Jordan saw it, the Japanese draft was primarily designed to gain for Japan the commercial and judicial advantages which she had been denied when negotiating with China in 1871. The proposals about transit dues, he thought, would be valuable as a means of improving Peking's financial credit and hence facilitating Chinese borrowing overseas. A reduction on dues in the coastal trade, as embodied in Article 17, would give an impetus to trading 'between the Treaty Ports'. On the other hand, the abolition of export duty on raw cotton and silk cocoons, 'evidently a sop to the owners of mills in Japan', would encounter opposition. It was not likely to be conceded without 'a severe struggle'. China was much more likely 'to throw difficulties in the way even of the foreign mills on her own soil procuring a free supply of the raw material'.[11]

The Chinese counter-proposals, presented to Hayashi in November,[12] were at least as 'severe' as Jordan had expected. They took the form of an alternative treaty draft in which the numbering of the articles was different from that of the Japanese version, even where the items themselves were in substance the same. There was no disagreement on most of the points concerning extra-territoriality, or on technical matters like the language of the text or the exchange of ratifications. For the rest, differences were of three kinds. In several instances, where Japan had proposed new regulations, or a significant revision of old ones, to cover privileges which she had in principle acquired by the Treaty of Shimonoseki, China sought to bring these within the scope of arrangements already in force for other powers.

Traffic on additional stretches of China's river system was one example. Another was that Japanese imports and exports, for which Japan had proposed specific tariff rates favourable to herself, were in the Chinese draft to pay duty 'in accordance with the tariffs now in force between China and Western countries'. In effect, China expected Japan to be bound by the rules which the Maritime Customs had worked out for others.

On the specific question of manufacturing in the foreign settlements there was complete disagreement. The Japanese draft (Article XV) had assumed that goods produced by foreign factories in the treaty ports would be free of import duty, but on being shipped to the interior would pay a three per cent levy as commutation of transit tax. By contrast, China now proposed that the location of any Japanese factories should be subject to the approval of Chinese officials; that the goods they produced should pay tax at ten per cent *ad valorem* when sold in the treaty ports; and that they should then pay another five per cent if shipped to the interior or exported. This difference was to prove in the end incapable of reconciliation.

Finally, China insisted, as she had done in 1871, that the treaty must be reciprocal. There were detailed instances of this throughout the Chinese draft, but the claim was stated as a general proposition in Articles XXXIV and XXXV, giving China most-favoured-nation treatment in Japan with respect to all matters concerning the administration of justice (extra-territoriality) and trade. Saionji Kimmochi, Japan's new Foreign Minister, rejected these sections of the document entirely. The whole basis of the West's treaties, he observed, was 'intercourse with China in China'.[13] Japan would accept no less. In a later telegram he made it clear that national pride was at stake: 'Under no circumstances will Japanese Government consent to be placed in any respect on less favourable footing than most favoured European Power'.[14]

If pride was to be a crucial issue between China and Japan, it was trade, and the taxing of it, which most engaged the attention of other powers. Britain, whose stake was the largest, was sceptical about the desirability, as well as the practicality, of much that Japan proposed. True, the simplification and where possible the reduction of Chinese imposts on trade was likely to lead to an expansion in its scale, which was desirable. On the other hand, customs receipts were the most reliable ingredient in China's revenue. The foreign loans which had been negotiated to provide the indemnity due to Japan under the Shimonoseki treaty – they were in large part British – were secured on those receipts, which were also the most likely source of funds for fiscal and administrative reforms. In the eyes of most Western governments such reforms were necessary for the sake of China's stability, and hence her long term economic prospects as a field for investment. To Jordan, indeed, this made the commutation of transit dues the most important of the measures put forward by Japan. Since almost the whole of existing customs revenue was mortgaged to the servicing of China's foreign debt, he wrote, her government – since it was unlikely to agree 'to place the management of her finances in capable foreign hands', as many foreigners would have preferred – was bound to turn to transit dues as an alternative, thereby hampering 'the circulation of foreign goods'. In these circumstances, commutation would provide a means of increasing revenue without undue penalty to trade.[15] Robert Hart, speaking as a Chinese official, came more briefly to the same conclusion: 'We want revenue and cannot afford to lose a penny'.[16]

Such considerations gave a particular importance to Chinese plans for taxing goods manufactured by foreign-owned companies in the treaty ports, about which opinion among non-Chinese proved to be divided. Merchants in Shanghai, Jordan reported,[17] had moved quickly to invest in spinning-mills, counting upon the Shimonoseki agreement to ensure 'an unrestricted market for their products'. Against that, China's desire to charge a duty of ten per cent and a transit tax of five per cent on all such products – twice what was payable on imports – would presumably be welcome to manufacturers in Britain and India, or even those in Japan. After all, he commented on another occasion, it might 'have the effect of enabling our Manchester and India trade to compete for a time at least with the products of Chinese mills', serving 'as an excise tax upon [China's] home manufactures which would act as a sort of indirect protection to foreign imports'.[18]

Jordan's argument found ready support in London. The Board of Trade's first response to the Japanese treaty draft had been not unfavourable. While recognising that Japanese industry in the treaty ports 'may compete seriously with our imports into China', it accepted that it might also help to create 'a greater demand for more than the bare necessaries of life', which would ultimately be to the advantage of Britain's trade.[19] Second thoughts, however, led to a different emphasis. In March 1896, replying to a Foreign Office letter which asked whether the British minister in Peking should be instructed to support his Japanese colleague in the disagreement over taxing manufactures, the Board wrote as follows:

> There is . . . considerable conflict between the British interests involved, for while on the one side there might be a profitable opening for the investment of capital as a result of any additional encouragement being given by China to the establishment of manufactures, the interests of home manufacturers and exporters (especially of textile goods) are in the

main directly opposed to any such encouragement being given. The larger and more prominent interest at the present time is in every way that of the home manufacturer . . . .[20]

The conclusion, that no pressure 'be brought to bear upon the Chinese Government . . . in the direction of supporting the Japanese demands', was duly conveyed to the legation in Peking.

Nor did Japanese business circles differ significantly in their attitude. At a later stage in the proceedings, when the commercial treaty had been signed but further disputes were delaying ratification, the Shanghai Chamber of Commerce took up the question. At a meeting in September 1896 the complaint was voiced that the tax China planned to levy on manufactures from the treaty ports 'would mean that spinners in Japan would be in a far more favourable position than those in Shanghai'.[21] However, when the chairman pointed out that little by way of help could be expected from Whitehall – 'Bombay has a strong voice in the matter', he said, while it had to be recognised that 'a [British] government so strongly supported by conservative members from manufacturing districts in Lancashire and Yorkshire which may view China mills as competitors will not be too willing to grant us over much' – it was finally agreed to accept something less than the rights embodied in the Treaty of Shimonoseki, provided that Chinese firms were put on the same footing as foreign ones. Partly by way of comment on this meeting, Japan's leading entrepreneur, Shibusawa Eiichi, acting in his capacity as President of the Tokyo Chamber of Commerce, sent a memorandum to the Foreign Ministry in Japan a few weeks later. The proposed tax, he agreed, would be damaging to the development of manufacturing industry in China, bearing hard on both existing silk filatures and prospective cotton mills. Japanese investors there would suffer as a result. Yet it was not by any means certain that this would be to Japan's disadvantage overall. The growth of a textile industry in China would mean for Japan 'the simultaneous loss of a major eastern market and the creation of a major competitor'. Few Japanese businessmen wanted that. It would be better by far 'to prevent as far as possible the growth of manufacturing industry in China, while greatly developing our own manufacturing industry'.[22]

Given this background, it is not surprising that the question of taxing manufactures figured largely in the discussions of a commercial treaty, nor that Japan in the end failed to get her way. Indeed, it was one of the points on which there were moments of acrimony. At a meeting in January 1896 Hayashi told Li Hung-chang that the way to develop China's wealth, in order to support her foreign borrowing, was to follow Japan's example of encouraging industry by *not* taxing its products. Li's reply was that in China it would be foreigners who would carry on industry, not the Chinese; and as for the Japanese, they would do better to 'stay at home and find in Japan itself a field for their industrial activity'.[23] It should be said that he was equally acerbic on the subject of extra-territoriality. The Chinese had remained loyal to their long-established laws, he pointed out on one occasion. They did not constantly tinker with them like the Japanese, 'English in the morning, and French in the afternoon.'[24]

As these incidents demonstrate, the negotiation of a treaty was not easy. The instructions which Saionji sent to Hayashi in Peking in December 1895 on the subject of China's counter-proposals were that he was to insist on holding to the stipulations of the Shimonoseki treaty and following the precedents to be found in European agreements with China.[25] The Chinese draft, he maintained, ran counter to the Shimonoseki terms with respect to manufactures, as well as the regulations to be observed at the new open ports and on inland water routes; by referring to 'Western' countries rather than 'European' ones it presumably had in view the possibility of exploiting the differences between the European and American treaties with China; and it introduced an unacceptable claim to give Chinese in Japan similar rights to those enjoyed by Japanese in China. For all these reasons the draft was to be rejected, as was any future one of the same kind.

In subsequent talks with Li Hung-chang, starting on 29 December, Hayashi found it difficult to gain any ground on this footing. Li stood upon his own interpretation of the Shimonoseki treaty, which, he claimed, did not deny China the right to impose a tax on manufactures. As to the commutation of transit dues, he held by the narrower agreement embodied in the Chefoo Convention of 1876 (a permit for specific destinations). On 5 February 1896 Saionji reiterated his own position, namely, that at Shimonoseki 'manufactures were expressly and unconditionally assimilated to imports in the matter of internal taxation of all kinds'.[26] There was to be no departure from this principle, he said. The result was deadlock on the point, though Hayashi continued discussion of other items.

At the end of March came a fresh initiative from Tokyo, reflecting the fact that the Itō government was under political pressure at home, which made an early success in China highly desirable. Saionji now agreed that he would accept taxation of manufactures at half the level proposed by Li Hung-chang – that is, at five per cent tax, plus a further two-and-a-half per cent for commutation of transit dues – providing China accepted in substance the rest of Japan's demands and guaranteed most-favoured-nation treatment for Japanese goods. Hayashi was also told to seek compensation in the form of the abolition of export duty on Chinese raw cotton, should that be possible. As to other tariff matters, if he were unable to secure improvements over existing rates he should abandon all claims for a separate tariff, relying on the most-favoured-nation clause and amending the Japanese draft accordingly.[27]

During April and May, when Mutsu Munemitsu briefly returned to office as Foreign Minister, further obstacles emerged. Li Hung-chang continued to insist on reciprocity, Mutsu to refuse it, especially with respect to extra-territoriality. No progress was made on tariffs. Accordingly Saionji, back at his desk from 30 May, decided to press China harder. Following an exchange of telegrams with Hayashi, the latter summarised the position that had been reached in the talks on 10 June 1896.[28] He had given Chang Yiu-huan (replacing Li Hung-chang as China's plenipotentiary) a memorandum setting out Japan's 'final' concessions. This omitted the question of tax on manufactures altogether. China, he said, was adamant that she could not afford the loss of revenue that would occur if the combination of foreign capital with cheap Chinese labour brought a rise in domestic textile production to the detriment of imports. Without British support Japan was unlikely to move her from that position. Any question about interpretation of the Shimonoseki text in this context was best left to be settled if and when a dispute arose, since Japan would in the meantime enjoy most-favoured-nation rights. He had made it clear that in the last resort she was willing to rest on these, preferring no treaty at all to a bad one. However, he had made concessions on other points. On both tariffs and inland waterways he had accepted the regulations already in force, as China wanted. On transit dues he had agreed to commutation as set out in the Chefoo Convention: a surcharge of half the relevant customs duty, or two-and-a-half per cent *ad valorem,* giving foreigners exemption from *likin.*

On 26 June a meeting at the Tsungli Yamen reached a settlement on this basis, except for one or two points of detail. The most troublesome of these was the position of Chinese in Japan. Peking wanted some public assurance that its citizens would receive 'fair and equitable treatment'. Tokyo, though not opposed to this in principle, was reluctant to concede any form of words which might imply 'right of admission into interior of Japan'. A solution was found in a letter, which Hayashi handed to Chang Yui-huan when the treaty was signed on 21 July, setting out Japan's reasons for refusing to grant most-favoured-nation status to the Chinese. Because Japan had recently concluded new treaties with the Western powers on a basis of equality, it said, within a few years 'the entire country of Japan will be opened to the residence, trade and travels of the subjects and citizens of these countries'. Under a most-favoured-nation clause China would be able to claim the same, but the arrangement would not in fact be reciprocal, since 'your country is as yet not opened entirely and Japanese subjects enjoy only a limited liberty of residence and trade in the ports which are opened to foreign trade'. Hence Japan would undertake nothing more than to ensure 'equitable' treatment for Chinese in Japan.[29]

Such a form of words was far removed from Saionji's declaration in December that the purpose of a commercial treaty was to regulate 'intercourse with China in China', excluding any kind of reciprocity. Nevertheless, Japan was in practice successful in excluding reciprocity with respect to all the principal legal and commercial privileges, as well as from the most-favoured-nation clause of the agreement. Only in the matter of rights of refuge for merchant vessels in distress did China succeed in retaining it. Rights of visit for warships, which China had also tried to make reciprocal, vanished from the final text altogether. On other points both sides could claim a number of victories. The question of taxing manufactures from the treaty ports was simply set aside to be dealt with in a wider context. The regulation of trade, harbour dues and river traffic was to be governed by the existing rules of the Maritime Customs, as China had always insisted, while import and export tariffs were to be those 'existing between China and the Western Powers', despite Japan's preference for 'European'. Japan gained no advantages on tea, seaweed, silk and cotton, though there was agreement to put Japanese ginseng on the same footing as American ginseng. Satow, commenting from Tokyo, thought that the decision about cotton was relatively unimportant. The workings of the most-favoured-nation clause, he said, plus Japan's own abolition of import dues on raw cotton, would guarantee that 'Japanese spinning mills will be placed on as favourable a footing as if cotton exported from China had been placed on the list of duty-free goods, as originally proposed by Japan'.[30]

Robert Hart gave the credit for much of this to China's stubbornness: 'There is really something very strong in China's "non possumus" – people give in to it in the end'.[31] All the same, this was not quite the end of the story. For example, it was still not clear what rate of tax China would succeed in imposing on manufactures from the treaty port settlements, which had become a matter for more general discussion. At the end of September Japan's new Foreign Minister, Ōkuma Shigenobu, sent a secret telegram to Hayashi, agreeing to accept a tax of ten per cent, in view of China's financial difficulties, but requiring as a *quid pro quo* the creation of separate Japanese settlements 'with rights of police and control of roads' at Shanghai, Tientsin, Amoy and Hankow. He later made it clear that this was to be in addition to any compensation the powers acting collectively were able to secure. Hayashi was sceptical. Other countries would certainly not allow Japan to have it both ways, he believed, while China was likely to 'refuse us who are weakest'.[32] Ōkuma, unconvinced, instructed Hayashi on 8 October to negotiate separately with the Tsungli Yamen concerning the tax on manufactures and Japanese rights in foreign settlements, cooperating with other foreign representatives only in so far as such action was 'not inconsistent with or detrimental to our separate demand'.[33] To strengthen his bargaining position he should threaten – as Hayashi himself had suggested – to withhold ratification of the commercial treaty unless a satisfactory settlement could be reached. A week later Ōkuma won cabinet approval to make this threat formal.

The foreign representatives in Peking, meeting without Hayashi, proved unable to agree on the question of manufactures, which was therefore referred to their governments at home. By contrast, Hayashi, acting independently, was able to secure everything else that Ōkuma had demanded. On 19 October the Tsungli Yamen promised to grant separate Japanese settlements at the newly opened ports, as well as at Shanghai, Tientsin, Amoy and Hankow; to discuss fresh regulations for river traffic to Soochow and Hangchow; and to withdraw Chinese troops from a disputed zone at Weihaiwei (still occupied by Japan against final payment of the Shimonoseki indemnity). In return, Japan ended her opposition to the tax on manufactures.[34] This having been settled, ratifications were exchanged on 21 October 1896.

These negotiations, the first which Japan conducted as a treaty power in China, are instructive in a number of ways. Most important, perhaps, was the demonstration of how far Japan still had to rely on the goodwill and cooperation of the major powers there, especially Britain, despite her military victory in 1894–5. In this respect the commercial treaty marks the beginning of the phase of 'dependent imperialism', in which for some twenty years she accepted Anglo–American domination of the treaty port system as the price of her own opportunity to profit from it. There was also, however, a hint of different things to come. From the beginning Tokyo had shown itself willing to pursue a number of Japanese interests separate from those of the treaty powers as a whole. Under Saionji these were clearly subordinate. Later – that is, between the signature of the treaty and its ratification – Ōkuma showed himself much more willing to put relations with the powers at risk for the sake of Japanese interests. It is tempting to see in this some forerunner of the Twenty-One Demands (which were produced by Ōkuma's cabinet in 1914–15, when Japanese official opinion was becoming more restive about Anglo–American influence). Certainly it underlines the fact that there was a continuing division in Japanese political life between those, like Saionji, who put emphasis on the advantages of 'international co-operation' in China, and those – the Army's leaders in the twentieth century, much more than Ōkuma – who saw 'autonomy' as a more attractive goal.

NOTES

1. English texts of the Japanese demands of 1 April 1895 and of the Shimonoseki Treaty of 17 April 1895 are to be found in M. Kajima, *The Diplomacy of Japan 1894–1922*, 3 vols (Tokyo, 1976–80), vol. I, pp 220–2, 262–71. I have discussed the peace negotiations briefly in *Japanese Imperialism 1894–1945* (Oxford, 1987), chapter 5.
2. Japan, Foreign Ministry, *Nihon Gaikō Bunsho*, vol. 26, p. 484. The correspondence concerning the dispute generally is in ibid., pp. 454–85. (Series hereafter cited as *NGB*).
3. Ibid., pp. 492–5.
4. Ōkoshi to Foreign Ministry, 30 March 1894, ibid., pp. 495–6.
5. Kajima, *Diplomacy*, vol. I, pp. 229–30.
6. Foreign Ministry file, 2. 2. 1. 1.
7. Kajima, *Diplomacy*, vol. I, p. 242.
8. Robert Hart, Inspector General of China's Maritime Customs, commented in December 1895 that Japan's slow progress in the commercial negotiations was 'owing to the Russo–French background of intervention': see J. K. Fairbank et al, *The I.G. in Peking*, 2 vols (Cambridge, Mass. and London, 1975), vol. II, p. 1043.
9. Texts of the draft and of the instructions to Hayashi are in *NGB*, 28.1, pp. 200–14.
10. O'Conor to Salisbury, no. 329, 28 August 1895, Foreign Office, China Correspondence (FO 17), vol. 1238.
11. O'Conor to Salisbury, no. 379, 8 October 1895, enclosing Jordan's memorandum of the same date, FO 17/1239.
12. Forwarded in Hayashi to Foreign Ministry, secret, no. 75, 21 November 1895, *NGB*, 28.1, pp. 230–42.
13. Saionji to Hayashi, telegram of 14 December 1895, *NGB*, 28.1, pp. 260–1. He reiterated the argument in a despatch of 23 December (ibid., 28.1, pp. 262–3).
14. Saionji to Hayashi, telegram of 31 March 1896, *NGB*, 29, pp. 436–7.
15. Jordan memorandum in Beauclerk to Salisbury, secret, no. 102, 17 March 1896, FO 17/1276.
16. Fairbank, *The I.G. in Peking*, vol. II, p. 1048.
17. Jordan memorandum in Beauclerk to Salisbury, confidential, no. 486, 5 December 1895, FO 17/1240.

18. Jordan memorandum in Beauclerk to Salisbury, most confidential, no. 29, 20 January 1896, FO 17/1275.
19. Board of Trade to Foreign Office, 16 December 1895, FO 17/1256.
20. Board of Trade to Foreign Office, immediate and confidential, 27 March 1896, FO 17/1287.
21. Minutes of meeting forwarded to Tokyo by Japanese Consul General in Shanghai, *NGB*, 29, pp. 530–49.
22. Shibusawa memorandum, 8 October 1896, *NGB*, 29, pp. 518–20.
23. The incident is recounted in a memorandum by Jordan, enclosed in Beauclerk to Salisbury, most confidential, no. 29, 20 January 1896, FO 17/1275.
24. Jordan memorandum in Beauclerk to Salisbury, secret, no. 80, 5 March 1896, FO 17/1275.
25. Telegram of 14 December and despatch of 23 December 1895, *NGB*, 28.1, pp. 260–3.
26. Telegram of 5 February 1896, *NGB*, 29, pp. 389–90.
27. Saionji to Hayashi, telegram, 31 March 1896, *NGB*, 29, pp. 436–7.
28. *NGB*, 29, pp. 476–82.
29. *NGB*, 29, pp. 494–5. The text of the treaty (in Chinese, Japanese, and English) is in Japan, Foreign Ministry, *Nisshi-kan narabi Shina ni kansuru Nihon oyobi takoku-kan no jōyaku* (Tokyo, 1923), pp. 36–59.
30. Satow to Salisbury, no. 150, 29 July 1896, Foreign Office, Japan Correspondence (FO 46), vol. 469.
31. Fairbank, *The I.G. in Peking,* vol. II, p. 1076.
32. Ōkuma telegram of 29 September 1896, and Hayashi replies of 4 and 6 October, *NGB*, 29, pp. 512–17.
33. *NGB*, 29, pp. 520–1.
34. *NGB*, 29, pp. 527–9.

2 Tanaka Diplomacy and Its Pro-British Orientation 1927–29

Hosoya Chihiro

The Washington system, instituted as a regional cooperative system between Japan, Britain and the United States to cope with the rise of Chinese nationalism and the threat of Soviet Bolshevism, did not work well after the mid-twenties. There was serious Anglo–American discord. It surfaced at the Peking Tariff Conference in 1925. Professor Ian Nish argues that 'Britain and the United States did not see eye to eye after the Nanking incidents in 1927 and over tariff concessions in the following year', and 'Anglo–American co-operation could not be relied on in east Asian affairs'.[1]

It was against this background of Anglo–American dissension that Shidehara diplomacy was conducted over the period from June 1924 to April 1927, followed by Tanaka diplomacy until July 1929. Tanaka diplomacy was distinct from Shidehara diplomacy in various ways as has been discussed by many historians. However, much attention has not been paid to the following point: whereas Shidehara placed an emphasis on maintaining the Washington system of cooperation, promoting friendly relations with the US, Tanaka had a tendency to opt for bilateral diplomacy, in particular to develop close cooperative relations with Britain. Such a feature of Tanaka diplomacy will be discussed here.[2]

The outbreak of the Nanking Incident on 24 March 1927 came as a great shock to all the powers. Both the United States and Britain responded by bombarding the shore from warships, in an attempt to protect foreign residents. Japanese gunboats did not participate at that time, but when the Hankow Incident occurred on 3 April, Japan landed a two hundred man naval brigade, to protect the lives of Japanese residents. They set up an armed guard around the Japanese settlement.

A series of meetings was held in Peking, primarily among the ministers of the three powers, to discuss punitive measures for the Nanking Incident. They were quick to agree on demanding that the Kuomintang punish the responsible leaders, issue a public apology, and give guarantees for the damage. But there was controversy over whom the demand should be presented to and the time limit for its execution. The most serious disagreement among the three countries, Japan, Britain and the US, was engendered by the question of sanctions – how should they respond if demands did not receive compliance? The British were the most adamant in their insistence on harsh sanctions. Measures brought up for discussion included occupation of the Woosung fortress, seizure of ships in Canton Harbour, and gradual intensification of bombardment on selected areas along the Yangtze River, destruction of the arsenal in Hankow, and blockade of the treaty ports.[3]

The United States was strongly opposed to the implementation of these measures, and this position was supported by Foreign Minister Shidehara Kijuro, who maintained that the sanctions would accomplish little. On 6 April Matsudaira Tsuneo, the Japanese ambassador to the United States, met with Joseph Grew, US under-secretary of state, to express opposition to any punitive measures that would jeopardise the foreign communities and possibly bring counter-effective results.[4] Shidehara was afraid that punitive sanctions would weaken the political position of Chiang Kai-shek.

The Japanese army, on the other hand, took a more positive stand supporting sanctions, stating to the Foreign Ministry that a stern warning should be sent to the revolutionaries, demanding that they demonstrate deep reflection and keen awareness of what they have done' and 'try themselves to wipe out the source of evil', and that if they failed to do all this Japan would have to take defensive measures together with the other powers.[5] The army went ahead on their own, preparing to send one division to implement sanctions.

Following the Hankow Incident the army lodged a vehement demand that Japanese diplomacy be reorientated. It was submitted to the prime minister and foreign minister in the form of a memorandum from Minister of War Ugaki Kazushige on 7 April. If, it began, 'the powers simply stood by to watch the communist movement in China gain influence as it is now it is only a matter of time before it spreads directly into Manchuria and Mongolia'. The memorandum then proposed the following three policy measures:

First, to strengthen even further cooperation among the powers in their approach to China and to establish a fully integrated system of cooperation centred around Japan. Second, to work out a cooperative plan to encircle communism, and third, to supply weapons and funds to the moderate elements in both the southern and northern factions, subject to approval by and with the cooperation of the powers, thereby charging those elements with the task of wiping out the communist forces in the upper basin of the Changchiang River and in the South thereof.[6]

After the Nanking Incident, Shidehara diplomacy was roundly criticized at home and the government was scorchingly condemned by the Seiyukai (party in opposition). It was against this background that Shidehara, still refusing to give Japanese agreement to the sanctions urged by the British, met with John Tilley, the British ambassador, on 6 April. At that meeting he stated his opposition to the idea of collective sanctions by the powers, and said, 'I am not opposed to the principle [of collective sanctions] but I cannot think of any appropriate and effective means to carry them out'.[7]

The British ambassador was under the impression that Shidehara's attitude had been modified. Tilley reported that he 'went, expecting to be told that his Excellency would have nothing to do with sanctions, but he made no objections to the proposal that it should be left to the admirals to formulate a scheme for the approval of their Governments'. He added, 'I had a faint impression that Baron Shidehara might, after all, find himself in our camp'.[8]

The British, finding themselves able to get a 'concession' from the Japanese government, began to work on the United States. On 9 April the Americans agreed to sanctions if certain demands were not met by the Chinese.[9] Thus, a protest note from the five Powers was handed both to Chiang Kai-shek and Chou Yu-jen on 11 April. It contained three demands. If these were not met, it asserted, 'the said Governments will find themselves compelled to take such measures as they consider appropriate', giving clear warning that sanctions would very likely be carried out in the case of non-compliance.[10]

Upon receiving the totally unsatisfactory reply from the Kuomintang, the ministers of the five countries decided on 15 April to send a second note of protest. The wording was harsher this time in threatening sanctions. The United States alone refused to be party to the second note – but Shidehara had no notable opposition.[11]

If we look carefully at the process of settling the issue of sanctions among the three powers, there emerges a delicate but clear shift in 'Shidehara diplomacy' compared with the stand that the Japanese foreign minister took in January toward the British proposal to send a joint force to Shanghai. He continued to place priority on maintaining the cooperative system, but by giving approval to a limited level of joint military action his diplomacy began slowly revolving toward the British side.

By this time, however, Japan, the US and the UK were gradually moving toward the same position *vis-à-vis* support and protection of the moderate faction within the Kuomintang, led by Chiang Kai-shek. The Japanese Foreign Ministry and army, moreover, converged on this policy orientation. When Shidehara opposed joint sanctions, he explained to the British that sanctions would only weaken the position of the moderates, and the British agreed, saying that they 'fully appreciate' the force of the view.[12] Secretary of State Frank B. Kellogg in refusing to take part in submitting the second note threatening sanctions, claimed that such pressure 'might tend to drive Chiang Kai-shek and the moderates into the arms of the radicals and would really do no good'.[13] The Nanking government was established on 18 April. The three governments all took steps to support the new regime and ultimately withdrew their representatives stationed in Wuhan.

Tanaka Giichi took over as prime minister on 20 April 1927, replacing Wakatsuki Reijiro. Tanaka concurrently held the post of foreign minister, beginning the era of 'Tanaka diplomacy'. The more militant nature of that diplomacy emerged when the dispatch of troops to Shantung was begun on 28 May, impressing observers with the sharp difference from the previous Shidehara diplomacy.

In the spring of 1927, with the steady advance of the Northern Expedition and the outbreak of the Nanking Incident, the foreign powers became increasingly concerned about the situation in North China. It appeared ominous enough for them to begin to consider plans for evacuating foreign residents of Peking and Tientsin and the possible withdrawal of the Peking legations, as well as increasing the number of soldiers. At that point the British took the initiative again in arranging for a joint force to be sent north. On 14 April the British government submitted to Washington a proposal to protect the Tientsin area and the traffic route by placing at least two divisions there. Britain had already made the largest contribution to the military guard at Shanghai, and thus they requested that the US and Japan take responsibility to supply troops this time, to 'do their share in the defence of common interests'. In the meantime, the British said, they were prepared to send one brigade of soldiers north. They finally stated that if it seemed impossible to increase the number of soldiers for the proposed guard, then it might be necessary to withdraw both residents and legations from the north.[14] The following day an identical proposal was delivered to the Japanese government.[15]

Vice-Minister for Foreign Affairs Debuchi Katsuji conveyed the government response: 'the Japanese government does not regard the situation in the north as very serious. Thus, while we do not consider an additional two divisions necessary, we are nevertheless ready to double the number of our troops already in the north, to station a total of eight companies'.[16]

When the Tanaka cabinet came in, the tilt of Japanese foreign policy toward the UK position accelerated. During the initial period, the cabinet followed its predecessor on the issue of sending troops to North China, as can be seen in the Japanese response of 12 April, but the tendency toward cooperation with Britain grew visibly stronger thereafter. On 3 May, for example, in his first meeting with Ambassador Tilley, Tanaka, was friendly and welcoming, making an effort to maintain the 'spirit of the Anglo–Japanese Alliance'. Tilley was favourably impressed, reporting that the China policies as outlined by Tanaka were 'of a less negative quality than those of his predecessor',[17] and that the British government was well-inclined toward the new Tanaka government.

At the 13 May meeting Tanaka was even friendlier toward Tilley, saying that rather than talking with 'a paper screen [*shoji*] between them' he wanted to continue 'without the screen'.[18] At the meeting that day Tilley conveyed the wishes of the British foreign minister to the effect that 'Britain and Japan should reach some sort of understanding or agreement' concerning the China issue, so that the two countries could take joint action there. Tanaka's response was not positive, however, since he was not prepared to elevate Anglo–Japanese cooperation to a level of general understanding.[19]

The Tanaka cabinet's decision to send troops to Shantung on 28 May and to dispatch two thousand Japanese soldiers from Port Arthur to Tsingtao must be understood in the context of the 'common understanding' that seemed to have grown between Britain and Japan. Certainly the main gist of sending troops was to give the Japanese residents in the Shantung area military protection, but it also meant Japan's consent to the British-initiated proposal for a joint dispatch of forces to north China.

On 26 May, two days before the Japanese statement announcing its decision to dispatch troops to China, the British Chief of Staff, General Sir George Milne, expressed his satisfaction over 'the Japanese decision to send its army to Shantung, which will greatly improve the situation there', at a meeting of the British cabinet.[20] This seems to imply that Britain had been informed in advance of Japan's decision to send troops to Shantung and had apparently given her blessing.

The British were naturally gratified when Tanaka ordered the first troops to Shantung. At a meeting on 2 June with the ambassador to England, Matsui Keishirō, Foreign Secretary Austen Chamberlain expressed his satisfaction with the Tanaka policy. 'Our minds were moving very much along the same lines', he said, and hoping that relations could grow steadily closer he stated his desire for 'some more formal agreement though not indeed a renewal of the alliance'.[21] The British side thereupon ordered more troops sent to north China, one objective being to set up a defence of the consulates in Peking.

The American minister, John V. A. MacMurray, believed that additional Japanese troops in Shantung would be effective in calming down the troubled northern situation:

> the Japanese Government's long delayed avowal of its determination to take military measures of a precautionary character to protect Japanese interests in North China put a wholly new light upon the various questions. This decision has the effect of serving notice on all the Chinese factions concerned that the Government of Japan is prepared to take measures against any menacing condition of affairs in North China.[22]

The Secretary of State, Kellogg, was also in favour of the way Tanaka was handling Japan's foreign affairs and gave his consent to the dispatch of Japanese soldiers to Shantung.[23] The United States on its part strengthened its marine force in the area around Tientsin.

Tanaka was less interested in maintaining the Washington system of co-operation than his predecessor, rather he had an inclination toward conducting diplomacy along bilateral lines. This tendency could be discerned in his diplomacy to deal with the mounting threat of Chinese nationalism.

In the first place, Tanaka demonstrated an eagerness to improve relations with the USSR. At the end of October 1927 he sent an influential leader of the Seiyukai, Kuhara Fusanosuke, on a special mission for the Japanese government to the Soviet Union and Germany, ostensibly to observe economic developments there. While in Moscow, Kuhara met with Stalin; they discussed the Japanese proposal to establish a buffer zone in North-East Asia as one way to stabilize their relations. Then on December 1927 Gotō Shimpei, former Foreign Minister, was sent to Moscow. His precise mission is not clear but Gotō's plan for Japanese–Soviet cooperation is said to have had a 'degree of understanding' from the government.[24] In Moscow he met with Stalin, Georgii Chicherin and other Soviet government officials and party leaders. Based on his long-cherished dream, Gotō told them that 'Japanese diplomacy, now being forced to shake off the yoke of American and British foreign policy', should shift to a policy of developing close ties with the Soviet Union and China. He also proposed that for the immediate future, 'Russia and Japan form an entente and try to settle the China problem in full mutual understanding'. Gotō went further still in sounding out the possibility of some kind of understanding with the Soviet Union on the issue of the 'expanding of communism in China'.[25] It seems safe to say from this episode that the Tanaka diplomacy was inclined to the idea of checking the radicalisation of Chinese nationalism by means of an understanding with the Soviet Union.

Perhaps the most significant event in Japanese relations with the United States at this time was an attempt to draw US funds into the Manchurian Railway. In early October 1927 Thomas Lamont, from the Morgan Trust Company, came to Japan to discuss with Inoue Junnosuke, president of the Bank of Japan, the possibility of underwriting a Manchurian Railway bond. They negotiated an amount of $30 million that Lamont agreed Morgan would underwrite. The loan negotiation was an important element in Tanaka's diplomacy, for it was directly related to the construction of the five railway lines in Manchuria and Mongolia. Tanaka assured the American government that Japan had no intention of trying to keep Manchuria and Mongolia as an exclusively 'Japanese sphere of interest', but would allow the area to be open to the enterprise of other nations. Lamont requested the State Department to approve the loan contract.[26]

If the underwriting of the bond issue by Morgan that was negotiated by Inoue and Lamont had materialised, it would have assumed a unique significance in the history of Japanese–American relations as the first American investment in the Manchurian Railway. The effort was, in any case, symbolic of the bilateral orientation of 'Tanaka Diplomacy'.

In his conduct of bilateral diplomacy Tanaka placed considerable emphasis on cooperation with the United Kingdom. A document entitled 'Opinions Concerning Policy Toward Manchuria and Mongolia', which was drawn up on 1 June 1927 by the Headquarters of the Kwantung army as a working paper for the 'General Outline of Japan's China Policy', which was submitted at Tōhō Kaigi (Eastern Conference), states that 'with regard to the revolutionary activities of Soviet Russia in China proper it is best to counter them in collaboration with Great Britain, and to sweep out the radicals'.

That opinion represented the base of 'Army Diplomacy' – the conviction that cooperation with Britain would be the most effective to deal with China. That thinking was closely related to the image that prevailed among the Japanese army, an image of their country encircled by the United States, the Soviet Union and China. (See, for example, 25 September 1929 entry in Ugaki's diary.[27]) The idea of cooperation with Britain was perhaps a product of a psychological mechanism to find an effective countermeasure to the encirclement of Japan by these three countries.

Faced with the resumption of the Northern Expedition in the spring of 1928, Tanaka deemed that the only remaining alternative was an armed intervention by Japan. Evidence seems to indicate that at that time the Japanese government considered the possibilities of a joint intervention by an Anglo–Japanese or Anglo–American–Japanese force. On 28 April 1928 Mr L. R. Hill from the British Embassy met with Major General Tatekawa Yoshitsugu, who had been appointed military attaché to the Japanese Embassy in Peking. Tatekawa conveyed to Hill the intention of Prime Minister Tanaka to intervene jointly against the Northern Expeditionary Army. In the course of discussion Tatekawa leaked certain ideas, representing them as his personal opinion. He suggested that Japan send troops to North China, taking control there, the United States establish military control in Central China, and Britain send its forces to the regions south of the Yangtze River. 'At least,' he said, 'Japan and Great Britain, who had the greatest interests at stake, should continue to give a lead and let those follow who would.'[28] There was strong army support for an Anglo–Japanese coalition, a position that was shared by some Foreign Ministry officials, including the Minister to China, Yoshizawa Kenkichi, Consul-General at Mukden, Yoshida Shigeru, and the Ambassador to Turkey, Obata Yukichi.[29] One of the most enthusiastic was a powerful member of the Seiyukai and parliamentary Vice-Minister for Foreign Affairs, Mori Kaku. Mori was probably very influential in the development of strong inclination in 'Tanaka Diplomacy' toward close accord with Britain. An interesting report on a Mori–Hill meeting written in December 1928 by British Consul Davidson, shows that Mori was strongly critical of Shidehara's diplomacy for its failure to effect conciliation with Britain. He commented, according to the Davidson report, that Shidehara had a 'deep-rooted distrust of British diplomacy', whereas Tanaka and the Seiyukai were 'genuinely anxious that England and Japan, and, if practicable, America also, should act in close cooperation in China', thus representing a positive change from the Shidehara era. Mori is also reported to have stated that for both Japan and Britain, interest in China is 'purely of a commercial nature and therefore identical', clearly revealing his own conceptual basis of Japan's foreign policy.[30]

Tanaka's inclination toward Anglo–Japanese cooperation is symbolised in the special mission to Britain by former Foreign Minister Uchida Yasuya. Uchida had represented Japan in signing the Kellogg–Briand Peace Pact in Paris on 27 August 1928. He was entrusted with the important mission of contacting Britain, 'the most appropriate partner in the protection of our interests', to sound out possible ways to work together on the 'China problem'.[31]

The US had already taken preliminary unilateral steps to approve Chinese tariff autonomy, and the Japanese government considered it most desirable to move in accord with Britain on this controversial issue. Several Foreign Ministry documents attest to the serious concern being given the possibility of cooperation with Britain. A paper dated 20 July was entitled 'The Issue of Anglo–Japanese Cooperation vis-à-vis China', while a document of 12 October is called the 'Problem of Anglo–Japanese Cooperation', and one more, dated November, is entitled 'Policy on Anglo–Japanese Cooperation'. In all of these documents one can trace the basic policy line that Japan and Britain should take steps together in settling the problems of tariff autonomy, abolition of extra-territorial rights and approval of the Kuomintang Government under Chiang Kai-shek. The latter document, 'Policy on Anglo–Japanese Cooperation', is especially forceful on these points.[32]

Uchida met with Lord Cushendun, acting foreign minister, in London on 8 September. The Japanese special envoy recommended that cooperative efforts between Japan and Britain in dealing with the Chinese demand for revision of the unequal treaties would be the most feasible, although, he said, Japan could not accept the unilateral abrogation of the trade agreements or other radical changes but was aware of the necessity for some adjustment. Uchida cited the common interests of Japan and Britain and proposed 'to consider a policy most appropriate to the current situation in China'.[33] Uchida stopped in San Francisco on his way home to see Foreign Minister Chamberlain, who was recuperating from an illness there.

Reviewing the developments in Tanaka diplomacy, it is clear that the tendency toward bilateral diplomacy marks a change from the era of 'Shidehara Diplomacy'. It also smacks of a tendency to go back to the 'Old Diplomacy', bearing a tradition built up during the days of the Anglo–Japanese Alliance when Japan sought to confront the threat of Russia and uphold Japanese interests in Manchuria and Mongolia through cooperation with England. Now, that tradition was being called upon to counter nationalism in China. In many ways, Tanaka seemed to have availed himself far more than did Shidehara of the tools of the 'Old Diplomacy'. Tanaka must have found it more comfortable to rely on the pre-World War I methods of the 'Alliance-Entente system' that produced the Anglo–Japanese Alliance and the Russo–Japanese Entente, and which encouraged continental expansion. His extensive use of secret diplomacy, reliance on multiple information channels, special envoys, and willingness to employ armed force as a means of enforcement combined to create a strong image of the 'Old Diplomacy' in both the style and content of Japan's foreign policy under Tanaka Giichi.

Tanaka's diplomacy clearly reflected significant change in the international system in East Asia, but more important, it was during the Tanaka era that the Chinese nationalist challenge to Japanese interests in Manchuria and Mongolia became a reality. The Washington cooperative system provided no mechanism by which to defuse the conflict over those interests when it began to intensify. When the wave of Chinese nationalism swept over the 'lifeline' of Japan, the Washington system could not function against new problems beyond its capacity to handle. In a sense, Tanaka diplomacy developed as a series of responses to this deficiency in the Washington system and growing Chinese nationalism.

The United States government was at this time also responsible for initiating an important change in the international system in East Asia. On 25 July 1928 the US unilaterally recognised the right of the Chinese to tariff autonomy, an action which implied the eventual recognition of the Nationalist government. On 3 March that year the US and the Nanking Nationalist government had exchanged official notes to settle, unilaterally, the Nanking Incident, and on 7 July the Nanking government announced the end of civil war and the completion of the task of unification. They declared that it was now time to enter into negotiations to replace the unequal treaties with new ones. Thus, shortly afterward on the 25th, the US and China concluded a new tariff agreement by which America recognised tariff autonomy.

When the Chinese notified Japan that they had abrogated the Sino–Japanese treaty of commerce, the Japanese government denounced the unilateral action and stated that they were ready to enter into negotiations for treaty revision but they would not accept unilateral abolition. While the American government had judged that a stable government existed in China, the Japanese were sceptical – they were not convinced that the US was being realistic in their appraisal of affairs in China.

While opposing the American action in recognising Chinese tariff autonomy the Japanese government was still eager to maintain international cooperation on such issues as the abolition of territorial rights. Special Envoy Uchida and Secretary of State Kellogg met on 29 September 1928, at which time Uchida handed the secretary a memorandum to the effect that Japan wished to maintain cooperation among the Washington treaty powers with regard to the China problem.[34]

Kellogg's reply to Uchida is revealing; he pointed out that the co-operative system was still alive, and it had, still, its *raison d'être*. It was still possible, he said, to make it operative. Kellogg continued,

> one of the greatest dangers that confronted the Powers out in China at this time was the danger of communist activities inspired by Russia, that the present Nationalist Government appeared to be making every effort to build up a stable and ordered government in China and that all the Powers should cooperate to strengthen the efforts of the present government of China in so far as it was possible to the end that a stable government might be built up there.[35]

Needless to say, Tanaka diplomacy also shared the assumption that Bolshevism was a distinct threat. Carrying over one of the basic lines from the Shidehara era, Tanaka continued to support the moderate faction in the Nationalist government. Kellogg's statement above, however, not only declared the possibility of maintaining the trilateral system of cooperation but also suggested a new alternative for American foreign policy which would seek cooperation among Japan, America, Britain and China without including the Soviet Union. This posed severe difficulties for Japan with regard to its own interests, at least as long as the Nationalist government made no clear guarantee of Japan's special position and privileges in Manchuria and Mongolia. Factors militating against Japanese acceptance of such an alternative were the domestic political situation, public opinion, and above all, the opposition of the military – the strongest single political force. Japanese foreign policy lost much of its flexibility because of the fact that for so long it was so deeply committed to maintaining its special interests in Manchuria and Mongolia.

As far as Japan's rights in those areas were concerned, a relatively smooth *quid pro quo* could have been carried off with the United Kingdom. And, as we have seen, Tanaka diplomacy put top priority on rebuilding the strong bilateral relationship with Britain. As it turned out, however, while Britain appeared to be enthusiastic about close ties with Japan as of May 1927, by the end of 1928 they had lost much of the former fervour and had gone as far as to sign a new treaty on tariffs with China. On 20 December Britain approved tariff autonomy and recognised the Nationalist government.

The United States and Britain took similar steps in their response to Chinese nationalism during the late twenties. It was at this point in post-World War I history that Japanese diplomacy began to show the symptoms of isolation, the pattern which was to dominate the East Asian political system in the next decade.

There were several alternatives for the Japanese foreign policy of this period, in coping with the newly developing situation in East Asia. One was to turn toward a fully functioning trilateral system of cooperation as set up within the framework of the Washington system. It would have been a dead end, however, for Chinese nationalism was trying to break through the dominant–subordinate structure of relations, and as soon as Japan's privileges in Manchuria and Mongolia became the target of a movement to rectify inequality, it was this very real issue to Japan that rendered the trilateral system incapable of functioning. The second alternative was to shift emphasis to bilateral diplomacy, as in Tanaka's efforts to create new ties with Britain, and confront Chinese nationalism on that basis. But we have seen how methods of the Old Diplomacy that once functioned very well – alliances, secret treaties, the division of power – were no longer applicable to East Asia during the twenties. The diplomatic style that Tanaka embraced, leaning toward the old approach, thus grew bankrupt and was finally completely ineffective. The third choice was to make China a new partner and work to reform the old dominant–subordinate relationship, revising the Washington system to create a four-power system of cooperation. American foreign policy-makers had given this alternative very ser-ious consideration, but Japan's interests and special status in Manchuria and Mongolia presented an obstacle too big to overcome.

From 1929 onward the pattern of Japan's isolation in East Asia became increasingly clear. It was about this time that Ugaki wrote in his diary of the suspicion that Japan was encircled by three powers – the United States, China and the Soviet Union. It is safe to assume that the Washington system of trilateral cooperation was on the verge of collapse by this time, at least on the issue of China.

There grew in Japan, especially among the military, the conviction that there was no choice but to unilaterally use military force to solve once and for all the problem of Japan's rights in Manchuria and Mongolia. With the Manchurian Incident and the subsequent note from Secretary of State Henry L. Stimson, a relationship that embodied a spirit of cooperation became one of confrontation. Japan left the League of Nations, and after American recognition of the Soviet Union, it withdrew from the Washington Naval Treaty. The Washington system had broken down completely. The outbreak of the China Incident in 1937 fixed the pattern of Japanese isolation in the context of East Asian politics. Thus, the process of transformation that the Washington system began to undergo came around to its final conclusion.

NOTES

1.   Ian Nish, 'Japan in Britain's View of the International System, 1919–37', in Ian Nish (ed.), *Anglo–Japanese Alienation, 1915–1952* (Cambridge, 1982), p. 36.
2.   Hosoya Chihiro, 'Britain and the US in Japan's View, 1919–37', in Nish (ed.), *Anglo–Japanese Alienation*, pp. 11–15.
3.   *Foreign Relations of the United States* (hereafter *FRUS*), 1927, vol. II, p. 178
4.   Ibid., pp. 183–4.
5.   Matsui Iwane (Head of the Second Division of the Army Staff) to the Ministry of Foreign Affairs, 28 March 1927, Japanese Foreign Ministry Archives (hereafter JFMA), *Teikoku no Tai-shi Gaikō Kankei Ikken* (Documents relating to Japan's policy towards China).
6.   *Ugaki Kakushige Nikki* (Ugaki's Diary). (Tokyo, 1968), vol. I, pp. 568–70.
7.   Shidehara to Yoshizawa, 7 April 1927, no. 175; Yoshizawa to Shidehara, 13 April 1927, no. 199, JFMA, *Nankin ni okeru Shina-hei no Bōkō Kankei* (Documents relating to the violent acts committed by the Chinese soldiers in Nanking) and *Teikoku no Tai-shi Gaikō Kankei Ikken*.
8.   Tilley to Chamberlain, 7 April 1927, FO 4284/1530/10.
9.   *FRUS*, 1927, vol. II, pp. 186–7.
10.   Ibid., pp. 189–90.
11.   Ibid., pp. 196–8.
12.   Howard to Kellogg, 5 April 1927, ibid., pp. 179–80.
13.   Kellogg Memorandum, 20 April 1927, ibid., pp. 204–5.
14.   Howard to Kellogg, 14 April 1927, ibid., pp. 188–9.
15.   Usui, Katsumi, *Ni-Chu Gaiko-shi* (History of Sino–Japanese Diplomatic Relations), (Tokyo, 1971), p. 51.
16.   Tilley to Chamberlain, 22 April 1927, F 4958/2731/10.
17.   Tilley to Chamberlain, 5 May 1927, F 5532/2/10.
18.   Tilley to Chamberlain, 17 May 1927, F 5539/2/10.
19.   Tanaka's talk with Tilley, 13 May 1927, JFMA, *Eikoku Shina Gaikō Kankei Zassan*. (Documents relating British Policy towards China).
20.   Conclusion of second meeting of the Committee on China, 26 May 1927, CAB 27/337; Hosoya, op. cit., Nish (ed.) *Anglo–Japanese Alienation*, p. 13.
21.   Chamberlain to Tilley, 2 June 1927, F 5202/201/23.
22.   MacMurray to Kellogg, 31 May 1927, *FRUS*, 1927, vol. II, pp. 124–6.
23.   Kellogg's talk with Thomas Lamont, 29 September 1927, Lamont Papers.
24.   Tsurumi, Yusuke (ed.), *Gotō Shimpei Den* (Biography of Goto Shimpei), (Tokyo, 1937), vol. IV, p. 872.
25.   Ibid., pp. 864–77.
26.   Usui, op. cit., p. 87; Mitani Taichiro, 'Wall Street to Manmo (Wall Street, Manchuria and Mongolia)', Hosoya and Saitou Makoto (eds) *Washington Taisei to Nichi-Bei Kankei* (Washington System and Japan–US Relations), (Tokyo, 1978), pp. 335–45.
27.   *Ugaki Nikki*, vol. I, p. 735.
28.   Hill to Dormer, 12 April 1928, F 2582/7/10.
29.   Dormer to Chamberlain, 18 April 1928, F 2582/7/10.
30.   Davidson Memorandum, 17 December 1928, F 369/3/10.

31. Uchida Yasuya Denki Hensan Iinkai (Editorial Committee for the Biography of Uchida Yasuya (ed.) *Uchida Yasuya*, (Tokyo, 1965), pp. 283–4.
32. Ibid.
33. Ibid., pp. 284–6.
34. *FRUS*, 1928, vol. II, pp. 425–30.
35. Ibid., p. 430.

3 The Road to Singapore: Japan's View of Britain, 1922–41

Ikeda Kiyoshi

The news of the signing of the alliance with Britain, announced by the Japanese government on 12 February 1902 was received in Japan with great excitement and stimulated a 'festive outburst', which soon swept across the country. One of the opinion-leading magazines, *Tōyō Keizai Zasshi*, pointed out in an editorial that as the nation was being 'carried away in euphoria . . . the prices of the national flags of Great Britain and Japan as well as those of champagne have doubled', and recorded that 'the people, both in government and civilian life, are busy congratulating one another constantly'.[1] Another magazine, *Jiji Shimpo*, expressed its delight on the signing of the alliance as follows:

> It was only forty or so years since Japan had opened its doors to the world community, and barely five or six years earlier that it had demonstrated its power to the world in the Sino–Japanese War; it was now able to attain, quite suddenly, full status as a world entity among the most powerful nations. It looks as though it is but a captivating dream. Is it really so?[2]

Within less than forty years of the 'festive outburst', on 14 July 1939 Tokyo citizens who had expressed their enthusiasm in 1902, adopted a resolution full of extraordinary hostility toward Britain at a Tokyo citizens' anti-British meeting in Hibaya Public Hall. The resolution was aimed against the Anglo–Japanese negotiations between the British ambassador, Sir Robert Craigie, and the Japanese foreign minister, Arita Hachirō, which were expected to take place the next day. The resolution reads:

> We, the seven million citizens of Tokyo, embodying the rising aspirations of Asian peoples, have determined upon a thorough bombing of Britain, the enemy of justice and humanity. Britain must abandon all its mistaken beliefs, return the concessions to China, and without delay leave the land of East Asia.[3]

In retrospect, Anglo–Japanese alienation after the First World War gradually changed from the aftermath of the alliance, through the competition and conflict of interests in China, deepening mutual hostility, to the last clash in December 1941. It must be stressed that 1936 was one of the turning points in the growth of alienation; the Japanese government's announcement of withdrawal from the London naval disarmament conference (15 January); the military coup d'état of 26 February and its effects upon domestic politics; the adoption of the 'Guideline of National Policy' by Hirota Koki's government (7 August); the conclusion of the German–Japanese Anti-Comintern pact (25 November). These developments, linking each other, dragged the United States into the final stage of confrontation with Japan. Britain had to follow American policy gradually and then completely in 1941: some reluctance had been felt in London because of the gap between the prestige of the empire and the vulnerability of British defences in the Far East.

This paper attempts to re-examine mainly the Japanese view of Britain during the interwar era, centring on the development of Japanese southward policy and the Sino–Japanese war. Let us begin with the aftermath of the Anglo–Japanese alliance and reaction to it.

The late Professor Richard Storry (1913–82), a brilliant Japanologist, once described an 'average Englishman's view of Japan' as follows: A Lotus Land 1870–1895, Japan The Gallant Ally 1895–1921, The Menace of Japan 1922–1945, Japan The Prize Winner 1946–1975. He wrote 'During Phase Three the clouds begin to gather, although very slowly at first . . . indeed they are not prominent at all until about halfway through this period, until the early spring of 1933, when Mr. Matsuoka Yōsuke leads his delegation out of the League of Nations at Geneva'.[4] After that the skies darkened until the storm broke.

In the first half of the 1930s, Britain viewed Japan with a mixture of optimism and caution as a country dominated by the military. Britain, the world-wide empire whose interests in Asia had been biggest among the Powers, believed that Japan was a Power whose ambition was more likely to be checked if she stayed within the world community of Powers than if she was alienated from them.[5] Although the British Foreign Office under Austen Chamberlain (1924–9) and Sir John Simon (1931–5), never regarded a clash of the two countries as inevitable in the near future, there was vigilance as regards the future:

If Japan was to attempt to annex Manchuria, the question would become an international affair, so long as the Four Power Treaty was in force, and Great Britain would have to act in concert with the other Powers. Only if treaties failed to act and British interests were vitally affected would a casus belli arise between this country and Japan alone. This is a possibility which seems exceedingly remote.[6]

Meanwhile, Japanese attitudes to Britain contrasted quite sharply with those of Britain towards Japan – a mixture of optimism and pessimism. Anti-British feeling among Japanese had grown since the abrogation of the alliance in 1922. One cause of this feeling was intense Japanese anxiety over Britain's policy of fortifying the naval base at Singapore. The shift of sentiment among military circles from pro-British to anti-British is well summarised by the following comment made by a Japanese general who had previously been very friendly to Britain: 'You British signed an alliance pact with us on Sunday, broke it on Monday, and started building a military base on Tuesday. It is clear that you no longer trust us'.[7]

The response of the Japanese in general to the abrogation of the alliance was, as Professor Ian Nish described, 'One of nostalgia, tinged with respect'.[8] There was, however, particularly among the military, a sense of disgust, much more serious than mere sentimental nostalgia.[9] Vice-Admiral Katō Hiroharu, who headed the navy delegation to the Washington conference, vehemently criticised unfriendly British behaviour which forced Japan to accept the ratio 5:5:3 at the conference:

Behind the Anglo–American principle of naval disarmament which is based on each other's existing strength, they conceal their intentions to gain supremacy over the world, which is not only irrational, but also does not accord with the principle of disarmament, thus does not assist the peace of the world.[10]

The termination of the alliance, the enforced 'inferiority' ratio of 5:5:3 and the construction of the Singapore naval base, all of these were to be manipulated as symbols to arouse anti-British feeling in the second half of the 1930s. It must be stressed here and will be important to underline that anti-British feeling was more severe than that of anti-American feeling, because of 'crafty British diplomacy'; Britain 'helped the US both directly and indirectly, taking a hostile attitude towards Japan, her ally in the Anglo–Japanese Alliance, and finally succeeded in abandoning the alliance, on conditions favourable to themselves'.[11]

Among the Imperial Japanese Navy there emerged an anti-Anglo-Saxon faction, called 'Kantaiha', headed by Admiral Katō, vice-chief of the navy's general staff, and Captain Suetsugu Nobumasa, who assisted Katō at the Washington conference. Both were infuriated by what they saw as the Anglo-Saxons' 'high-handed' and 'oppressive attitude toward Japan'.[12] Upon returning to Japan Katō and Suetsugu advocated a policy of overthrowing Britain and the United States which gained popularity among young officers. I should like to draw particular attention to the fact that among those young officers we can find several names of those who were to press strongly for the southward policy of the navy in the latter half of the 1930s. They responded naturally to young Prince Konoe Fumimaro's aggressive claim, 'Ei-Bei hon'i no heiwa shugi o haisu' ('Down with the Anglo–American peace principles') (1918). One of the radical groups of young officers in the navy, Ōshi Kai (Emperor's War Society) established in 1928, revealed their angry xenophobia in its proclamation:

> Now faced with the loud voices of hostility to Japan all over the world, and with the tightening oppression towards us . . . Japan, anxious about the serious shortage of food, resulting from its inadequate land and increase in population, is on the verge of self-ruin or expansion abroad . . . We have to advance and exploit Asia to emancipate the Asian races expelling the tyrannical white men.[13]

While anti-Anglo-Saxon feeling had fermented among the young officers, the mainstream of military circles advocated the pro-Anglo-Saxon attitude, the so-called Shidehara (Kijūrō) diplomacy which bears the marks of the old Anglo–Japanese alliance within the framework of international order in Asia established at the Washington conference. The top leaders of the army recognised the utility of continued cooperation with Britain in the face of rising nationalism in China and with an increased 'Bolshevik threat' there. The minister of war, Ugaki Kazunari, wrote in his diary about the necessity of Anglo–Japanese rapprochement: 'It would be useful to include the United States in this (Anglo–Japanese) rapprochement. If this co-operation can be achieved the Chinese issue can be solved before it becomes a critical worldwide problem (5 December 1926)'.[14] His intention aimed at the localisation of the China problem within the regional cooperation between Japan, Britain, and the United States against Chinese nationalism and Soviet Bolshevism. The prime minister, Tanaka Giichi, a leading figure from the army, also maintained Ugaki's pro-British attitude in contrast with Shidehara's rather pro-American inclination in dealing with the China problems, for example in the case of sending a Japanese force to Shantung in May 1927.

On the other hand, the leading figures in the navy also advocated co-operation with Britain and the United States as necessary because of the realities of Japanese national power compared with theirs. Admiral Katō Tomosaburō, one of the plenipotentiaries in the Japanese delegation at the Washington conference, described the reasons why Japan must accept the so-called inferior ratio of 5:5:3, as follows:

> National defence is too serious a business to be borne only on the soldiers' shoulders. War also cannot be carried out by soldiers alone. Without money we cannot conduct war . . . In the case of possible war with the US in future, Japanese would have to wage the war independently against this terrible enemy who overwhelms us in its national power . . . We cannot expect any aid from Britain or France, whose resources had been exhausted by the last War . . . thus, it seems, in view of avoiding a clash with the US in future, more fruitful for Japan to accept the 10:10:6 ratio.[15]

Among the leaders of public opinion in those days we can find many advocates of the Washington treaties system, for example, retired Captain Mizuno Hironori wrote an article in which, illustrating the background of the Russo–Japanese war, he stressed 'the more vital factor of economic power than that of military in modern war'. He warned Japan of her isolation politically and economically in the contingency of a Japanese–American clash. He criticised especially the policy of breaking with Britain and the United States led by Katō Hiroharu and Suetsugu in clear contrast with his high appreciation of Katō Tomosaburo who 'overcame a crisis within the Japanese navy by abandoning of an old naval building plan, Hachi Hachi Kantai Keikaku (Eight Eight Fleet Program)'.[16]

As for naval affairs, the policy of cooperation with Britain and the United States within the framework of the 'Washington system', represented by such as Katō Tomosaburo and Mizuno, had constituted the mainstream inside the Japanese navy, through the preliminary disarmament negotiations at Geneva in 1928 until just after the naval disarmament conference in London in 1930.

The opening of military action by Japan in Manchuria on 18 September 1931, the ensuing outbreak of the Shanghai Incident on 28 January 1932, and Japan's proclamation of Manchukuo on 1 March 1932, all of these marked Japan as a power hoping to force a change in the status quo in the Far East. Britain and the United States saw all of these as a challenge to the Washington System, though the former's attitude towards Japan was milder compared with that of the United States embodied in the famous Stimson doctrine of 'non-recognition'. I should like to mention briefly here several attempts at rapprochement within both Britain and Japan. The pro-Japanese group centred around Neville Chamberlain, the chancellor of the exchequer; this proposed concluding an 'Anglo–Japanese Non-aggression Pact' in 1934. In connection with this move they sent to Japan a mission led by Lord Barnby in September 1934 for the purpose of cooperating with Japan with regard to various economic problems in China. The dispatch of a mission headed by Sir Frederick Leith-Ross to Japan in September 1935 was the last attempt at rapprochement by the British government. The mission was entrusted with the task of establishing British and Japanese cooperation in extension of a joint credit facility to the Chinese and forcing the Kuomintang government to acquiesce in *de facto* recognition of Manchukuo, an important step towards rapprochement between Japan and China.[17] Both missions met with a negative reception in Japan, especially among the army; thus the idea of developing economic cooperation between the two countries ended in failure.

Lastly, it is worth mentioning the final, if unsuccessful, attempt at rapprochement on the side of the Japanese government. On 16 April 1937 the cabinet of Hayashi Senjūrō approved a new China policy which placed much emphasis on economic cooperation with Britain and the United States in China, to 'respect the vested interests of the third nations and, if necessary, to operate jointly the facilities of these countries and even make use of their capital goods'.[18] The new China policy was based on the ideas of the foreign minister, Satō Naotake, who had long held the view that the China problem could not be settled without Anglo–Japanese rapprochement.[19] In response to the Barnby mission Satō dispatched the mission of the Federation of Japanese Economic Organisation headed by Kadono Jukūrō for the purpose of promoting Anglo–Japanese economic cooperation in the Chinese market on the base of mutual concessions. Unfortunately the Kadono mission arrived in London too late, that is, two days before the outbreak of the Marco Polo Bridge Incident on 7 July 1937.

The origins of Japan's southward move can be traced back to just after the Russo–Japanese war of 1904–5. In sharp contrast with the Japanese army which had already started the continental (and northward) policy as Japan's advance in future, the navy had envisaged a southward advance. Some of the leading admirals, such as Yamamoto Gombei and Satō Tetsutarō, advocated the southern advance in future as more beneficial for national defence and development, criticising the army's policy of expansion into Manchuria and Mongolia.[20] Although their romantic expectations were too vague to be formed into a concrete national policy, it might be interesting to remark here on a gloomy prophesy by Takegoshi Yosaburō, one of the famous journalists, on the probable Anglo–Japanese clash in the event of Japan's move southward:

> We, the Japanese, who stemmed originally from the south, must here-after advance to and exploit the great riches of the southern regions. Under the Anglo–Japanese Alliance Britain exploited us with the result of wasting our national resources on Manchuria and Mongolia. The clash between Japan and Britain would not be escapable in future when Japan dared to move to the south.[21]

It was not until the middle of 1934 that the Japanese navy began to formu-late concretely a policy of advancing into South-East Asia. In September 1934, when a Japan–India–Britain conference on the cotton trade had been deliberating in Simla, intensifying anti-British feelings among Japanese, the navy ministry approved a 'Guideline dealing with China':

> Faced with the military penetration by the powers into the south of China, Japan must be more intensively watchful of them, and try to prevent their aggressive moves. It is now inevitable for Japan to adopt a more active strategy in this area within the very near future.[22]

The document above-mentioned was the first announcement on a south-ward advance that the navy made formally. In March 1936, the navy ministry organised a new committee for the purpose of formulating a new southward naval policy, which comprised several influential middle-echelon figures from both the navy ministry and the naval chief staff (NCS). It is worth noting the name of Captain Nakahara Yoshimasa among the committee members, who was the foremost exponent of a southward advance. Nakahara, nicknamed 'King of the South Seas', had persuasively canvassed among his colleagues his conviction that Japan's destiny lay to the south. In this context he later described the outbreak of war between Britain and Germany in September 1939 as 'the golden opportunity for Japan's southward advance'. Nakahara exulted in his diary as follows:

> Finally the time has come. Japan must be brought back to its maritime tradition, placing the main emphasis on the development of the navy. We should not hesitate even to fight the United States and Britain to attain that end. This marine nation, Japan, should today commence her advance to the Bay of Bengal! Moss-covered tundras, vast barren deserts . . . of what use are they? Today people should begin to follow the grand strategy of the navy, altering their old bad habits.[23]

The proposed plan of southward strategy by the committee (April 1936) was aimed to penetrate peacefully into the Outer South Seas from the bases in Taiwan and the Inner South Seas, 'utilising the complicated political situation in Europe, and taking advantage of British defence vulnerability in the Far East'. They envisaged southward expansion through peaceful means, 'For the time being through increasing trade and emigration'.[24] The reason for the proposed southern strategy was essentially two-fold. In part it was the navy's desire to contend with the army for an increased share of armaments and budgetary appropriations. Secondly, there was economic motivation behind the southern strategy. The navy was worried about a shortage of strategic materials, especially petroleum for its fleets and of aviation fuel for its air force. Thus, to conduct research on the oil question, the navy established a research committee for southern policy (July 1935) and began to make a systematic investigation of petroleum and other resources in South-East Asia.

On 8 August 1936 Hirota Kōki's government adopted the now famous 'Fundamentals of National Policy', which was an easy compromise on paper between the army's continental (northward) policy and the navy's southward advance. Although this policy paper expressed a policy of gradual advance to the south 'through peaceful means' and 'carefully avoiding hostilities with Britain', it was of decisive significance in placing a southward advance on a par with continental expansion at the centre of Japanese foreign policy:

> Japan expects her national and economic advance into the Outer South Seas to occur through gradual and peaceful means, avoiding the hostilities of other nations in order to consolidate her national power as well as the strengthening of Manchukuo.[25]

The first move towards the south started with the incident at Peihai on the coast of Kwangtung, south China (3 September 1936). The navy's third fleet at the China station dispatched a group of vessels there to demonstrate its aggressive attitude. Captain Nakahara, head of the bellicose section in the NCS, found his 'golden chance towards the south', in the incident envisaging the occupation of Hainan. He wrote in his diary: 'To change the situation radically, there remains nothing but to force down Britain. Thus the occupation of Hainan! We should occupy Hainan while Britain is unprepared'.[26] The Sino–Japanese war, which broke out in July 1937, soon escalated into full-scale hostilities, so that the navy's southward strategy came to be subordinated to the army's continental policy for a while. A group of middle-echelon officers such as Captain Nakahara, Commanders

Ishikawa Shingo and Chudō Kan'ei, radical exponents of the southward strategy, took advantage of the Sino–Japanese war to control the south China coast and islands in the South China Sea.[27] In February 1939 the navy brought Hainan under occupation – overriding the army's hesitation – and a month later took the Spratly Islands.

It was a natural and logical result that the Japanese military and government had to revise its 'Fundamentals of National Defence' under the drastically changing international situation after Japan's withdrawal from the League of Nations in 1933 and from the naval disarmament conference in 1936. Since the first decision in developing 'Fundamentals of National Defence' in 1906, proposed by Yamagata Aritomo, potential enemies of Japan had long been dual – Russia for the army, the United States for the navy. Traditionally the navy had built and trained its fleets and air forces preparing against the counterparts of the United States alone, because they did not possess enough power to prepare against two sea powers combined. The naval chief staff recognised fully that it was almost impossible for the navy to wage war against the United States and Britain simultaneously, keeping in mind the 5:5:3 ratio.[28]

The supreme command decided to include on paper Britain among Japan's potential enemies for the first time, although ranked next to Russia, the United States and China. On 3 June 1936 the emperor sanctioned the new 'Fundamentals of National Defence' (the third revision) finally, though he expressed some anxiety over including Britain among potential enemies, asking Prince Fushimi, chief of the naval staff, for an explanation.[29] It was not until September 1938, a year after the outbreak of the Sino–Japanese war, that the navy prepared a concrete military operation scheme against Britain, in which the naval chief staff gave priority to the occupation of Hong Kong and Singapore immediately, after a Japanese fleet defeated a British-dispatched fleet to the Far East.[30] Strategically the Japanese military considered that the United States would not willingly be made a cats-paw of Britain on the assumption that Japan had no conflict with the United States. As late as the autumn of 1940, they judged that Britain and the United States were politically and strategically separable. Even Shigemitsu Mamoru, the ambassador in London (1938–41) sent his observation on 5 August 1940 to Tokyo saying 'the policies of Britain and the US are not joint but parallel. So far these policies have not necessarily been in accord in aim or conduct'.[31]

On 25 November 1936, six months after the third revision of Japan's 'Fundamentals of National Defence', Japan concluded an Anti-Comintern pact with Germany, marking a first step towards involvement in worldwide antagonism between 'Have-Nations', including Britain, and 'Have-Not-Nations' like Germany and Italy. In any case, in the wider perspective of

Anglo–Japanese relations, the inclusion of Britain in the list of Japan's potential enemies, as well as the signing of the Anti-Comintern pact with Nazi Germany within the same year, suggested a significant change in Japan's political shift from pro-British to anti-British and pro-German, although important pockets of pro-British feelings still remained.

Just after the Sino–Japanese war started at Marco Polo Bridge on 7 July 1937 with Japanese military action developing successfully, the British government under Neville Chamberlain, now prime minister, did not, it seems, take events in north China very seriously for a while. The abrupt change of her attitude to Japan was the result of the spread of Japanese military action to Shanghai on 13 August, then over the Yangtze River region and the landing of one army corps at Hangchow-wan on 5 November 1937. Faced with the drastically changing political situation in Europe – Nazi Germany's advance into the Rhineland in March 1936, absorption of Ethiopia by Italy in May and the outbreak of the Spanish civil war in July 1936 – Chamberlain had no defence resources to spare for the Far East. He adopted a policy of rapprochement with Japan to earn time and sent Sir Robert Craigie as ambassador to Tokyo for the purpose of peaceful negotiations on pending serious issues between the two countries in China: Craigie arrived in Tokyo in September 1937.

During his stay in Tokyo until the start of the Pacific war in December 1941, he continued strenuously to negotiate with Japanese foreign ministers; Hirota–Craigie talks in September 1937, Ugaki–Craigie talks in July 1938, Arita–Craigie talks in July 1939, Toyota–Craigie talks in August 1941, none of which was successful, leading to the final catastrophe. Anglo–Japanese friction was too deep to be mitigated.

Faced with China's resistance being stronger than anticipated, the Japanese government, military, and public opinion turned their eyes on Britain and the Soviet Union as the backers of Chinese resistance. Thus anti-British feelings grew rapidly so that the war in China 'was not simply a war between China and Japan, but . . . between Britain and Japan in its essence'.[32] Craigie found anti-British feelings 'still very strong even in naval circles' in the spring of 1938 and at the end of the year he could report that the 'Japanese Navy – and particularly in its younger officers – are manifesting such strong anti-British sentiments.'[33] A clear instance of anti-British feelings will be found in a document prepared by the investigation bureau of the naval chief staff (1 September 1938), which was entitled, 'Why have our anti-British feelings been so stimulated?":

It is certain that British support or instigation lie behind the contemptu-
ous and anti-Japanese tendencies now prevailing among the Chinese
people and the unfriendly policies adopted by the Dutch East Indies
government in recent years.[34]

After the famous announcement of the creation of the 'New Order in East
Asia' by the prime minister, Konoe Fumimaro (3 November 1938), anti-
British feelings increasingly grew among the civilian right-wing, middle-
echelon officers in military circles and radical pro-Axis officials in the
Foreign Office. They viewed the Sino–Japanese war as part of a global
battle between 'Have-Not nations' like Japan and 'Have-Nations' with
Britain as champion of the existing world order. One of the influential
foreign-relations journals, *Gaikō Jihō,* criticised severely 'British-style out-
look on the world and British-style racial attitudes which dominate the
entire world', emphasising Japan's determination to break up the status quo
dominated by Anglo-Saxons:

> A hundred million proud people [Japanese] are by no means ready so
> easily to starve or suffocate. Inevitably they seek to maintain a life line
> in neighbouring China, and the present situation in China itself is the
> explosion of a people's vitality.[35]

The tremendous movement of anti-British fever during the Sino–Japanese
war, in brief, aimed to demonstrate that the war was basically a process of
breaking up the world order that Britain stood for. Correctly speaking, the
fever was virulent twice, the first was from October 1937 to February 1938,
the second, most violent, from July to September 1939. While the former
was led by the civilian right wing focused on the dual targets of hostility to
Russia and Britain, the latter concerned the Craigie–Arita talks on the
Tientsin blockade by the Japanese army (June 1939) and constituted the
first nationwide mass movement in its scale of mobilisation modern Japan
had experienced. The second 'fever', although manipulated indirectly by
the Home Ministry and the military behind the screen, shifted its target to
concentrating on Britain alone. An anti-British conference held on 14 July
1939 in Ōsaka, for example, demanded that Britain suspend her economic
and military aid to Chiang Kai-shek's China through Hong Kong and the
Burma Road, Indian independence, and the liberation of Asia from the
fetters of British imperialism. The conference concluded its resolution as
follows:

> Japan should force Britain not to aid the Kuomintang government who
> continues to resist us and to return her settlements to China. When

Britain refuses our demands, we should break off relations with Britain and punish her.[36]

The ideology of a 'Holy War', that the true aim of the Sino–Japanese war lay in building up a new order in Asia, had permeated deeply among world opinion. Ten press companies in Tokyo announced jointly the meaning of 'Holy War' on 14 July, though in a milder tone:

> Since the outbreak of the Sino–Japanese war, Britain misunderstood Imperial Japan's fair aim and dared to aid Chiang Kai-shek's government behind the screen . . . We, the Japanese, hold the firm belief that we should remove all obstacles in the way of conducting our holy war . . . We want Britain to revise her recognition of the present state of Asia and to co-operate with us realistically in establishing a new order in Asia so as to promote peace all over the world.[37]

The reorientation of Japan's foreign policy, which began with the Nazi–Soviet non-aggression pact in August and the ensuing German invasion of Poland in September 1939 had been followed by Japan's more friendly attitude to Britain for a while. Initially, Abe Nobuyuki's government adopted a policy of non-intervention in the European war, which was followed by that of Yonai Mitsumasa's government until the outcome of European developments became clear. Yonai, with his foreign minister Arita, was fearful of war with Britain and the United States if Japan concluded a military alliance with Germany as well as the repercussions of a Japanese move into South-East Asia.[38] This attitude lasted until the fall of Yonai's government in July, which occurred soon after the collapse of France and the tragedy for Britain at Dunkirk.

Upon the fall of France, the navy's southward strategy, which had been subordinated to the army's successful execution of the Sino–Japanese war, obtained support quickly even within the army, which had been negative to it before. They held an illusory expectation that the downfall of Britain was fated to occur in the very near future with German predominance all over Europe. It was in such a situation that the Supreme Command Government Liaison Conference (established in December 1937) adopted a basic national policy entitled 'Outline of the Main Principles for Coping with the Changing World Situation' (27 July 1940), in which the further southward advance policy and military alliance with the Axis were stipulated. 'The Outline of the Main Principles', which had been drafted before by key officers in the military, both navy and army, depended upon an assumption that Britain and the United States could be separated strategically. The military was prepared for an advance to the south and ready to use armed force if necessary, 'restricting in so far as is possible its operations to Britain alone, though it might be impossible to avoid war with the US'.[39]

On 22 September 1940 a Japanese army corps in China began to advance into northern Indo-China by agreement with the Vichy government, which was followed by Japan's signature of the tripartite pact with Germany and Italy on 27 September. In the course of a broadcast the prime minister, Prince Konoe, proudly announced a 'Greater East Asia':

> Germany and Italy intended to establish a New Order in Europe and Japan will do likewise in Greater East Asia. It is natural that Germany and Italy should occupy leading positions in the respective spheres, and the attempt to obstruct historical evolution has produced a second European war and tension in the Far East approaching a state of war. Therefore, it is inevitable that Japan, Germany and Italy should assist one another, and the pact may acquire the force of military alliance according to circumstances.[40]

It became increasingly clear after the entry of Japanese troops into northern Indo-China that those elements which favoured southward expansion were gaining the day. The navy established a new first Committee in December 1940, which was composed of energetic middle-echelon officers. The Committee was part of a broader institutional reorganisation in the navy designed to gain a greater voice in national policy. Captain Ishikawa Shingō, the leading figure among them and foremost exponent of a southward strategy, was full of energy and politically minded; he dominated the Committee. He held quite vehement anti-British and pro-German feelings since his short trip to Europe in 1935–6. As early as 1937, he had grasped the international situation as follows:

> 1. Since the Manchurian Incident in 1931 Japan has been encircled by Britain and the US and the encirclement has been increasingly tightened; how to escape will be the most important problem in the near future. Japan's naval policy must be guided by this consideration.
> 2. The revival of Germany in Europe has been impressive and she will protest against the established European order around 1940 when it may be the most suitable opportunity for Japan to escape from her present encirclement.[41]

There is no doubt that members of the First Committee, most of whom were pro-German and led by Captain Ishikawa, were determined to assert the navy's policy toward South-East Asia, though some Japanese historians, for example Professor Nomura Minoru, have questioned the role of the Committee.[42] On 30 January 1941 the Supreme Command Government Liaison Conference approved the 'Outline of Policy toward French Indo-China and Thailand', which envisaged strengthening Japan's control, if necessary with 'coercive actions'; this began after the end of January by means of increasing occupation troops in northern Indo-China while the navy concentrated its vessels and aircraft in the region of Hainan island, engaging in 'demonstration', dispatching one cruiser, *Natori,* and one destroyer to Saigon and another destroyer to Bangkok on 28 January.

One possible reason for the navy's sudden militancy at this time can be found in intelligence warfare – the 'Automedon affair' of December 1940. The navy had come into possession of a copy of the British war cabinet minutes of 8 August 1940, portraying an extremely pessimistic evaluation of far eastern defence, in which the chiefs of staff concluded that since Britain was 'unable to send the fleet to the Far East', it 'must avoid an open clash' with Japan.[43] The Japanese naval leaders regarded this information, it seems now, as confirming British vulnerability. Admiral Oikawa Koshirō, the navy minister, at the liaison conference on 27 December stated, 'According to our intelligence document, it is estimated that Britain would not go to war as long as Japan confines itself to advancing into French Indo-China but war would become inevitable if Japan advances into the Dutch East Indies'.[44]

At the end of May 1941 the foremost exponents of southward advance in the navy rapidly became more hawkish and inclined to a pro-war position even against Britain and the United States combined, because of the failure of the Dutch–Japanese negotiations on oil. In June 1941 the First Committee stated that:

> In the present critical situation the Imperial Japanese Navy has to decide quickly and clearly its will for war (including engagement with the US) and to conduct every policy with an aggressive attitude.[45]

On 2 July at the imperial conference in the presence of the emperor Konoe proposed the adoption of the 'Guideline of Imperial Japan's Policy in coping with the Changing Situation', which decided clearly that Japan should establish the 'Greater East Asia Co-Prosperity Sphere' regardless of the changing world situation'.[46]

Admiral Nagano Osami, the chief of the naval staff, presented a new policy on the base of army–navy negotiations to the liaison conference on 12 July, which stipulated that Japan should carry out its southern advance 'without a day's delay' to demand bases and the stationing of troops in southern Indo-China to the Vichy government and if this demand should meet resistance, it should use force. Receiving the information that Vichy had agreed to admit Japan to a joint protectorate of Indo-China, the reaction in Washington was swift. On 26 July President Roosevelt issued an executive order freezing Japan's assets in the United States and halting all trade with Japan including the highly important oil exports. This all-out embargo of Japan was followed by Britain and Holland to the results of perfect 'A-B-C-D encirclement' against Japan. On 28 July Japanese troops advanced into southern Indo-China to break through the encirclement. It was the fateful step toward hostilities on 8 December 1941.

The Japanese government and military devoted no serious attention to how the United States and Britain would react to Japan's advance into southern Indo-China nor was any doubt expressed as to the creation of a new order in Europe under German hegemony. Japan's final will to engage in war with the United States, Britain and Holland at the conference in the presence of the emperor on 5 November was based upon one obsessive assumption, that is, Britain would be compelled to submit to Germany in the near future. On 15 November the liaison conference adopted a blueprint for future strategy in bringing the war to an early end, which was entitled 'Plan for Promoting Cease-fire'. In short, the Japanese leaders – government as well as military – grasped the situation that Japan would hardly be able to defeat the United States in direct military clashes. So what they earnestly hoped for was to achieve a negotiated peace after a limited short-term war. They envisaged three contingencies of cease-fire; when they achieved a state of self-sufficiency by securing an adequate supply of resources in the south; when Chiang Kai-shek's regime had collapsed; or when Britain was forced to sue for peace as a result of her military defeat by the Axis powers. Among these the last case was seen to be the most probable one.[47]

> Japan should find the way for her survival by quickly overthrowing the outposts of Britain, the US and Holland in the Far East, and by adopting some active measures to facilitate the collapse of Chiang Kai-shek's regime, while trying in close co-operation with Germany and Italy to put down Britain first so as to induce the US to withdraw from the war.[48]

To cite a passage from Professor Ian Nish, 'the Road to Singapore might be a tempting path'[49] for the Japanese after the First World War. The Japanese decision-makers in 1940–1, obsessed with an illusion of Britain's probable ruin, dared to challenge the 'old order' in the east dominated by the British empire. In this sense they were preoccupied with too biased a view to grasp international relations with a sense of proportion. In retrospect it is quite suggestive that the Japanese troops landed on the Malay coast one hour before Japan's attack on Pearl Harbor, illustrating, at least, one of the paths to the Pacific war.

NOTES

1. *Tōyō Keizai Zasshi*, editorial on 'Determination of the people', by Ryukotsu (under a pseudonym), 22 February 1922.
2. *Jiji Shimpō*, editorial on 'The effects of the Anglo–Japanese Accord', 14 February 1902.
3. Tokyo *Asahi Shinbun*, editorial on 'Anglo–Japanese negotiation', 15 July 1939.
4. Richard Storry, 'The Image of Japan in England', 27 February 1970, cited in *Bulletin of the International House of Japan*, May 1970.
5. Ian Nish, 'Japan in Britain's View, 1919–37', in Nish (ed.), *Anglo–Japanese Alienation*, p. 43.
6. *Documents on British Foreign Policy, 1919–1939* (hereafter DBFP), series 1a, vol, I, p. 875, cited in ibid., p. 34.
7. F.S.G. Piggott, *Broken Thread*, (Aldershot, 1950), p. 271.
8. Ian Nish, *Alliance in Decline: A Study in Anglo–Japanese Relations, 1908–1923*, (London, 1972), p. 384.
9. Nish, *Anglo–Japanese Alienation*, p. 8.
10. *Katō Hiroharu Denki-Hensan-Kai, Katō Hiroharu Taishō Denki* (Biography of Admiral Katō Hiroharu), (Tokyo, 1941), pp. 741–2.
11. Lt-General Tanaka Kunishige's letter to Field Marshal Uehara Yusaku, 20 December 1921, cited in *Uehara Yusaku Kankei Bunsho*, (Papers related to Uehara), pp. 258–9.
12. Biography of Katō, pp. 743–4.
13. Misuzu Shobo (ed.), *Gendai Shi Shiryo*, (Documents on Modern History of Japan), (Tokyo, 1963), series 4, p. 44.
14. *Ugaki Kazushige Nikki*, (Ugaki's Diary), (Tokyo, 1968), vol. I, p. 556.
15. Letter from Admiral Katō Tomosaburō to Vice-Admiral Ide Kenji, January 1922, cited in Ikeda Kiyoshi, *Nihon no Kaigun* (The History of the Japanese Navy), (Asahi Sonorama, 1986), vol. II, pp. 84–5.
16. Mizuno Hironori, 'Analysis of the New Policy of National Defence', *Chuokoron*, April 1926.
17. Hosoya Chihiro, 'Britain and the US in Japanese View, 1919–37', in Nish (ed.), *Anglo–Japanese Alienation*, p. 21.
18. Japanese Ministry of Foreign Affairs (JMFA) (ed.), *Nihon Gaikō Nenpyō narabini Shuyō-Bunsho* (Chronology of Japanese Foreign Policy and Important Documents), (Tokyo, 1955), vol. II, pp. 361–2.
19. Satō Naotake, *Kaiko Hachijūnen* (Eighty Years of My Life), (Tokyo, 1963), p. 375.
20. Satō Tetsutarō, *Teikoku Kokubō Shi-Ron* (On the Defence of Imperial Japan), (Tokyo, 1908), Preface.

21. Takegoshi Yosaburō, *Nangoku-Ki*, (The Story of Southern Area), (Tokyo, 1910), cited in Ikeda Kiyoshi, *Kaigun to Nippon*, (The Navy and Japan), (Chukōshinsho, 1979), p. 88.
22. Misuzu Shobō (ed.), op. cit., series 10, *Nitchū Sensō* (Sino–Japanese War), vol. I, p. 10.
23. September 1939, *Nakahara Yoshimasa Chujō Nisshi* (Diary of Rear-Admiral Nakahara), cited in Japanese Self-Defence Agency (JDAA) papers.
24. Misuzu Shobō, op. cit., *Nitchū Sensō*, vol. I, pp. 354–5.
25. JMFA (ed.), *Gaikō Nenpyo*, pp. 344–5.
26. September 1936, in Nakahara Diary, see note 23.
27. Sumio Hatano and Sadao Asada, 'The Japanese Decision to Move South (1939–1941)', cited in R. Boyce and E. M. Robertson (eds), *Paths to War* (London, 1989), p. 385.
28. Bōeichō Bōeikenshujo (National Defence Research Institute) (ed.), *Dai honei Kaigunbu Rengō-kantai*, (Supreme Command and the Combined Fleet), vol. I, pp. 320–1.
29. Ibid., p. 323.
30. Ibid., p. 376.
31. *Gaikō Nenpyō*, pp. 489–90.
32. Yokoi Tadao, 'Nichi-Ei Kaidan Naiyō ni Kansuru Iken', (Opinion on Anglo–Japanese talks), cited in JDAA unpublished papers.
33. Craigie to Foreign Office, 7 May 1938, Craigie to Halifax, 14 December 1938, FO 371/21521; ADM1/9909, cited in A. Marder, *Old Friends, New Enemies*, (Oxford, 1981), p. 25.
34. Misuzu Shobō (ed.), op. cit., *Nitchū Sensō*, vol. III, pp. 339–40.
35. 'Nichi-Ei Kankei no Kinjō', (Recent Trends of Anglo–Japanese relations), *Gaikō Jihō*, 15 January 1938.
36. Osaka *Asahi Shinbun*, 17 July 1939.
37. Tokyo *Asahi Shinbun*, 14 July 1939.
38. Takamiya Tahei, *Yonai Mitsumasa*, (Tokyo, 1948), p. 137.
39. Misuzu Shobō, op. cit., *Nitchū Sensō*, vol. III, pp. 504–5.
40. Tokyo *Asahi Shinbun*, 28 September 1940.
41. Ishikawa Shingo, *Shinjuwan eno Keii*, (The Road to Pearl Harbor), (Jiji Tsūshinsha, 1960), p. 114.
42. *Daihonei Kaigunbu*, vol. I, pp. 495–6.
43. John W.M. Chapman (ed. and translator), *The Price of Admiralty: The War Diary of the German Naval Attaché in Japan, 1939–43*, (Sussex, 1985), vol. II, p. 338.
44. Sanbōhonbu (ed.), *Sugiyama Memo*, (The Memoirs of Sugiyama), (Hara Shobo, 1967), vol. I, p. 157.
45. *Daihonei Kaigunbu*, p. 527.
46. Inoki Masamichi (ed.), *Nihon Seiji Gaikō Shiryō Sen*, (Selected documents on Japan's domestic and foreign policy), (Yūshindō, 1967), p. 276.
47. Bōeichō Bōeikenshujo, *Daihonei Rikugunbu Kaisen Keii*, (Supreme Command – Army, Origins of the War), vol. II, pp. 642–4.
48. *Sugiyama Memo*, vol. I, p. 523.
49. I. H. Nish (ed.), *Anglo–Japanese Alienation*, p. 53.

4 Culture in Japanese Foreign Affairs

Akira Iriye

In a recent issue of the *Journal of American History,* nine historians contribute essays on different approaches to the study of American foreign affairs, ranging from 'ideology' and 'national security' to 'gender' and 'psychology.' As one of the contributors, I write about the 'cultural' approach. To illustrate what I mean by this, I refer to US–Japanese relations in the 1930s:

> First, one may analyze the contrasting ideologies and value systems of the two countries that enhanced a sense of crisis across the Pacific. Second, one may document the exchange of persons, goods, and services that continued up to the attack on Pearl Harbor and discuss their place in the deterioration of the bilateral relationship. Third, one may put the relationship in the global context and consider how American–Japanese relations fitted into the cultural climate of the time, exemplified by such developments as the vogue of geopolitics, the crisis of modern liberalism, the rise of totalitarianism, and the worldwide search for a new ideology.[1]

This essay will elaborate on the above passage, in the hope that it will shed light on both Japanese foreign affairs of the 1930s and on the 'cultural' aspects of those affairs. What follows, then, may be considered a footnote to the above article. It may, I hope, also be viewed as a modest footnote to Ian Nish's impressive corpus of writings in the field of modern Japanese diplomacy. He has mostly dealt with political, military, and economic issues. What I offer is a series of observations on less tangible, more informal aspects of Japanese foreign relations.

Because 'culture' is a vague term, it seems important to note, as the above quote suggests, that in the study of international relations it refers at least to three kinds of phenomena or activities. First, there is national culture: traditional ways of life, ideas, beliefs, etc. shared by people living within a national boundary. They become linked to external affairs inasmuch as national leaders as well as public opinion relate themselves to the

47

rest of the world in certain comprehensible frameworks (a set of values, priorities, and the like). These frameworks are products of the national culture. Second, there is the intermingling of national cultures through individuals (tourists, merchants, soldiers, missionaries), ideas, and goods. The intermingling may be voluntary, or it may be promoted officially. In the latter case, propaganda and intelligence work will be involved. Third, we must go beyond national cultures individually or as they interact with one another, and consider whether or not the world at large (the international system) has a cultural dimension, in addition to its power and economic dimensions. In other words, besides power balances and economic exchanges, are there cultural activities that define the international order at a given moment in time? If not, why not?

The study of Japanese foreign affairs may be enriched by raising such questions. I shall focus on the 1930s and discuss these issues as they help in understanding Japan's road to the Second World War.

First of all, regarding Japanese national culture, the key to modern Japanese foreign affairs was the priority the country's leaders gave to military strengthening, including arms build-ups, alliances, and overseas bases and colonies. That had been the consensus since the 1870s, if not earlier, and it did not change significantly in the 1930s. In that decade, however, as James Crowley, Michael Barnhart, and others have demonstrated, military strengthening came to have even more geopolitical implications than earlier, so that the military and their civilian collaborators paid particular attention to controlling natural resources in nearby countries. Whereas earlier military strengthening had been visualised as indispensable for national defence and for obtaining the respect of other countries, now the goal was to prepare the nation for 'total war.' Japan, after all, had achieved the status of a great power, and its security was well ensured. But to the men of the 1930s it was not enough to stop here; Japan must go on to develop a 'national defence state', with its people and resources fully mobilised for war.[2]

It may be observed that there was nothing 'Japanese' about such ideas. As will be noted, conceptions of total war and national mobilisation were widespread throughout the world in the 1930s. But that, too, was part of Japanese culture: to reflect trends elsewhere. In a more immediate sense, however, some Japanese were aware of the need to couch their construction of a national defence state on more national cultural grounds. That was why, as Mark Peattie has shown, Colonel Ishiwara Kanji's ideas about Japan's 'ultimate war' was so influential. One of the conspirators who engineered the Manchurian incident of 1931, Ishiwara was fond of saying that mankind's final war was to be fought between Japan and the United States, the former representing the East and the latter the West. As a result of such a war, the world would enter its golden age, exemplifying mankind's 'common aspirations'. Japan was destined to win the final war because it had amalgamated the essences of other civilisations and would continue to do so. The world's civilisation in the future must be built upon a unity of all civilisations. Hence, it was Japan's mission to prepare for the last battle and lead the way for the eternal peace.[3]

Rather abstract and unbelievably naive, such ideas were apparently taken quite seriously then. For instance, the Ministry of Education's guide to school teachers, known as 'The Essences of the Nation' (Kokutai no hongi, 1937), contained similar ideas about Japan's unique role as a mediator and amalgamator of cultures. The relationship between such a role and the need for war was never quite clear, but at least these ideas served to sanctify war when it came. By linking war to Japan's cultural tradition and mission, it was possible to assert that a war in which the nation became engaged was a 'Japanese' war, unlike other countries' wars, and was presumably nobler or more justifiable. For the Japanese, the above booklet pointed out, war had never been fought for its own sake; it had always been waged for harmony and for peace. For Japan 'war is not for destroying, controlling, or conquering others; it is to create in accordance with certain principles, to realise the great peace'.[4]

This sort of vocabulary was an important aspect of Japanese culture as it went to war in the 1930s. Of course, for Japan's opponents – first the Chinese and then other Asians as well as Americans and Europeans – this was sheer hypocrisy and propaganda, cloaking aggressive acts and atrocities the Japanese military were committing all over Asia. However, this still does not alter the fact the Japanese chose to go to war not only on traditional grounds but also on the basis of a vocabulary of culture. The problem is to try to understand why they did so, or, to be more precise, why they engaged in such self-deception. Certainly, some of them knew that despite the pious language of going to war for cultural ends, the actual fighting was as brutal as any war, and that the Japanese had not become noticeably nobler just because their leaders told them they were carrying on a holy war against the West. As Nagao Yoshirō, the literary critic, wrote in January 1942, the Japanese must take care not to behave even more arrogantly than the British or the Americans in Asia. The Chinese, he wrote, had long been accustomed to Japanese ruffians and exploiters in their midst, and their counterpart in the rest of Asia might now take advantage of the military victories to engage in unethical deeds. Could such people really be expected to promote the cause of Asian unity?[5] Nagayo was being frank, and few expressed such ideas so openly. For the bulk of the population, it would seem that the slogan of pan-Asianism and Asian liberation from the West was taken seriously, even sincerely.

This in itself is a cultural phenomenon. How could one espouse noble visions when in fact there was nothing noble about the war? Of course, other nations have also tended to develop such a duality of perception and reality, but it seems possible to argue that in the Japanese case the gap between the two was particularly noticeable, for even in private diaries and personal letters, one sees expressions of satisfaction that Japan's cause is right, and that the nation is really fighting for selfless ends. This isolation from reality may be attributable to the country's traditional insularity and the people's lack of exposure to other peoples. The well-known in-groupness of the Japanese, in which extreme politeness to one another existed side by side with suspicion of, even hostility toward, outsiders, coexisted with a naivety which made them believe that somehow other Asians would accept their definition of the reality.

Distancing oneself from reality took on fatal significance when Japan's top leaders persuaded themselves that despite all the objective indications to the contrary, which suggested the United States was far superior to Japan in agricultural, mineral, and industrial output, somehow Japan had a chance to win a war against that nation, or at least to so shake the Americans' will that they would desist from retaliating. Some political scientists use the term 'strategic culture' to indicate this sort of mentality; in purely strategic terms, a war against America made no sense, but there was a culture that overcame such calculations and launched the nation on a war course. Or, to use a psychoanalytic concept, the Japanese may have been victims of 'compensatory grandiosity.' Because they knew they were inadequate compared with America and other countries, they wanted to act grandiosely to compensate for this inferiority, and what better way was there to do so than to strike at the mightiest power in the world?

These are all cultural phenomena, and it is clear that to understand Japan's war decision or any other act at that time, or at any time, it is important to understand them. For that matter, the whole structure of decision-making is also a cultural production. Like other countries, Japan had a decision-making system that was uniquely its own, and the way discussions were held, opposing views expressed, and final decisions reached must be understood in relation to the cultural setting. To examine this, it is important not only to study official transcripts of meetings but also personal records that document informal conversations among leaders. Private diaries and personal writings of men close to the seat of power are particularly valuable in this respect. The recently published diaries of two men who were very close to the Shōwa emperor, Makino Nobuaki and Irie Sukemasa, are good examples. Makino, who was lord keeper of the privy seal during 1925–35, and Irie, who became one of the emperor's chamberlains in 1934 and assumed the post of grand chamberlain after the war, both recorded in detail what they did and heard at the Imperial Palace. Their diaries enable us to have some idea of where the emperor stood on a number of critical issues, and on the whole it would seem, on the basis of these and other publications, that the Shōwa emperor was extensively involved in decision-making, especially with regard to Japan's external affairs. For instance, Makino records that in 1929 the emperor was very concerned with properly punishing those officers responsible for the assassination of Chang Tso-lin in the preceding year. Makino actively supported the emperor in this, and the affair ultimately brought about the resignation of Prime Minister Tanaka Giichi. The emperor told Makino he was very pleased with the membership of the succeeding cabinet of Hamaguchi Osachi.[6] Irie was too junior a court official before the war to be fully aware of developments of comparable importance, but his diary is valuable as it chronicles in detail his meetings with individuals who came into contact with him. Here again, one notes a sense of isolation from the real world. The court circle, those who were around the emperor, consisted primarily of men who were concerned with preserving good relations with the United States and Britain, and there is little doubt that the emperor shared their sentiment.

But the real puzzle is why they thought they could maintain amicable relations with these countries while the nation went on its aggressive war on the continent. Here again was a case of aloofness from the real world. For instance, in 1933 the emperor instructed the foreign minister to maintain friendly relations with the Anglo–American powers in the wake of Japan's withdrawal from the League of Nations.[7] It would have been much easier to do so if the nation had not withdrawn from the League. Likewise, the Irie diary shows how the very same men who had professed their friendship with America and Britain were elated at the news of the successful attack on their possessions in December 1941.[8] Again, in April 1945, when news of President Franklin D. Roosevelt's death reached Tokyo, Irie expressed his satisfaction ('It is great news,' he wrote in his diary), and proceeded to prophesy that the position of the United Nations would now become much more difficult thereafter.[9] In reality, of course, nothing of the sort happened. The ultimate unrealism, perhaps, was the emperor's and the court circle's last-minute faith in the Soviet Union; in the spring of 1945 they persuaded themselves that the latter would somehow agree to mediate between Japan and the Anglo–American nations to end the war on a basis other than an unconditional surrender. Like the Pearl Harbor attack, this made no geo-political or strategic sense, and therefore must be considered a product of a certain mentality. To inquire into it should provide another agenda for the study of the cultural aspect of Japanese foreign affairs.

Apart from Japanese psychology and mentality, however, there may be another answer to the question of why the slogan of pan-Asianism was taken so seriously. It served as an ideology to fill the gap between Japan's military ambitions and economic achievements. Michael Hunt defines 'foreign policy ideologies' as 'sets of beliefs and values . . . that make international relations intelligible and decision making possible.'[10] That will do as a broad definition, but the definition says little about different types of beliefs and values. On one hand, there are more traditional and easily comprehensible ideas such as balance of power and trade expansion. On the other hand, there are much more abstract notions that are nevertheless taken as seriously. Pan-Asianism is a good example, and in order to understand it as an ideology of Japanese foreign affairs, it may be well to postulate that in international relations ideologies often play a role as a link between a nation's military power and economic resources. Ideally, the two should go hand in hand; 'ends' and 'means' should somehow be in balance. The fact was, however, that in the Japanese case there had steadily developed a serious gap between its military power and its economic performance. By the end of the First World War, the nation had emerged as one of the top three military powers in the world, the position it maintained throughout the interwar period. In 1939, in fact, it had more military aircraft than even the United States, and as late as 1941 its combined naval power was greater than that the United States stationed in the Pacific. The picture, however, was quite otherwise in the economic sphere. Japan's national income of about $2 billion at the end of the First World War, although nearly double what it had been before the war, was still behind that of the United States and that of most European countries, despite the wartime devastation suffered by the latter. Twenty years later, although the United States had suffered more severely than Japan from the Depression, the former's national income of $90 billion was about thirteen times as much as the latter's. A nation whose income was ¥31 billion (about $7 billion) would fight a war that would ultimately cost over ¥65 billion. Clearly, if such a country was to go to war to maintain and even augment its military power, it needed an ideology to justify it to the people who must do the fighting and who must pay for the endeavour. But what sort of ideology would it be? Here the

Japanese self-perception as an Asian country that had absorbed the essences of the West suggested an answer. Japan would go to war to lead Asians in their struggle for liberation from Western domination. But the content of the ideology is less important than that an ideology was thought to be required. In such a perspective, the war almost by necessity was a 'war of ideas,' as an American observer put it, or a cultural phenomenon.[11]

Enough has been said about the cultural approach to Japanese foreign affairs in the framework of national culture. Next we may briefly consider the second dimension, the intermingling of national cultures through individuals, ideas and goods. Whereas the first dimension focused on cultural developments inside Japan, this second looks at Japanese overseas, what they did, what impact they had on the people they came into contact with – as well as foreigners in Japan and their impact on Japanese. Of course, Japanese soldiers were all over China, but their collective action belongs more to formal military history. What is equally important is to examine how they behaved as individuals, what impressions they obtained of Chinese, and vice versa. Strangely enough, we seem to have more information on this last item than on the first. Not only are there Chinese publications that chronicle the country's perception of, and resistance to, Japanese aggression, but books like Edgar Snow's *Red Star Over China* (London, Gollancz, 1937) provided ample information on how the Chinese portrayed the Japanese invaders. Likewise, *One Day In China: May 21st 1936,* a collection of individual Chinese reports on what they did and thought about on that day in 1936, which has been edited and translated by Sherman Cochran (London: Yale, 1983), is extremely valuable as it shows how ordinary Chinese in various parts of the country steadily developed a national sense of resistance to Japanese aggression. There is relatively less of this type of literature on the Japanese side. It is to be hoped that the kind of collaborative work that has begun to be undertaken by Chinese and Japanese researchers into the Marco Polo bridge incident or the 'rape of Nanking' will yield much fresh information. But quite apart from Japanese atrocities and battles, one should recall that there were many, less heinous (if no less aggressive, from the Chinese point of view) encounters between individual Chinese and Japanese, especially in the occupied areas. Thousands of Japanese who worked as merchants, teachers, policemen, and so forth, came into daily contact with Chinese. A minority of Chinese even collaborated with Japanese propagandists in establishing information centres and schools to spread the gospel of pan-Asianism.[12] Matsumoto Shigeharu's memoirs note that as a Dōmei newsagency correspondent he was in close touch with Chinese political and intellectual leaders.[13] What he and other journalists said and did to the Chinese, and how the latter responded, are topics that await scholarly research.

But it was not China alone that attracted Japanese visitors, armed or otherwise. Even as the war went on in Asia, Japanese scholars, artists, students, journalists, businessmen, and many others went to Europe, North America, and elsewhere. Some, like Yabe Teiji, the political science professor at the University of Tokyo who studied in Germany, kept a detailed diary after their return, while others, like Maruyama Kumao, who studied French literature in Paris, have published their reminiscences.[14] From these writings it is possible to gain an insight into Japan's cultural interactions with the world before the war. Such accounts may not properly belong in the study of Japanese foreign affairs, but they are nevertheless important as they show that, contrary to official propaganda about Asian resurgence and Western decadence, Japanese continued to be fascinated with, and eager to learn from, the West. Add to this the fact that men and women who studied in Europe and America in the 1930s went on to emerge after the war – provided that they survived the war – as intellectual and sometimes political leaders in postwar Japan, then we shall realise the value of understanding such individual encounters.

Just as Japanese continued to go abroad in the 1930s, foreigners did not stop coming to Japan. And their cultural impact would seem to have remained strong, despite the official ideology of pan-Asianism. After all, baseball was still popular, and Hollywood movies were shown up to the last moment before Pearl Harbor. In 1943, Shimizu Ikutarō, then a young sociologist, wrote, 'much of the machinery and technology that we have in our lives was either invented in America or mass-produced there and then brought to Japan. Movies, cars, the radio . . . these things that we cannot cast off from our life are fundamentally American products; they were produced out of American life and express what we call Americanism'.[15] Such a view, expressed in the middle of the war, gives clear evidence that even then American products, visible and invisible, dominated Japanese life. The obverse was not the case, and we must recognise that cultural influences at this level were virtually unidirectional. It was because of the pervasive influence of American culture that the Japanese government tried so hard to counter this by espousing pan-Asianism. In a sense, it was an attempt to narrow the gap between Japan's formal, geopolitically-oriented quest for Asian empire and its informal cultural ties to the West.

There were, however, attempts by the Japanese government in the pre-war period to do something about the situation, in particular about making Japanese culture better known in the West. It is interesting to note that in

1934, the year the British Council was established to promote cultural contact overseas, the Japan Society for the Promotion of International Culture (Kokusai Bunka Shinkokai) was also founded, with a view to making Japan better known abroad and to encouraging cultural cooperation with other countries. Although officially inspired and funded (at least partially), the KBS was initially a private organisation and tried to steer clear of official diplomacy so that it would not be branded a propaganda agency. Nevertheless, its goal was to promote cross-cultural dialogue with other countries in order to have Japanese policy better understood. In order to carry out such an objective, it established an office in New York, several branches in China, and also joined forces with German and Italian cultural agencies to develop bicultural associations. The New York office was particularly important in view of the deteriorating relations with the United States. Organised in 1938, it donated books on Japan to various American libraries, held tea ceremonies and flower arrangement classes, sent instructors to teach Japanese, and sponsored discussion sessions on current affairs. It is difficult to judge how effective such activities were. The effort was too little and came too late, and the Japanese staff of the New York office ended their American days on Ellis island, before being shipped back to their country in exchange for Americans detained in Japan after Pearl Harbor. A full story of this and other similar organisations is yet to be told.[16]

The third dimension of culture in international affairs is what may be termed shared global consciousness. Going beyond what Shimizu called 'Americanism' which he saw spreading throughout the world, and beyond the growing animosity among nations in the 1930s, it is possible to argue that certain perceptions about global and national affairs were held in many countries regardless of their temporal relationships. After all, there was agreement among officials and intellectual leaders in most nations that something profound had shaken international order and that familiar conceptions of world or national issues were losing their relevance. Whether this transformation was due to the Depression or to deeper causes, conditions within nation-states as well as their interrelationships could no longer be comprehended in a vocabulary that had defined these phenomena for decades. As Reinhold Niebuhr wrote in 1934, a familiar world was passing but as yet there was little understanding what shape the coming world would take.[17] The consequent search for new meaning cut across national boundaries. To be sure, the search was to be consummated in a ringing reaffirmation of such traditional values as freedom, democracy, and justice on the part of the Anglo–American nations, whereas among the Axis powers those values would be rejected as no longer valid. Instead, they would look for the establishment of a new order at home and abroad on alternative conceptual foundations. But the fact remains that the search for new meaning was a transnational phenomenon. In that sense, then, Japanese efforts in the 1930s to provide some ideological underpinnings for what they were doing abroad were not an isolated development. An international order based on the observance of the territorial status quo, arms control agreements, and the exchange of goods and capital appeared to have broken down, as had a domestic order that had sustained it. Cooperation, understanding, and 'other vacuous nouns are vain', an American scholar wrote in 1934.[18] Japanese (and, for that matter, German, British, and many other countries') writers could have readily agreed.

Out of this search for a new vocabulary, there steadily grew the acceptance of power in international (and domestic) affairs. Although power politics had always provided a basic definition of international relations, something was unique about its acceptance in the 1930s, for there was greater self-consciousness about it. This was because during the 1920s the emphasis had been on turning away from military power toward a vision of economic interdependence and political cooperation. Now, however, once again power appeared to be the key. It is easy to see this in the case of Japan or Germany, but one should also note that traditional geopolitics as a worthy conceptualisation made a comeback in America and Britain as well. That was why the alliance with the Soviet Union was so popular when it was formed in 1941. The Japanese and the Anglo–Americans were engaged in the same game that year, the game of geopolitics, when they both tried to entice the Soviets to side with one against the other. The Russians, on their part, played their cards well and ended up befriending both the Japanese and the Anglo–Americans, again for geopolitical reasons. (The Soviet decision in August 1945 to forsake the Japanese neutrality treaty and to go to war against the nearly defeated Japan was also a geopolitical one, and it is interesting to note that only in 1990, when principles such as justice and human rights are once again taken seriously in the world, have Soviet writers begun openly expressing their misgivings about the decision.[19])

I have elsewhere argued that the blurring of the distinction between war and peace was an important conceptual development of the 1930s.[20] 'The distinction between periods of peace and war is lost,' an economist at the University of Tokyo wrote.[21] There was no such thing as peace separate from war, or vice versa. This was because both were aspects of national development which was essentially 'spiritual' and 'cultural'. Though writers in the democratic countries hesitated to equate war with culture so easily, they, too, tended to see war and peace as much more organically linked than had been the custom. The fact that the wartime alliance, the United Nations, automatically became the postwar international organisation, also called the United Nations, is typical. As an American writer noted on the eve of Pearl Harbor, the worldwide anti-Axis alliance must continue to function after the war to promote cooperation in 'the economic and social fields' in order to 'organize the world'.[22] This was, at least in theory, little different from the Japanese view that fighting and reconstructing China must be undertaken simultaneously, or that war against the Anglo–American powers meant a more beneficial peace for the inhabitants of South-East Asia. No matter how self-deceptive such thinking was, one understands it better by putting it in a comparative, global context.

That, in conclusion, would be the value in studying the cultural aspect of Japanese foreign affairs. By raising the kinds of question this essay has enumerated, one becomes aware of global developments, not merely geo-politically or economically but also culturally. It does not mean that culture is always the key to foreign affairs. A knowledge of Japanese culture, for instance, does not necessarily enable one to predict the country's response to a specific foreign policy issue, any more than would be the case with other countries. Neither can it be said that two countries with a cultural affinity will not develop serious economic crises or even military conflicts. What the cultural approach does do is to sensitise us to human conscious-ness – aspirations, dreams, ambitions, prejudices. In a case of a country like Japan, whose external affairs were characterised by military strengthening, imperialism, and aggressive wars during the first half of its modern century, and then, quite abruptly, by economic growth without military involvement overseas during the next half century, the cultural approach should shed light on the question of continuities and discontinuities in the nation's dealings with others. Has Japan changed? What cultural factors have brought about the change? If the nation has changed little culturally, then how does one explain its contrasting behaviour before and after the Second World War? Should it be linked to the international environment? What have been the cultural forces in that environment that have tolerated a Japan playing an economic but not a military world? How have the Japanese themselves defined their country's position in the international system? Questions can be multiplied, and of course similar ones can be raised with respect to other countries. By examining them one comes to a better understanding of the forces that have made the world what it is.

NOTES

1. *Journal of American History*, vol. 77, no. 1, June 1990, pp. 100–1.
2. See James B. Crowley, *Japan's Quest for Autonomy*, (Princeton, 1966); Michael Barnhart, *Japan Prepares for Total War*, (Ithaca, 1986).
3. See Mark Peattie, *Ishiwara Kanji*, (Princeton, 1975).
4. Irie Akira, *Nijjuseiki no sensō to heiwa*, (War and peace in the twentieth century), (Tokyo, 1986), pp. 125–8.
5. Okuno Takeo et al. (eds), *Taiheiyo kaisen*, (The coming of war in the Pacific), (Tokyo, 1964), pp. 244–5.
6. *Chuokoron*, (Central Monthly), vol. 1, no. 8, August 1990, pp. 342–67.
7. Ibid., vol. 105, no. 9, September 1990, p. 360.
8. *Irie Sukemasa nikki*, (Irie Sukemasa diary), (Tokyo, 1990).
9. Ibid.
10. *JAH*, vol. 77, no. 1, p. 108.
11. *New Republic*.
12. See Akira Iriye, 'Toward a New Cultural Order: The Hsin-min Hui', in Akira Iriye (ed.), *The Chinese and the Japanese*, (Princeton, 1980), pp. 254–74.
13. Matsumoto Shigeharu, *Shanghai Jidai*, (The Shanghai years), (Tokyo, 1974–5).
14. *Yabe Teiji nikki*, (Yabe Teiji diary), (Tokyo, 1975); Maruyama Kumao, *Senkyuhyaku sanjunendai no Paris to watakushi*, (Paris and I in the 1930s), (Tokyo, 1986).
15. Reprinted in *Chuokoron*, vol. 104, no. 4, April 1989, p. 494.
16. A good source for the study of KBS activities is its monthly publication, *Kokusai bunka*, (International Culture).
17. Reinhold Niebuhr, *Reflections on the End of an Era*, (New York, 1934).
18. *Harper*, vol. 169 (August 1934), p. 268.
19. *Asahi*, 17 June 1990.
20. Akira Iriye, 'War as Peace, Peace as War', in Nobutoshi Hagihara et al. (eds), *Experiencing the Twentieth Century*, (Tokyo, 1985), pp. 31–54.
21. For a discussion of Japanese ideas of war and peace, see *Nijjuseiki no sensō to heiwa* (War and peace in the twentieth century; Tokyo, 1986), chap. 4.
22. *New Republic*, 105.8 (25 August 1941), p. 238.

5 An Absence of Change: Women in the Japanese Labour Force, 1937–45[1]

Janet Hunter

The part played by Japanese women in economic development has until recently received little attention from most economic historians of Japan. Writers on the war period, too, have given the bulk of their attention to technological, structural and institutional developments, and the ultimate inadequacy of raw materials, fuel, manpower and functioning machinery to sustain the prolonged campaign against the United States. Takafusa Nakamura has stressed the significance for postwar development of, for example, welfare measures, technological advances and labour skills, and the spread of subcontracting. With others, he has identified the control associations used by the state to coordinate private enterprise and achieve production targets as the forerunners of postwar industrial policy.[2] 'Patriotic' labour unions assisted the later dominance of the now famed company unions.[3] Likewise, the economic developments of 1937–45 were equally the product of earlier developments. The China and Pacific Wars, notwithstanding the prostration of the economy in August 1945, did not produce in Japan's economic history the dramatic discontinuity which some historians have identified as characterising developments in social or political history.

This paper is concerned to locate wartime female labour force participation patterns in the context of Japan's longer-term economic development, with the aim of shedding some light on to what the American historian, Thomas Havens, in a seminal article on women and war in Japan, called the 'relative persistence of prewar female work trends in Japan compared with her allies and enemies'.[4] The statement that one of the reasons for the inadequacy of the labour force was the need to resort to the increasing use of women, students and Koreans is often made without comment. There is no question that in as far as these groups often lacked the necessary skills and commitment for the tasks assigned to them, the quality of their work was seriously impaired. They also increasingly lacked physical strength – malnutrition was widespread by 1944. Labour productivity dropped rapidly during the last two years of the conflict not just for this reason, but also because of shortages of fuel and raw materials, and capital goods inadequacies. Yet policy-makers did not turn to adult women to sustain labour supply. Far greater dependence was placed on a policy of drafting school and university students, and bringing in workers from the colonies, especially Korea, whose inhabitants were not normally admitted to the ranks of the fighting forces.[5]

I

The National General Mobilisation Law, passed by the Diet in April 1938, some nine months after the start of full-scale hostilities with China, was the key legislation in the state's attempt to mobilise Japan's resources for war. The law gave the government sweeping powers to control all factors of production, effectively allowing the authorities carte blanche to arrogate to themselves whatever powers they deemed necessary at any stage during the emergency. A succession of regulations issued under the provisions of the law over subsequent years brought a growing element of compulsion in the mobilisation of labour, and mobilisation plans over successive years of the war increasingly looked to the female labour supply.[6] From 1939 onwards workers began to be pushed into 'essential' industries or banned from moving out of them. In November 1941, compulsory registration of labour for certain groups was introduced. Cabinet measures for future war planning in February 1944 included total student mobilisation. Much of this operation was poorly coordinated, however. Regulations were piecemeal, and the national labour mobilisation system was not synthesised into a single law until March 1945, only five months before Japan's surrender. Some women were affected by the restrictions and registration gave the state access to many more. Some were channelled from 'non-essential' industries, such as textiles, into the production of items such as aeroplanes, while others were frozen in their jobs. Protective legislation, for example that which prohibited night working by women, was suspended for the duration of the emergency, and as early as August 1939 the Welfare Ministry allowed women over twenty-five again to work underground in mines.[7] At the beginning of 1944 women were encouraged to form 'volunteer groups' (*teishintai*).[8] These succeeded the women's patriotic labour groups (*kinrō hōkokukai*), which had sought to employ married women on a part-time basis for up to six months, and had not been conspicuously successful. In the final stages of the war those between seventeen and forty years of age were organised into national militia units (*kokumin giyūtai*) with a view to defending Japanese soil to the last man or woman.[9]

Yet mobilisation of women, even of unmarried women, was never made compulsory, despite complaints of a labour shortage from before the onset of the Pacific War. A leader in the *Oriental Economist* in August 1941 talked of the need to cope with a shortage of labour, but made virtually no mention at all of the possibility of mobilising women.[10] In September 1943 the Conference of Vice-Ministers passed a resolution recognising that women were an underutilised workforce needed at a time of national crisis, and urging that means of tapping the supply should be investigated. Measures should include the investigation of areas of work 'especially suited to women's characteristics' in the priority industries such as aircraft manu-facture, as well as in government workshops and offices to replace drafted men, and in areas where male employment was now prohibited or restricted. Major groups to be targeted were new school graduates, unmarried girls over fourteen, and students in non-essential schools. Local organisations were enjoined to promote mobilisation, and businesses to ensure that measures were taken in the factories to accommodate women, for example by establishing separate washing facilities, giving special consideration for hours of work and holidays, and opening up greater chances of promotion.[11] In June 1944, *Outline Measures for the Reception of Women's Volunteer Corps* enjoined enterprises further to adapt themselves to receive these groups by improving working conditions (this included the provision of music to ease the burden of work), creating more women supervisors and providing better training.[12] By this time, however, resources were unavail-able to fulfil these requirements, and such central coordination and planning as had existed were rapidly disintegrating.

If we look at the number of women actually mobilised during the conflict, it is apparent that relatively fewer new women workers were brought into the labour force than was the case in Britain and the United States. Numbers of women in the labour force, their occupational distribution and the proportion of the labour force they made up are indicated in Tables 1–3. International comparison of the female share of the labour force is given in Table 4. The most detailed estimates in English on female labour force participation in Japan at this time are given in Jerome Cohen's *Japan's Economy in War and Reconstruction*.[13] One problem lies in the absence of comprehensive data for the eighteen months after February 1944, a period during which there was initially a substantial increase in mobilisation, and later a decline in the workforce through shortages, bombing, evacuation and other increasingly insurmountable problems. A widespread black market in labour from late 1944 exacerbated the problem, and the labour market was in chaos by the spring of 1945. The official statistics used by Cohen show that the female civilian labour force increased from 12.8 million in October 1940, to 14.0 million in February 1944, while civilian male labour remained more or less static at around 19.5 million. This marked an increase from women's share of the total civilian labour force from 39 per cent to 42 per cent. However, if one looks at the labour force as a whole, including those drafted into the armed forces, we find that in 1940 women were 37.3 per cent of the total labour force, and in 1944 still only 37.4 per cent, an insignificant increase. Mobilisation accelerated during the latter half of 1944, and Ministry of Welfare estimates suggest that in the year from March 1944, 1.4 million women entered the civilian labour force,[14] but numbers declined rapidly thereafter. The women's volunteer corps, the main vehicle of female mobilisation, comprised nearly 300 000 women by mid-1944,[15] but little more than 200 000 had been sent into industry – mostly armaments, aeroplane production and other manufacturing. Many of these 'volunteers' were new graduates, who were in any case likely to have entered the workforce. By March 1945, the number had risen to 472 000, but around half of these had been working elsewhere previously, and were not new additions to the workforce.[16] In theory all those registered (by 1945 all unmarried women of ages 12–39) were liable to be drafted as 'volunteers', but exemptions were many, and broad exclusions, such as of those who were 'the axis of the family', opened the way for many others.[17]

Table 5.1   Population and labour force, Japan proper (000s)

	October 1940		February 1944	
	Male	*Female*	*Male*	*Female*
Population	36 566	36 548	38 605	38 439
Labour force	21 424	12 753	23 395	14 012
Armed forces	1 694		3 980	
Civilian labour force	19 730	12 753	19 415	14 012

Source: J.B. Cohen, *Japan's Economy in War and Reconstruction* (Minneapolis, 1949), p. 288.

Table 5.2   Distribution of civilian labour force, per cent

| | October 1940 | | February 1944 | |
	Male	Female	Male*	Female
Agriculture and forestry	33.5	56.6	30.3	59.0
Fishing	2.4	0.5	2.1	0.6
Mining	2.7	0.6	3.1	1.0
Manufacturing and construction	31.3	15.3	39.3	17.0
Commerce	15.2	14.7	6.1	9.3
Communication and transport	6.2	1.2	7.5	2.0
Government and professional	7.7	5.3	10.3	7.6
Domestic service	0.2	5.3	0.3	3.1
Miscellaneous	0.8	0.5	0.4	0.4
Total	100.0	100.0	100.0	100.0

From: J.B. Cohen, *Japan's Economy in War and Reconstruction* (Minneapolis, 1949), pp. 288, 290.

Table 5.3   Distribution of female labour force, per cent

	1947*	1950*	1955
Agriculture and forestry	68.3	60.7	51.6
Fishing	0.8	0.5	0.9
Mining	0.8	0.5	0.3
Manufacturing and construction	11.9	12.8	14.7
Commerce	6.1	12.2	15.8
Communications and transport	1.6	1.5	1.6
Service industries	8.2	10.2	13.7
Government and professional	1.4	1.6	1.4
Miscellaneous	1.1	0.1	0.0
Total	100.0	100.0	100.0

Source: Takenaka Emiko, *Sengo Joshi Rōdō Shiron* (Tokyo 1989), p. 173 (amended).

*Columns do not add precisely, due to rounding.

Table 5.4 Female share of labour force, per cent

	Japan	Britain	Germany	United States
1920	37.6	29.5 [1921]		20.4
1925			35.9	
1930	35.7	29.8 [1931]		21.9
1933			35.5	
1939			37.1[a]	
1940	37.3[b]		40.0[a]	25.8[a]
1943	37.4[b] [1944]	38.8[a]	40.5[a]	34.1[a]
1947	38.1			38.6[a]
1950	38.7	30.8 [1951]		30.0[a]
1955	39.1			
1957				33.0[a]
1960		33.5		

[a] As percentage of total civilian labour force.
[b] As percentage of total labour force, including armed forces.

Sources: J.B. Cohen, *Japan's Economy in War & Reconstruction* (Minneapolis, 1949), p. 288; P. Summerfield, *Women Workers in the Second World War* (London, 1984) p. 196; L. Rupp, *Mobilising Women for War* (Princeton, 1978) pp. 185–6; Deutsche Institut für Wirtschaftsforschung, *Die Deutsche Industrie im Kriege 1939–45* (Berlin, 1954), p. 139.

II

A. J. Grajdanzev, a US expert on Asian economies, noted in mid-1943 that the mobilisation of women 'is only being postponed until all male labour power is absorbed,[18] but clearly the authorities had a considerable reluctance to introduce a greater degree of compulsion in the mobilisation of women. More than anything else, this lack of compulsion stemmed from a reluctance to infringe the 'domestic' status of women. Official propaganda and social conservatism had for many years acted to promote the role of women as pre-eminently that of wife and mother. This social role had become ideologically integrated into the overall socio-political ideology of the Japanese state, which made any infringement potentially undermining of this ideology. Under the banner of army influence in politics motherhood in particular became an object of sanctity. To become *gunkoku no haha* (mother of the military nation) was depicted as the height of a woman's aspirations, and certificates were presented to those who produced the most children, stating that their recipient 'has made a significant contribution to the nurturing of the nation'.[19] If the children were boys who would be future soldiers and rulers of the empire, so much the better. That such considerations were important in decisions relating to the mobilisation of women is abundantly apparent from contemporary comments and justifications, and that the policy remained unchanged despite the severe shortage of labour in time of war supports the contention still further.

Wartime Japan's attempts to reconcile the widespread emphasis on women's domestic role with the economy's need for women's labour are suggested in a piece by the influential writer Kikuchi Kan, published in 1940, in which he argued that women were not being appropriately educated in the areas such as cooking and cleanliness required for their marital vocation. However, argued Kikuchi,

> Marriage is not a place of refuge for women who are tired of making their own living . . . Many modern men want working girls for wives so that they can work together. This is not because men have lost the grit to support their wives, but because economic conditions of modern society have made such cooperation necessary in order to maintain a decent living.[20]

Official statements spoke of the importance of bearing in mind the traditional family system of the country and the 'special characteristics' of women, which necessitated that in mobilisation there had to be particular 'adherence to public morality, elevation of character and attention to such things as health'.[21] The *Outline Measures for the Receipt of Women's Volunteers Corps* of June 1944, mentioned above, enjoined employers of such groups to give them at least two hours' instruction per week to aid 'the development of the special character of women and womanly virtues'.[22] Maki Kenichi, Director of the Bureau of Health of the Imperial Rule Assistance Association, wrote of the importance of not allowing work to undermine women's major task of procreation and augmentation of the Japanese race.[23] Professor Minoguchi Tokijirō of Hitotsubashi University commented that the major obstacle in using women in manufacturing was taking them away from family life, which was liable to promote later marriage and more widespread use of contraceptive measures in a Japan where population increase had to be a priority.[24] Certainly, the power of the domestic lobby is suggested by a resolution passed in the summer of 1939 by the most influential national federation of women's associations, entitled 'Women, Go Back to the Home', which complained that more and more women had other tasks which caused them to neglect their household duties, meaning that they could never be good wives and mothers. Criticism of this resolution by an influential 'progressive' magazine is indicative of a conflict between ideals of domesticity and labour force participation which had long existed, and which was now becoming more acute under pressure of war.

> This meaningless movement is eloquent evidence of the problem facing all Japanese women today – how to adjust and harmonize domestic duties with outside work, either at an office or a factory. The resolution is said to have been inspired by similar action in Germany, but such imitation without investigation seems indeed a thoughtless move on the part of the women advocating it. Those words – "Women, Go Back to the Home!" – somehow carry weight and sound logical. Coming from an influential women's organization, they may become an effective appeal to the women of the nation regardless of the present situation.[25]

Havens, writing in 1975, also acknowledged that the fact that 'nearly everyone in wartime Japan from military oligarchs on down appeared to hold static psychocultural views about the place of women in society . . . to some degree inhibited the state from legally requiring the services of all women as a part of its general national labour policy'.[26] He makes quite clear, however, that 'patriarchal officials' should not be blamed for the minimal rise in Japanese women's employment. Rather, it should be seen in the context of overall labour mobilisation policy, with its dependence on re-assignment from non-essential industries and voluntary inducements. In fact, only 1.5 million men were conscripted for civilian labour between 1939 and 1945. Cohen attributes the lack of compulsory conscription to 'the traditional aversion of upper-class women in Japan to industrial work', the fact that 'the upper class with prejudice against factory labour did not support the public opinion that women also should be conscripted to war production'. Greater emphasis on student mobilisation, said Cohen, 'was due to the traditional social stigma which in Japan attracted to women who worked, most of whom, in the past, had come from the poorer rural groups'.[27]

III

Ideology, self-interest and the deficiencies of the planning mechanism, however, are not in themselves adequate fully to understand the shifts in Japanese women's occupation patterns during the war years, or, rather, the relative absence of such shifts. Wartime mobilisation has to be seen in the longer-term context of broader factors operative in the labour market and the overall degree of industrialisation of the Japanese economy. The factors which are of concern to us here are the highly labour-intensive nature of the more traditional sectors of the economy, the continuing importance of the agricultural sector in the Japanese economy until well into the post-1945 era, and the relationship between movements in male and female labour.

That Japan was suffering a *de facto* labour shortage by the latter years of the war is widely acknowledged. Despite sporadic warnings earlier on, it only began to be officially acknowledged late in 1942, when Japan had already been at war for five years. Concern at the economic problems stemming from a protracted conflict had been submerged in the euphoria of the six months following Pearl Harbor. In Japan, and abroad, it was assumed that the country as a whole was in a position of abundant labour, and that absolute shortages would never be a problem. One writer in 1938, having visited an athletics display, commented, 'The mere sight of these young sports fans will serve to reassure the observer of Japan's abundant reserves of man-power apart from her large army now fighting in China'.[28]

Later commentators believed that this perspective continued to influence policymakers for much of the war. Cohen, writing in 1949, spoke of the basic assumption of Japan's having a plethora of labour,[29] and an article in the *International Labour Review* took a similar view the same year.[30] By 1941, though, there was no reserve of adult unemployed.[31] Through a combination of inefficiency and intransigence on the part of the civilian and military authorities, an acute shortage of skilled labour occurred, as skilled workers were indiscriminately drafted into the armed forces and insufficient training given to those who replaced them. This left industry ill-equipped to maintain existing production levels, let alone sustain the desired expansion in war-related production.

This labour shortage was at least in part a function of the inefficient methods still predominating in the primary sector, in farming, fishing and mining, and in commerce, which remained dominated by small-scale retail establishments, many of them family businesses. These sectors still accounted for a very substantial part of the working population, though contributing proportionately less to the nation's wealth.[32] The agricultural sector, dominated by its small family farms, was highly labour-intensive. In this sector, it was said, 'human labour counts more than machinery'.[33] Moreover, even the manufacturing sector was far from consisting exclusively of large-scale operations. Medium and small enterprises, many employing fewer than ten people, accounted for a substantial part of output and proportionately more of the manufacturing workforce. In 1939 well under half of all workers in metals, machinery and chemical production worked in plants of over 500 workers, and in foodstuff production it was only 3 per cent.[34] At the peak of production in October 1944, plants of up to 49 workers accounted for half of the million or so working in Tokyo, and even more elsewhere.[35] Many of these smaller plants were less mechanised and less efficient in terms of labour productivity than larger enterprises, though they had been given a new lease of life by the spread of electric motors over the preceding two decades. Many were not directly geared to war production, but produced essential consumer goods. Some small plants acted as feeders for larger ones, but the US Bombing Survey noted that their importance should not be exaggerated.[36] War production required overwhelmingly expansion in the large scale sector of manufacturing, but although some small enterprises were integrated into large-scale production through a system of subcontracting, this very subcontracting relationship with large companies, as well as the frequent lack of competition between small and large enterprises in terms of product, made a shift of labour out of the less productive into the more productive operations far from easy. Of importance, too, were household industries, many of which did not even qualify as 'small' enterprises. Domestic production of a variety of commodities either for direct sale or for middlemen, such as of chopsticks, matches and knick-knacks for export, had been undertaken on a considerable scale both by urban families and as rural by-employment throughout the 1930s. While much of this activity dried up for want of raw materials and markets after Pearl Harbor, its labour was not necessarily, nor easily, released into the modern sector, and as capital shortages in the war industries caused manufacturers to demand still more of their workers the pressure on available workers increased.[37]

Overall, the so-called 'traditional' sectors of the Japanese economy, which remained of huge importance throughout the war years, were engaged in highly labour intensive operations, and absorbed a quantity of labour far in excess of their contribution to output. The important point in respect of this discussion, though, is that it is these sectors which already employed substantial numbers of women. If we look at the distribution of the female labour force within the economy, we find that women accounted for well over half the agricultural labour force, and a very considerable proportion of those engaged in commercial activity (in 1940 55 per cent of workers in the service industries, and 36 per cent of those in retailing and finance[38]). Homeworkers were almost exclusively women. Such occupations were easier to combine with childcare and domestic activities than was factory work, and were dominated by married women. These sectors could only be made more efficient by substantial capital outlay or enforced rationalisation, or, in the case of those occupations deemed non-essential, wound down by depriving them of raw materials or other means. Many enforced mergers did, in fact, take place, and the number of workers employed in small enterprises decreased dramatically. For example, by August 1945, plants of up to 49 workers accounted for under 30 per cent of the Tokyo labour force, compared with around 50 per cent a year earlier.[39] However, the married women who accounted for a major part of the labour force in these small enterprises were, by their very status, exempt from the attempts to mobilise the female workforce more effectively, and were, if anything, more likely to replace their male colleagues who could be forcibly drawn off into other sectors. Thus a large number of women workers were already tied up in inefficient sectors which could not easily be run down or made more efficient, and remained so.

Closely connected with the point made above, we need to take into account the size of the agricultural sector in wartime Japan. The agricultural sector still accounted for 44 per cent of Japan's working population in 1940, although it contributed only 18.8 per cent of GNP.[40] It was increasingly worked by women,[41] and although there was no systematic policy to take the majority of conscripts from the countryside and exempt skilled male workers in essential industries, women's predominance in agriculture increased as some men were drafted into the armed forces. Where men were drafted, many women found themselves engaged on a full-time basis in what had hitherto been just part of their domestic duties. Some of these women, like many of their counterparts in small-scale peasant agriculture in other countries, had never appeared fully in the official statistics. Other farming women, who had previously been registered as engaging in handicraft production (i.e. manufacturing), were not necessarily released for factory production by the decline of their by-employment, but turned back to cultivation.

The state, realising the importance of the agricultural sector for the food requirements of the empire, and in particular for the Japanese islands, manifested an undiminishing concern with maintaining the agricultural labour force. It recognised that 'the duties of the women of the agricultural districts are of the greatest importance because of the fact that their menfolk have been called to the colours in large numbers'.[42] It did what it could to support women's agricultural activity, organising task forces to help at harvest time, promoting village groups to assist widowed women and those whose husbands were away at the front, and providing childcare to release them for agricultural work. However, as the war progressed it became more and more difficult to replenish supplies of fertiliser, repair tools, secure high quality strains of seeds or organise the seasonal requirements of manpower so essential to paddy rice production, particularly where heavy work was concerned. Workers were rendered increasingly less capable through inadequate nutrition, and with the majority of the workforce burdened by motherhood and other domestic responsibilities, agricultural labour became less and less productive. More women became involved in producing less food. Women were 52 per cent of the agricultural labour force in 1940, and 58 per cent in 1944. Nearly 600 000 more women were working in agriculture than four years earlier.[43] Their predominance grew even more in 1944–5. Significantly, agriculture, forestry and fishing accounted for a greater proportion of the total civilian labour force in 1944 than they had done in 1940, and that civilian labour had shrunk in absolute numbers.[44]

It thus appears that much of the growth in the female labour force that did occur was being directed toward the agricultural sector, and such was the size of this sector that it was absorbing most of the additional labour which could be drawn into the workforce without further degrees of compulsion. Meanwhile, in the urban sector, munitions, capital goods and peacetime industries were competing with each other for the available, limited supply of non-agricultural labour, and, given a choice, most girls would work in a department store rather than an aircraft factory or a mine. One writer remarked in July 1939, that the demand for female employees was increasing all round. Department stores were forced to readvertise vacancies, and to take primary-school, as opposed to secondary-school graduates.[45] A Western commentator on Japan's energy shortage in early 1940, nearly two years before the onset of war with the United States, mentioned the problems mines had in securing female labour, because women were offered more attractive jobs elsewhere.[46]

A characteristic of Japan's retention of a substantial agricultural sector, then, was that the overall participation rate of women in the economy, particularly of married women, was already high, allowing much less leeway to bring unoccupied women into production. Essentially, this is a further facet of the ways in which the relative lack of development of the industrial sector in Japan, by comparison with countries such as Britain, the United States and Germany, posed a fundamental obstacle to the country's ability to sustain a prolonged conflict. With pressure to marry and produce a large family stronger than ever before, and married women considered more 'exempt' from war work except in agriculture, the war industries were faced with a limited pool of unmarried women upon whom they felt they could justifiably call – hence the growing dependence on students and schoolchildren, who donned work-trousers (*monpe*) and *hinomaru* (rising sun) headbands over their sailor suits and were set to work.

The development of heavy industries in the 1930s had been primarily dependent on men moving out of agriculture and women increasingly taking their place. Higher industry/agriculture wage differentials for men had contributed to men's accounting for a far greater proportion of the factory labour force at the end of the decade than at the beginning. Development studies have suggested that in industrialising economies women tend to become concentrated in the 'traditional' sectors, including agriculture, and Japan is no exception to this. Throughout the decade of the 1930s female dominance of the agricultural workforce was gradually increasing, and this trend continued and even accelerated under the pressures of male conscription. Some agricultural men were conscripted directly into the armed forces, while many others were drafted into industry to help its expansion or to replace their conscripted colleagues. They, in turn, were replaced by women. Ministry of Agriculture and Forestry officials estimated the movement of farm labour into industry between July 1937 and February 1944 as 1.3 million men and only 650 000 women.[47] The increase in female manufacturing workers which did occur came to a substantial degree from redirected urban labour. In particular the textile industry was dramatically scaled down, with the redirection of over 80 000 workers.[48] Theatres were compulsorily closed in March 1944, and about 40 000 entertainers were drafted;[49] countless others were sent to 'comfort' troops at the front. Overall, though, the industrial expansion of the 1930s had depended largely on the flow out of agriculture of male labour, which in its turn was replaced by female labour. The draft reinforced this chain of flow. After the end of the war, when demobilisation, repatriation and the destruction of productive capacity promoted a substantial flow of labour back into the countryside, women lost out disproportionately in the shrunken manufacturing sector, but in the agricultural sector, too, their numerical dominance was initially reduced. However, the importance of agricultural work in women's employment rose dramatically, far exceeding that of men (see Table 5.3). This reversal of previous trends, however, was little more than a temporary 'blip' in a longer-term process. When the expanding manufacturing sector of the Korean War period began to reclaim some of the 'surplus' agricultural population, women again lagged behind men in being drawn into non-agricultural employment. While the average female wage in agriculture remained at around 80 per cent of the average male wage in agriculture throughout the 1950s, the differential in manufacturing was actually growing at the end of the decade, giving women a greater incentive than men to remain in the rural sector. When continuing high rates of growth and increased demand for labour began to reduce male:female wage differentials in manufacturing in the early 1960s, the flow of women out of agriculture accelerated.[50]

IV

Notwithstanding complaints of an overall labour shortage, there was a lesser flow of women into war work in Japan than was the case in Britain and the United States during World War II, though proportionately more women were mobilised than in Germany during those years. In both Germany and Japan ideological factors appear to have impeded the regimes' mobilisation of women, but it has been suggested here that longer term economic factors also played a major part in Japan. Significantly, Germany, too, had a substantial agricultural sector, which accounted for about 30 per cent of the labour force in 1944, and in which women by far outnumbered men.[51] Even in Britain and the United States, though, the flow of women into war work did not necessarily bring long-run change. Recent research into women's work in Britain during the Second World War has emphasised the longer-term continuity in patterns of women's labour force participation. It has been suggested that in Britain, as well as in the United States and Germany war failed to act as a social revolution for women.[52] Gail Braybon's study of British women in the First World War, though less concerned with economic development, highlights 'the remarkable consistency of male attitudes towards women's work, even in the exceptional time of the war'.[53] This consistency in attitudes of both men and women clearly continued to exert an important influence on the way in which women operated in the labour market.

In Japan, too, the participation of women in the labour market was not fundamentally altered by the wartime experience, which neither improved their conditions, nor enhanced their position in the market. Women workers in the wartime years were not paid more, nor were they given new opportunities of skill training or promotion, whatever economic rationale and national need might have dictated. The differential between male and female wages in manufacturing was marginally narrowed, but the average female manufacturing worker during the conflict still earned less than half the wage received by her male colleague.[54] The few critics who argued that it was courting national disaster for industrialists to argue at a time of crisis against training women workers in order to hold down their wages went largely unheeded. Problems with equipment, raw materials and shortage of skilled workers led Japanese manufacturers to make increasing demands on their labour force, but to have given women workers more training would have provoked demands for higher pay, and many employers feared changing their attitude to women workers would open a dangerous door. One 'patriotic' feminist commented that:

Capital not only attempts by means of cheap female labour to offset the diminution of its profits under national control, but would also use it as a provision against bad times, since female workers can be dismissed with less fear of their making a strong demand for a high dismissal allowance . . . Women are not innately incapable of training and intelligent understanding, but the aim of the industrialists is the dual one of making them efficient and at the same time to keep their wage value down to the lowest level.[55]

Ironically, the same writer stated that it was inappropriate to expect women's wages in the agricultural sector, where women workers were essentially supplementing the family income, to determine women's industrial wages, where conditions comparable to those which determined male industrial wages were operating.[56]

Women's participation in the labour force, too, shows little indication of substantive change. The war years accelerated some existing trends, like the flow of male labour out of agriculture, with its knock-on effects on women. Other existing features of women's participation, like the concentration of women in the traditional sectors of the economy, with their high labour intensity and low per capita productivity, impaired the ability of the authorities to mobilise women effectively, while their ideology kept them back from compulsion. Moreover, unlike Britain in World War I, increased women's participation generated no movements for political change or legal equality. There seemed to be no need for them. The radical political reforms brought by the Occupation seemed all that the most ardent feminists could want, and truly revolutionary to the majority of Japanese women. Among the starvation, poverty and abject misery of the early postwar years, equal employment opportunities were a very low priority. Any job was worth having. For Japanese women workers, therefore, the main significance of the war years lay in the additional burden which it placed upon them in conjunction with the very absence of change in their position in the workforce.

NOTES

1. An earlier version of this paper was given at a seminar at Manchester University. My thanks are due to those who made helpful comments (not all of which, I suspect, I acted upon!), and to Alan Milward for assistance with data on women in the German labour force during World War II.

2. T. Nakamura, *The Postwar Japanese Economy* (Tokyo, 1981), pp. 14–20.
3. A. Gordon, *The Evolution of Labour Relations in Japan: Heavy Industry 1853–1955*, (Cambridge, Mass., 1985), pp. 257–327.
4. T. R. H. Havens, 'Women and War in Japan, 1937–1945', *American Historical Review*, vol. 80, no. 4, October 1975, p. 919.
5. Japanese works on labour in the wartime period include Ōhara Shankai Mondai Kenkyujo, *Taiheiyō Sensōka no Rōdōsha Jōtai*, special edition of *Nihon Rōdō nenkan* (Tokyo, 1964); E. Takenaka, 'Kyōkō to Sensōka ni okeru Rōdō Shijo no Henbo, in I. Kawai et al., (eds), *Kyōkō kara Sensō e*, vol. 3 of *Kōza Nihon Shihonshugi Hattatsu Shiron* (Tokyo, 1968). However, one of the most comprehensive works on Japan's economy in this period in either language remains J. B. Cohen, *Japan's Economy in War and Reconstruction* (Minneapolis, 1949), which includes a substantive chapter on developments in the labour market.
6. For a full account of the development of labour mobilisation policy as it related to women, see J. B. Cohen, *Japan's Economy in War and Reconstruction*, pp. 271–352; also T. R. H. Haven's 'Women and War in Japan', pp. 916–27. The text of the National General Mobilisation of Law is in R. Akamatsu (ed.), *Nihon Fujin Mondai Shiryō Shūsei*, vol. 3, *Rōdō* (Tokyo, 1977), pp. 469–75.
7. ILO, 'A Survey of Economic and Social Conditions in Japan', *International Labour Review*, vol. LX, no. 1, July 1949, p. 9. Underground work for women had been prohibited since 1933, but the extent of exemptions had permitted its continuation in many smaller mines (R. Mathias, 'Mit Kohlenschlitten und Spitzhacke – Frauenarbeit im japanischen Kohlenbergbau', *Der Anschnitt*, vol. 42, no. 2, 1990, pp. 78–9).
8. Onnatchi no Shōwa Shi Henshū Iinkai, *Shashinshū Onnatachi no Shōwa Shi* (Tokyo, 1986), p. 55.
9. Ōhara Shankai Mondai Kenkyujo, *Taiheiyō Sensōka no Rōdōsha Jōtai*, p. 14.
10. 'Labour in Time of War', *Oriental Economist*, vol. VIII, no. 8 August 1941, p. 404.
11. 'Joshi Kinrō Dōin no Sokushin ni kansuru Ken', *Nihon Fujin Mondai Shiryō Shūsei*, pp. 478–80.
12. 'Joshi Teishintai Ukeiregawa Sochi Yōkō', issued by the Council of Vice Ministers, 21 June 1944, and reproduced in *Nihon Fujin Mondai Shiryō Shūsei*, pp. 481–4.
13. More recent work in Japan has produced T. Nakamura and K. Arai, 'Taiheiyō Sensōki ni okeru Yūgyō Jinkō no Suikei: 1940–1947', in *Shakaigaku Kiyō*, no. 27, but I have relied on Cohen's data here.
14. J. B. Cohen, *Japan's Economy in War and Reconstruction*, p. 288.
15. 'Joshi Teishintai no Kessei, Shukkin, Ukeire Jōkyō', *Nihon Fujin Mondai Shiryō Shūsei*, p. 487.
16. T. R. H. Havens, 'Women and War in Japan', p. 922.
17. 'Joshi Teishin Kinrō Rei', *Nihon Fujin Mondai Shiryō Shūsei*, p. 486.
18. A. J. Grajdanzev, 'Japan's Economy Since Pearl Harbour', pt. II, *Far Eastern Survey*, vol. 12, no. 13, June 1943, p. 129.
19. Onnatchi no Shōwa Shi Henshū Iinkai, *Shashinshū Onnatchi no Shōwa Shi*, p. 47.

20. K. Kikuchi, 'Women and Marriage', *Contemporary Japan*, vol. 9, no. 1, January 1940, p. 58.

21. 'Joshi Kinrō Dōin no Sokushin ni kansuru Ken', *Nihon Fujin Mondai Shiryō Shūsei*, p. 479.

22. 'Joshi Teishintai Ukeiregawa Sochi Yōkō', *Nihon Fujin Mondai Shiryō Shūsei*, p. 482.

23. K. Maki, 'Kinrō Bosei Hogo', *Nihon Fujin Mondai Shiryō Shūsei*, p. 489.

24. T. Minoguchi, 'Joshi Dōin Ron', originally published in Kaizō, vol. 25, no. 3, reprinted in *Nihon Fujin Mondai Shiryō Shūsei*, p. 493.

25. I. Tsubokawa, 'Women Back to the Home?', originally published in the journal *Kakushin*, translated in *Contemporary Japan*, vol. 8, no. 4, June 1939.

26. T. R. H. Havens, 'Women and War in Japan', p. 916.

27. J. B. Cohen, *Japan's Economy in War and Reconstruction, pp.* 273, 320, 324.

28. H. Aragaki, 'Japan's Home Front', *Contemporary Japan*, vol. 7, no. 2, September 1938, p. 289.

29. J. B. Cohen, *Japan's Economy in War and Reconstruction*, p. 271.

30. 'A Survey of Economic and Social Conditions in Japan', *International Labour Review*, vol. LX, no. 1, July 1949.

31. United States Strategic Bombing Survey, *Effects of Strategic Bombing on Japan's War Economy*, (Washington, 1946), p. 31.

32. In 1940 the primary and tertiary sectors together accounted for 73 per cent of the employed population (Y. Andō (ed.), *Kindai Nihon Keizaishi Yoran* (Tokyo, 1975), p. 6), but only 52 per cent of net domestic product (Ohkawa Kazushi et al. (eds), *Long Term Economic Statistics of Japan*, vol. 1, *National Income* (Tokyo, 1974), p. 202.

33. H. Aragaki, 'Japan's Home Front', p. 294.

34. Y. Andō, *Kindai Hihon Keizaishi Yōran*, p. 119.

35. US Strategic Bombing Survey, *Effects on the Urban Economy* (Washington, 1946), p. 29.

36. Ibid.

37. T. Watanabe, 'Wartime Industry and Female Labour', *Contemporary Japan*, vol. 8, no. 3, May 1939, p. 364.

38. Y. Andō, *Kindai Nihon Keizaishi Yōran*, p. 5.

39. US Bombing Survey, *Effects on the Urban Economy*, p. 29, Y. Ando, *Kindai Nihon Keizaishi Yoran*, p. 134, gives a table showing firm mergers 1940–43, which shows the accelerating pace of company amalgamations.

40. Y. Ando, *Kindai Nihon Keizaishi Yōran*, p. 6; Ohkawa et al., (eds), *Long Term Economic Statistics*. vol. 1, p. 202.

41. Since 1936 more women than men had worked in the agricultural sector (J. Hunter, 'Women's Labour Force Participation in Interwar Japan', *Japan Forum*, vol. 2, no. 1, April 1990, p. 110.

42. T. Miyao, 'Our Women in the Emergency', *Contemporary Japan*, vol. 8, no. 5, July 1939, p. 648.

43. J. B. Cohen, *Japan's Economy in War and Reconstruction*, p. 293.

44. US Strategic Bombing Survey, *Effects of Strategic Bombing upon Japan's War Economy*, p. 31.

45. T. Miyao, 'Our Women in the Emergency', p. 648.

46. K. Bloch, 'Coal and Power Shortage in Japan', *Far East Survey*, vol. 9, no. 4, 1940.

47.   The flow of labour out of agriculture is discussed in Ohara Shankai Mondai Kenkyujo, *Taiheiyō Sensōka no Rōdōsha Jōtai*, pp. 166ff.
48.   In fact it was argued that this process went too far. See J. B. Cohen, *Japan's Economy in War and Reconstruction*, p. 390.
49.   Ibid., p. 281.
50.   M. Umemura et al. (eds), *Long Term Economic Statistics of Japan*, vol. 9, *Agriculture and Forestry* (Tokyo, 1966), p. 221; T. Blumenthal, 'Scarcity of Labour and Wage Differentials in the Japanese Economy 1958–1964', in R. Kosobud and R. Minami, (eds), *Econometric Studies of Japan* (Urbana, Ill., 1977), p. 162.
51.   The situation in Germany is made more complex by the large number of non-Germans used in the labour force during the war years, but women accounted for 54.5 per cent of all Germans in agriculture in 1939, and 65.4 per cent by 1944 (US Strategic Bombing Survey, *The Effects of Strategic Bombing on the German War Economy* (Washington, 1945), p. 202; Deutsche Institut für Wirtschaftforschung, *Die Deutsche Industrie im Kriege, 1939–45* (Berlin, 1954), p. 139.
52.   P. Summerfield, *Women Workers in the Second World War* (London, 1984), pp. 185ff; L. Rupp, *Mobilising Women for War: German and American Propaganda 1939–1945* (Princeton, 1978), p. 181.
53.   G. Braybon, *Women Workers in the First World War: the British Experience* (London, 1981), p. 11.
54.   Ōhara Shankai Mondai Kenkyujo, *Taiheiyō Sensōka no Rōdōsha Jōtai*, pp. 68–9.
55.   T. Watanabe, 'Wartime Industry and Female Labour', *Contemporary Japan*, vol. 8, no. 3, May 1939, pp. 366, 368. Takenaka Emiko, ('Kyōkō to Sensōka niokeru Rōdō Shijō no Henbō', p. 305) cites a similar criticism by the contemporary feminist, Tanno Setsu.
56.   T. Watanabe, 'Wartime Industry and Female Labour', p. 368.

6 Wartime Japanese Planning: A Note on Akira Iriye

Louis Allen

In July 1979, the Imperial War Museum hosted an Anglo–Japanese conference, sponsored by the British Academy and the British National Committee for the History of the Second World War. The title 'on the history of the Second World War' – was somewhat deceptive, since most of the papers were concerned with diplomatic relations between Britain and Japan in the 1920s and 1930s, postwar planning and postwar relations. Professor Nish edited the English version of the papers, which appeared under the title *Anglo–Japanese Alienation 1919–1952*,[1] while the Japanese version, edited by Professor Hosoya Chihiro, was entitled simply *Nichi-Ei Kankei-shi* (The history of Anglo–Japanese relations) 1917–1949.[2]

It may be of some anecdotal interest to recall that this was not the first time such a conference had taken place. In the immediate aftermath of the Japanese surrender, XII Army Command in Burma held a conference between British generals and their staffs still in the Burma area, with the Japanese commanders on the other side. The British side was led by General (later Sir) Hugh Stockwell, GOC 82 West African Division, and the Japanese side by the former GOC Burma Area Army, General Kimura Hyōtarō, who had with him Lt-General Sakurai Shōzō (28 Army), Lt-General Honda Masaki (33 Army), and a number of divisional commanders. They met in February 1946 in a lecture theatre in the Rangoon University buildings which served as XII Army HQ, just as they had served the Japanese Burma Area Army GHQ until April 1945. The interpreter was a civilian, a Mr Saito who had already acted in that role during the surrender parleys of August and September 1945. Lt-Colonel McLachlan, GSO1 of XII Army, acted as major-domo, summoning in the Japanese generals, who took their seats behind a long table facing tiered rows of British officers under the benign surveillance of General Stockwell. It was a fairly formal occasion, the questions having been compiled beforehand and answers prepared. XII Army issued a bulletin of the questions, and the answers later formed another such bulletin which, like the SEATIC bulletins of 1945 and 1946 based on interrogations of Japanese officers elsewhere in South-East

Asia, served as the basis for many later accounts, and for Mount-batten's *Report*. At the end, although Brigadier E. F. E. Armstrong (Briga-dier, General Staff, XII Army) warned the assembled British officers to be circumspect in what they said to the Japanese, since some of the latter might in the event be arraigned for war crimes, General Stockwell, with character-istic decent human feeling, could not forbear to stand up and express the thanks of the British side to the Japanese generals for their willingness to answer questions. The great gap on the Japanese side was, of course, Lt-General Mutaguchi Renya, former GOC 15 Army, who had returned to Japan under a cloud long before, and who was to upset conventional wisdom on the Burma campaign twenty years later[3] in answer to enquiries by a British military historian, Lt-Colonel A. J. Barker, then writing *March on Delhi*.[4]

Brigadier Armstrong was right in one case: General Kimura, who had been Vice-Minister for War 1941–44, was arraigned as a Class A war criminal by the International Military Tribunal for the Far East in Tokyo, was found guilty and hanged in Sugamo Prison on 23 December 1948. The other generals were put in charge of various labour units made up from their former divisions and distributed round Burma until they were repatriated, most of them in 1947.

The conference was an interesting glimpse of the hitherto incompre-hensible enemy, face to face. It did not reveal any great secrets, nor, at that time, could it have been expected to. The crucial effect on the Burma campaign, for instance, of the fundamental disagreement between Mutaguchi and Satō, on how to conduct the Kohima battle, was something from which the Japanese needed to distance themselves in times before discussion, let alone evaluation. But on the tactical level, the answers were both informative and detailed, and the enthusiastic interest shown by the Japanese side is an indication of the powerful impact upon their minds of the Burma campaign, the importance of which is regularly undervalued by those who regard the conflict in the Far East as purely a 'Pacific War', waged by the Americans against the Japanese. No one, for instance, reading much of the US historiography on the subject, or those Japanese writings based on it, would suspect that it was in the battles for Imphal that the Japanese army sustained the greatest defeat in its history.

During the 1979 conference, Professor Akira Iriye, Professor of History at the University of Chicago, presented a paper on 'Wartime Japanese Planning for Postwar Asia.' Based mainly on Japanese sources such as *Shūsen shiroku, Sugiyama Memo,* and *Haisen no kiroku,* he claimed that there was 'little or no planning for "postwar" Asia'. There was, of course, planning for the administration of occupied areas, but in this as in much else there was a 'rift between military strategists with no interest in the future and civilians who were trying to formulate some definition of war and peace objectives.' Later in the war, attempts to make piecemeal concessions to Nationalist China and Russia in pursuit of chimeras of a separate peace modified the details of a new order in East Asia. Russia's intervention, and the war's speedy end, destroyed that order forever; or at least the military version of it. The note that follows is an extended comment on Professor Iriye's paper, in which the original conference format survives, though one or two more recent references have been added.

Professor Iriye's paper is both trenchant and sophisticated, as one would expect from him. It also bears an interesting relationship to Professor Thorne's,[5] since both of them appear to indicate that there was little on either side which might be termed postwar planning in the strict sense. On the British side, divided counsels and the pressure, implicit or explicit, of American interests, hampered clear-cut thinking on how the British Empire, lost to the Japanese in 1942, could be restored; on the Japanese side, the awareness that the postwar world would *not* be a world moulded by Japanese desires inhibited forward thinking beyond a certain point.

Yet those of us who spent the formative years of our lives translating endless wodges of Japanese plans of one kind and another will need convincing that there was, as Professor Iriye claims at the start of his paper, 'little or no wartime Japanese planning for "postwar" Asia.'[6] No doubt there is no real disagreement between us. It is largely a question of vocabulary. Plans there were, in plenty, as a glance at the administrative regulations for some of the occupied territories clearly shows: the dispositions of occupied Burma, for instance, reproduced as an appendix of historical documents to Ōta Tsunezō's *Biruma ni okeru Nihon gunseishi no kenkyū* (Tokyo, 1967)[7] which occupy nearly a hundred pages of text; or the documents relating to the government of the East Indies, including the very tardy and unwilling preparations for independence, published by Waseda University in 1958, *Indonesia ni okeru Nihon gunsei no kenkyu,* which Harry Benda made available in English as *Japanese Military Administration in Indonesia: Selected Documents* (Translation Series No. 6, Southeast Asia Studies, Yale University, 1965).

Professor Iriye is, of course, well aware of these, and has anticipated my comment by pointing out that the Japanese were preoccupied with the course of the war and only made plans for instant use, for military purposes. There is a presumption behind this which I would like to question. It is this: that our knowledge of what Japan would have liked Asia to be must be vitiated because all Japanese thinking on the matter is limited first by the fact that campaigns were in progress, second by the fact that the campaigns ended in defeat; and only a victorious nation can indulge in the delights of postwar planning. I am not sure that I would find it necessary to accept that the version of Japanese rule over Asia, exemplified in the wartime military government arrangements for occupied territories, would have been significantly altered once peace came, had Japan been victorious. A solution imposed by force tends to be realised, practically, by the instruments of force. That is precisely what happened in East Asia. Japan's military solution meant that the impact of Japanese ideas was felt by occupied countries, hostile or friendly, as a military impact. The vision of East Asia that Professor Iriye dismisses as official rhetoric was undoubtedly, for thousands of Japanese of all ranks in the Imperial forces, sincerely held, however wrong-headed it may seem in retrospect to modern Japanese, and however wrong-headed it did appear at the time to the Allies.

It is possible to interpret Professor Iriye's case in the following way. What planning *did* exist for the future of Asia – or what *vision* existed, for one glides over into the other – was a technique of propaganda-cum-mystification, concealing the real nature of Japanese motivation. Japan had a clear economic purpose, the seizure of raw materials and the lands which contained them. She also had a 'cover-story' for this seizure, which was entitled 'the liberation of East Asia'. When the possibility, then the certainty, of defeat approached, destroying the chance of achieving the first purpose permanently, plans nonetheless continued to be made, however unevenly, for the second purpose. The mystification was all the more powerful since it was intended to convince not merely new subject peoples but also the Japanese themselves.

To believe this, it is not necessary to believe in a conspiracy by a small ruling group, feeding their people on illusions while pursuing their own far from altruistic aims. By no means. The purpose is equally in terms of self-deception.

Whether we interpret events as the result of national self-deception, or whether we view them as the result, in Professor Iriye's terms, of the Japanese seeking to provide their militarism with an aura of sanctity and legitimacy, the upshot is the same. A successful Japan would extrude European and American interests from East Asia, and establish her own hegemony, which would be welcomed by peoples previously subject to the old colonial powers. Tojo's speech in the Diet, referred to in Professor Iriye's paper,[8] has therefore a recognisable genealogy. As if anticipating Tojo speaking of Japan liberating Asia from Western domination and constructing a new world order, the old field-marshal Yamagata Aritomo had written to Premier Okuma, in August 1914, that when the great conflict which had just begun in Europe was over, attention would be focused again on the Far East. 'When that day comes, the rivalry between the white and the non-white races will become violent, and who can say that the white races will not unite with one another to oppose the colored peoples?', the implication being that, as he said in a private conversation a year later, 'the racial problem is the key to the solution of the Asia problem . . . we must attempt the solution of our myriad problems on the premise of "Asia for the Asians" . . . Thus while the expansion of Japan into Manchuria may be a move for her own betterment and that of her people, it would also be a necessary move for the self-protection of Asians and for the co-existence and co-prosperity of China and Japan.'[9]

The terms of the argument of the Imperial Rescript of the Great East Asia War are there already. Are we to think the combination of apparent altruism and enlightened self-interest unbearably Pecksniffian? I believe Professor Iriye would have us think so, and his interpretation of the 10 March 1943 Liaison Conference seems to bear this out.[10] The conference dealt with the details of Burma's independence, and Professor Iriye interprets the clash in the conference between the Foreign Minister, Shigemitsu, and the military representatives, as one between on the one hand a broad idealistic framework and on the other holding the reins tight, under an appearance of granting freedom. So Professor Iriye speaks of an independent Burma being 'founded on moral righteousness',[11] a translation which has a sermonising Victorian flavour about it, and which seems to be unrelated to the issues under debate.

The term used is *dōgi,* which might as well be rendered 'justice' or simply 'morality' without hypocritical overtones.[12] There were good reasons for its use: the Japanese were trying to establish a case that their relations with Burma were not to be based on mere exploitation of Burmese resources, which was asserted to have been the case with British rule.

But Japanese military officials insisted on inserting the phrase 'co-existence and co-prosperity' into the sentence dealing with the development of East Asian countries, whereas Shigemitsu wanted merely a reference to 'mutual benefit' and 'reciprocity'. This may have been mere 'squabbling over words'[13] but Shigemitsu clearly did not think so. He rudely dismissed 'co-existence and co-prosperity' as politically meaningless phrases (*kyōson kyōei naru go wa seijiteki imi sukunashi*) and said that mutual benefit (*gōkei*) exactly correspond to the mood of the younger peoples of Asia (*gōkei wa jakusho minzoku no kimochi wa pittari hamarite yoshi* . . .).[14]

Nonetheless, those who objected to the use of *gōkei* and preferred *kyōson kyōei* had sense on their side, even if it was only a propaganda sense. The Imperial Rescript referring to Japan's initial war aims contains the well-worn phrase *jison jiei*, self-existence and self-defence. The introduction of a new phrase in a document conferring independence on another Asian nation, which paralleled the phrase with Rescript and at the same time morally improved upon it by implying collaboration and cooperation, which *kyō* does in *kyōson kyōei*, surely made very good sense. (Admittedly the *ei of jiei* means 'defence' and not 'prosperity', but the resonance of the phrase is undoubtedly parallel.)

Nor, if one looks at the minutes of the 19 July 1943 Liaison Conference, is it clear that the military alone are arguing with Shigemitsu. Apart from the Navy Minister's initial intervention, the speakers in this particular discussion are termed 'A. N. Other' (*soregashi*) so the *status* of the inter-vention is not clear. And although 'co-existence and co-prosperity' may be an 'obvious allusion to Tojo's and other militarists' wartime propaganda',[15] Tojo himself intervened to say that the draft should be studied by the drafting office and he wanted to leave the decision on wording to the Foreign Minister.[16]

But let us move away from questions of rhetoric to the practical planning shown in the annexe to the conference minutes.[17] Here the picture of a Japanese version of independence is made clear. Professor Iriye mentions two things which will restrict independence: the provision of Japanese advisers, and the behest to conduct foreign affairs in close cooperation with Japan.[18] But there is much more. Burma is, to start with, a truncated Burma, the Shan States and Karenni being under a different dispensation (and, of course, territory had already been annexed by Thailand with Jap-anese approval). The Burmese were made responsible for installations needed by the Japanese Army, and the Burma National Army would have to accept the supreme command of the C.-in-C. of Japanese forces in Burma. The economy would not be free but would be linked to 'the plan for the economic construction of Greater East Asia'; currency would be regu-lated in collaboration with the Japanese Empire; communications would be under Burmese authority with the proviso that nothing should hinder the operations of Japanese forces; enemy industrial installations should be transferred to Burma, with the exception of those required for the admin-istration of Greater East Asia and the completion of the Great Asia War.

As a blueprint for a new state, this is giving with one hand and taking away with the other. But there is something worse, in the details of planning, when we look at the way military government was to be carried on in Indonesia. The most trivial details of daily life are interfered with. A circular issued by the Regent of Luwu, Palopo, dated 27 December 1944, wears a terrible air of ostentatious industry and humourless deference:

> When returning a greeting we must not laugh, smoke, etc., but assume an energetic posture. If we encounter a person of higher rank while running, we must at once slow down and then salute. It is forbidden to greet a person while running.
>
> When walking with a superior we must not stay abreast of him but remain slightly behind him and always walk on his side.
>
> When addressing a superior we must stand at attention.
> When talking one must speak in a loud voice, not like a woman, and not squat.
>
> One must put on one's hat correctly, not at an angle. The hat should be two inches above the two ears.
>
> It is not permitted to sit with one's mouth open, lest one be considered empty-headed.
>
> When we have no work to do we must read regulations concerning our work.
>
> During every conversation in which the name *Tennō Heika* [His Imperial Majesty] occurs, one must stand at attention.[19]

A British wartime treatment of Japanese propaganda, Peter de Mendelssohn's *Japan's Political Warfare*,[20] gave considerable credit to the force of the phrase *Dai Tōa Kyōeiken* as a slogan. 'It is a brilliantly clever invention,' wrote Mendelssohn, 'concrete and real, yet suggestive and allowing full scope to imaginative embroider . . . Clothing, as it does, the frankly imperialistic ambitions of the Japanese military with an altruism which makes the concept of Empire palatable even to the most reluctant, the connotation of "cooperation" at the same time tends to make the people regard themselves as leaders, liberators and brothers rather than just another set of imperialist exploiters'.

I think he is right, and this emphasises what I said earlier about the slogan value of 'morality' in this connection. As further proof of this, and of the way in which Japanese notions of the future of Asia were envisaged by political thinkers of the time, as opposed to members of the Supreme Command, I would like to refer to an article by Tsurumi Yusuke, 'Sensō mokuteki ron' (A discussion of war aims) which appeared in the review *Nihon Hyōron* in June 1943,[21] i.e. roughly half way between the date of the Liaison Conference hesitantly giving independence to Burma and that of the enormous propaganda exercise of the Greater East Asia Conference in November 1943. It was written at a time when defeat was no doubt predictable, but the date and mode of defeat were uncertain, and there still seemed a possibility of ranging Asia with Japan against the West.

Tsurumi was a member of the House of Representatives, and Director of the Taiheiyō Kyōkai (Pacific Association). Japan's war aims, he wrote, were sufficiently shown in the Imperial Rescript: Japan was defending herself, establishing the stability of East Asia and aiming at 'enjoying with others the co-prosperity of all nations' (*manpō kyōei no raku wo kai ni* . . .).[22] People are bravest when defending their own lives, and Japan has done only this in 3000 years of existence. But Japan has also created the Greater East Asia Co-Prosperity Sphere, the most suitable form of regional organisation for mankind at its present stage. The world-view imposed by Great Britain was an attempt to rule the whole planet, the centre of which would be British industry, and the rest of the world would be its markets. The first British Empire based on the Atlantic failed with the American Revolution. The second, based on the Indian Ocean, could not be defended. Now the US and Great Britain were trying to establish a joint third world-empire. But, as James Burnham had pointed out in *The Managerial Revolution,* of the three heavy industry zones (Western Europe, the east coast of North America, Japan) which could form the nucleus of broad regional zones of development, the East Asia zone would centre on Japan, and be used not for individual profit, as hitherto, but for the common welfare of the public. This would exist alongside a Euro-African Co-Prosperity Sphere advocated by Germany and Italy. With the outbreak of the Great East Asia War, a spirit has surged up inside Japan, a recognition of a Japanese-type mission to the world. Japan has volunteered for this war with a moral and religious passion (*dōgiteki,* – the term used in the Liaison Conference on Burma – *shūkyōteki jōnetsu wo motte*)[23] because it is conscious of this basic war aim. As Hitler had proclaimed, man was not a being who threw away his life for economic interests. He always died for an ideal, and Japan's war aims had their foundations in such an idealism. A new society was being born in East Asia, with Japan as its centre, a Japan which had been newly born again. 'Without understanding this new concept, and the popular enthusiasm for this new concept, it is impossible to understand the basis of the Great East Asia War. That is the sublime war aim which the Japanese people can display to the world.'

We are, of course, over-familiar with this rhetoric. Where de Mendelssohn was right, so many years ago, and where I think Professor Iriye agrees with him, in the military's interpretation of the Greater East Asia Co-Prosperity Sphere as 'establishing Japanese domination over the rest of Asia',[24] is in the effect of the slogan. Where I am not sure I agree with Professor Iriye is in a division between military and civil opinion here.

But surely, if the reality of independence was, as the Burma plan showed it to be, a mere sop, with tight Japanese control remaining, the use of puppet regimes, and the splitting of territory (this applied later to Japanese planning for Indonesia and also to French Indo-China), then how could even Japanese puppet leaders proclaim their devotion to it? If we except Hayashi Fusao's egregious rehearsal of the case for Japan in the 1960s as the hundred years' war for the liberation of Asia, Japanese political historians by and large have refused to be taken in by the Co-Prosperity Sphere, from Ienaga Saburō's verdict of 1968 that it was a regime characterised not by coopera- tion but by brutalised compulsion[25] to Professor Yano Tōru's dismissal of it as 'the illusion of the Greater East Asia Co-Prosperity Sphere'.[26]

Their scepticism merely reinforces our own. Nonetheless, if it was so hollow, if the Conference of November 1943 which was its shopfront was a sham, if the rhetoric Japan used was becoming, in Kiyosawa Kiyoshi's words, quoted by Professor Iriye, 'more universalistic and less pan-Asian',[27] why did it have the effect it did on certain non-Japanese Asian leaders? With every allowance made for hindsight, and for covering one's rear, how, if Professor Iriye is right, do we account for the *terms* used by Ba Maw in Tokyo in November 1943?

> On an occasion like this it is only natural that there should be only one thought in our minds . . . It is impossible to exaggerate the feelings which are born out of an occasion like this. For years in Burma I dreamt my Asiatic dreams. My Asiatic blood has always called to other Asiatics. In my dreams, both sleeping and waking, I have heard the voice of Asia calling to her children . . . the voice of Asia gathering her children together. It is the call of our Asiatic blood. This is not the time to think with our minds; this is the time to think with our blood, and it is this thinking with the blood which has brought me all the way from Burma to Japan . . . We have once more discovered that we are Asiatics, discovered our Asiatic blood, and it is this Asiatic blood which will redeem us and give us back Asia.[28]

The factor here, which Japan could use, and which the Western allies could not use, is the potent one of race. In spite of the bogus D. H. Lawrence rhetoric with which Ba Maw clothes these aspirations, the message is clear enough and was consecrated in one of the phrases published in the Joint Proclamation of 6 November: one of the conference's five principles was 'the abolition of racial prejudice' (*jinshu sabetsu no teppai*). As Professor Thorne and W. Roger Louis and other writers, including the present writer, have stressed, the factor of race, explicit or otherwise, needs constant emphasis if we are to understand not the ideas, but the strength of the appeal, of the Co-Prosperity Sphere, for those people who had been the victims of racial prejudice at the hands of colonial powers.[29] There is little logic in this, because Japan herself could put up a considerable showing as a racist power; but in the immediate situation of 1942–45 this hardly mattered.

If we can move next to the power-political considerations put by Professor Iriye, it does not seem that British historians would have much to quarrel with in his interpretation of Japan's changing relations with the Chungking regime. We have long been accustomed to the notion that Kuomintang Chinese were perfectly prepared to treat with the Japanese, as circumstances demanded, and J. H. Boyle has traced the vicissitudes of the deals and counter-deals of the process.[30] What is curious about this process is that it produces a circular argument. Japan went to war with the Western powers to ensure a supply of oil for her industry. She needed oil to prosecute her war with China, and the hostility of the Western powers towards her was largely a product of that war. Yet we find Tojo expressing the view, quoted by Professor Iriye on p. 17, that 'it was necessary to shake hands with Chungking' in order to crush America and Britain.[31] Certain personal reminiscences emphasise the confidence some Japanese military leaders seem to have had that it was always possible to do a deal with China. The confidence of the egregious Tsuji Masanobu, for instance, after the surrender of 1945, that his services would be welcomed by Chiang Kai-shek and his secret police, was fully justified in the event.[32] And there was the curious episode at the Japanese surrender ceremony at Nanking, when the Chinese had prepared a round table for the discussions with the Japanese envoys, and were only persuaded by the insistence of the Americans to have a long rectangular table instead. They would have preferred the circular form, since it did not oppose the two sides as antagonists, victor and vanquished,

but enabled them all to sit round and discuss matters on terms – more or less
– of equality between Asians (many of the Chinese officers having been
trained in Japanese military academies anyway).[33]

So there was a basis for confidence in the possibility of a rapprochement
as far as China was concerned. But that the same confidence, or hope, could
have been entertained as far as Soviet Russia is concerned is perhaps the
most startling item in Professor Iriye's paper. Because it turns Japan's
whole vision of the future of East Asia, and her war aims, topsy-turvy.

Shigemitsu was no doubt right to assume that sooner or later there would
be friction between the Soviets and the Anglo–Americans.[34] But both he and
Kido were only on safe ground when it was a question of using the Soviet
Union as a mediator in bringing peace.[35] What seems to have happened is
that a kind of glide took place between the idea of inviting the Soviet Union
to act as a go-between or peacemaker and that of the Soviet Union as an
active partner in an East Asian power system devised by the Japanese to
save their own bacon. Professor Iriye mentions the offer of concessions to
the Soviets, with variations on a theme, in 1944.[36] But certain items must
have been seen by the Soviets as highly speculative. How could Japan offer
tin and rubber, when it was becoming increasingly difficult, if not impossible, to maintain a shipping line between the southern regions – source of
that tin and rubber – and Japanese ports? Even the far-going territorial
concessions referred to later – retrocession of Southern Sakhalin, the northern
Kuriles and the Chinese Eastern Railway – and which are dated 6 September
1944 (a Foreign Office draft) must have seemed gestures of despair.[37]

That is why I think, even with inverted commas, it is difficult to speak,
as Professor Iriye does, of a 'plan' to 'help augment Soviet power in Asia
so that Japan and Russia would somehow become united in opposition to
the Anglo–American powers.[38] The term 'plan' glorifies a *pis-aller,* a set of
last desperate throws, and easily recognisable as such. Japan too, though
Professor Iriye does not stress this, was prepared to offer more startling and
less realisable goals: the *besshi* of the 7 September 1944 Liaison Conference
contains references to cooperation with Russia in an advance to India and
the Indian Ocean; the move southward by the Russians was one of those
predicted – wrongly – by officials of the War Ministry some months later.[39]

The conditions laid down for China are as unreal as those laid down for
attracting the Soviets. 'Japan would facilitate [Chiang's] return to Nanking,'
says Professor Iriye, 'where he would establish a unified government. There
would, thereafter, be no Japanese interference with internal Chinese politics'.[40] But the source for this information shows the matter was not so
simple.[41] A unified government meant agreement with Wang Ching-wei,

but that was left to 'direct negotiations between the two'.[42] Hong Kong was to be handed over to China, and, provided Britain and America withdrew their forces from China, Japan would do the same. But the status of Manchuria was to remain unaltered.[43] In other words, in spite of occasional favourable indications, the thing was a pipe-dream.

In terms of the Soviets, the same is true, and it is intriguing to notice that the minister in Spain, Suma Yakichirō, is by this time thinking not along lines of diplomatic feasibility, but in terms of catastrophe reminiscent of science fiction. 'Relocating the nation on the Asian continent'[44] is an anticipation of the nightmares fermenting in the imagination – several decades later – of the SF novelist Komatsu Sakyō in *Nihon Chinbotsu* (Japan Sinks).

There was, it must be said, rather more to the policy of certain military circles in Japan, or rather in the Japanese forces, than either rapprochement with China or Russia. There were those who wished to shorten the lines of communication in South-East Asia, and establish a self-supplying redoubt there, which would maintain itself even if seaward communication with Japan became impossible. Although Burma had gone, most of the landmass of South-East Asia was still in Japanese hands, garrisoned by an undefeated army, and in addition it was still possible to frustrate the successful return of the colonial powers, even if they forced a military entry, by hastening the 'liberation' process. It is this which explains the hasty handing over of independence to the various countries of Indo-China in the spring of 1945, and to Indonesia in August 1945; an attempt, like that of the unjust steward, to acquire merit, however belatedly, in the postwar eyes of the new nations of South-East Asia. The staggered datings of independence meant, for South-East Asia, that the process was not the working of an overall plan but a series of *bricolages*. It is interesting that, in observing the results in one of these cases, that of Indonesia, in the few months after the surrender, the erstwhile China expert in the State Department, Stanley Hornbeck, then Ambassador to the Hague, continued to interpret the situation in racist terms:

> On one hand the 'white' peoples of the Occident together with those 'coloured' peoples in various parts of the world who remain under their influence and partake of their ways of thinking, and on the other hand those 'coloured' peoples who reject or escape from the influence of the 'white' and occidental peoples . . .[45]

Hornbeck was convinced the Japanese were, through the Indonesians, basically continuing their war: 'More and more the evidence indicates that the present situation in the Netherlands East Indies is a product of Japanese inspiration and a projection of the Japanese war effort'.[46]

The plan to grant independence before the Allies returned to South-East Asia had some chance of success, as history was to prove. But how could the Japanese have expected any kind of success with their overtures to Russia? As Professor Iriye points out the Yalta agreements ensured a sharing out in the East and in the Pacific between the USA and Russia.[47] The latter had nothing to gain from a volte-face on behalf of the Japanese. Russia was the traditional enemy, and even in the midst of Japan's struggles in the Pacific and South-East Asia, the Kwantung Army's operational plans for an anti-Soviet campaign were updated annually. There is, therefore, something totally unreal about the draft of a situation report by the Military Affairs Section (*Gunmuka*) of IGHQ (at the end of April 1945) speculating on the possibilities of a union (*ketsugō*) in East Asia between Japan, Russia and China, and the creation of 'alienation and antagonism' (*rikan kakushitsu*) between the US, Great Britain, Russia, Chungking and Yenan.[48]

The explanation is perhaps to be found in the jottings of the Vice-CGS, General Kawabe, dated 16 April 1945, the same day as the consulate-general at Chita sent to Tokyo accounts of Russian build-up in planes, tanks and assault formations:

> Firm reports have come in of the transport of units to the Soviet East, and that Stalin has finally made up his mind; yet for some reason or other I cannot believe that Stalin has reached this decision. Although I don't rely on his good feelings towards Japan or a spirit of non-cooperation as far as America is concerned, he is a past master in calculated self-interest (*dasan ni chozeru*) and I can only hazard a guess that he ought not now to be seeking fresh battlefields in the East – that is my one hope.[49]

There are three separate elements in the considerations about Russia. Can she be kept from making war against Japan? Can she be persuaded to act as peacemaker? Can she be persuaded to act as a party to a new order in East Asia? In none of these questions did Japan have any standing, and it is in this connection that I think a remark should be made to add a final note to Professor Iriye's observations. It is taken from a paper delivered by Richard Storry to the National Maritime Museum in 1974, on the subject of 'plans and reality'. He is discussing the beginnings of the war, and says,

> Intelligence in the broadest sense is obviously essential to good planning; and it was here that the Japanese displayed remarkable shortcomings. I refer in particular to their failure to calculate correctly the reactions of their potential opponents. It really does not seem to have entered the minds of Japan's military leaders that it would be on the question of China that the breach with the United States would occur.[50]

The substance of that comment applies precisely to Japanese suppositions about a rapprochement with the Soviet Union from autumn 1944 to the summer of 1945. Tokyo's attempts were 'doomed to disappointment' says Professor Iriye.[51] Indeed yes. But predictably so. Her initial aim of *jison jiei* was finally defeated in August 1945. The role she assumed, to achieve that aim of liberator of East Asia, had better luck. Both Japan's victory and subsequent defeat were necessary for the nations of South-East Asia to win their independence; an outcome which was, perhaps, in the end, not entirely the result of planning, but rather of the serendipity of war.

NOTES

1. Ian Nish (ed.), *Anglo–Japanese Alienation, 1919–1952* (Cambridge, 1982).
2. Tokyo University Press, 1982.
3. Mutaguchi Renya, *1944-nen U-go sakusen ni kansuru kokkai toshokan ni okeru setsumei shiryō*, (Explanatory historical materials in the National Diet Library concerning Operation U, 1944), privately published by Ihagaki Kikutarō, Tokyo, 1964).
4. A. J. Barker, *March on Delhi* (London, 1963).
5. Christopher Thorne, 'Wartime British planning for the Post-War Far East', *Anglo–Japanese Alienation*, pp. 199–225.
6. Iriye, in *Anglo–Japanese Alienation*, p. 177.
7. Quoted by Iriye, op. cit., p. 182.
8. *Anglo–Japanese Alienation*, pp. 179–81.
9. R. Tsunoda et al., *Sources of Japanese Tradition* (Columbia, 1958), vol. II, pp. 209–10.
10. *Anglo–Japanese Alienation*, p. 182.
11. Ibid.
12. *Sugiyama Memo*, vol. II, pp. 389 and 392.
13. *Anglo–Japanese Alienation*, p. 183.
14. Liaison Conference, 18 July 1943, *Sugiyama Memo*, vol. II, p. 441.
15. *Anglo–Japanese Alienation*, p. 182.
16. *Sugiyama Memo*, vol. II, p. 441.
17. Ibid., pp. 441–2.
18. *Anglo–Japanese Alienation*, p. 182.
19. Benda et al., *Japanese Military Administration in Indonesia: Selected Documents*, pp. 230–4. The overlaying of a sacral attitude on a purely political situation complicated Japan's role as an occupying power enormously. Cf. Suzuki Shizuom and Yokoyama Michoyoshi (eds) *Shinsei kokka Nippon to Ajiya – senryōka no han-Nichi no genshō* (Japan the divine nation and Asia – the roots of anti-Japanese feeling in the occupied territories), (Tokyo, 1984).

20. London, 1944, p. 143.
21. No. 6, vol. 18, pp. 72–81.
22. Tsurumi, Yusuke, *Sensō mokuteki ron* (A discussion of War Aims), *Nihon Hyōron*, vol. 18, no. 6, June 1943, pp. 72–81.
23. Ibid.
24. *Anglo–Japanese Alienation*, p. 183.
25. Citing evidence from Prince Mikasa downwards, cf. Ienaga Saburo, *Taiheiyō Senso* (Tokyo, 1968), pp. 181–208, '"Dai Tōa Kyōeiken" no jittai' (The reality of the Great East Asia Co-Prosperity Sphere).
26. *'Nanshin' no keifu*, (The genealogy of the southward advance), *Chuo Koron*, 1975, pp. 145–72.
27. *Anglo–Japanese Alienation*, p. 185.
28. Ba Maw, *Breakthrough in Burma* (Yale, 1968), pp. 342–44.
29. W. R. Louis, *British Strategy in the Far East* (London, 1973); C. Thorne, 'Racial Aspects of the Far Eastern War of 1941–45', *Proceedings of the British Academy*, vol. LXVI, 1980, pp. 329–77; L. Allen, *Singapore 1941–1942* (London, 1977), ch. xi, 'The Factor of Race'; L. Allen, *Burma the Longest War* (London, 1984), 'Race', pp. 604–16; Cedric Dover, *Hell in the Sunshine* (London, 1943).
30. J. H. Boyle, *China and Japan at War 1937–1945* (London, 1972).
31. *Anglo–Japanese Alienation*, p. 187.
32. Tsuji Masanobu, *Senkō sansenri* (Underground Escape), (Tokyo, 1952).
33. L. Allen, *End of the War in Asia*, p. 240.
34. *Anglo–Japanese Alienation*, pp. 188 and 192.
35. Ibid., p. 191.
36. Ibid., pp. 191–4.
37. Ibid., p. 192.
38. Ibid., pp. 192–3.
39. 10 April 1945, cf. *Dai Honei Rikugunbu*, vol. 10, p. 192.
40. *Anglo–Japanese Alienation*, p. 193.
41. *Haisen no Kiroku*, pp. 163–4.
42. Ibid., p. 163.
43. Ibid., p. 164.
44. *Anglo–Japanese Alienation*, p. 193.
45. *Foreign Relations of the United States*, 1945, vol. VI, p. 1166. For a more recent confirmation of this view, from Japanese evidence, cf. T. Fusuyama, *Nankai no akebono* (Dawn in the South Seas), (Tokyo, 1983).
46. Ibid., pp. 1176–7.
47. *Anglo–Japanese Alienation*, p. 194.
48. *Dai Honei Rikagunbu*, vol. 10, p. 195.
49. Ibid., p. 192.
50. *The Second World War in the Pacific: Plans and Reality*, Maritime Monographs and Reports, no. 9, 1974, p. 5.
51. *Anglo–Japanese Alienation*, p. 194.

7 Roosevelt and the Making of America's East Asian Policy, 1941–45*

T.G. Fraser

Every American of a certain generation remembers 7 December 1941, not as a 'date which will live in world history', but as one 'which will live in infamy'. That amendment, personally made by Franklin Roosevelt to the draft of his speech asking Congress for a declaration of war on Japan, set the tone of his country's war effort in the East, a struggle which was to be marked by racism and brought to an end by the total destruction of Hiroshima and Nagasaki. A week later, the President laid before Congress a summary of relations between the United States and Japan, a 'record', he concluded, 'for all history to read in amazement, in sorrow, in horror, and in disgust!'[1] In contrast to his response to the attack on Pearl Harbor, when Hitler and Mussolini declared war four days later, Roosevelt merely sent a brief note to Congress asking that a state of war be recognised. From that time until his sudden death on 12 April 1945, Roosevelt's clear priority was victory, first over the European Axis and then over Japan. But he was also a veteran of the Wilson administration who had seen his leader's hopes for a postwar world order collapse under the weight of misunderstanding, political intrigue and isolationist feeling. Roosevelt knew that this time things had to be very different and even as he waged war he was planning for its outcome. 'We are going to win the war and we are going to win the peace that follows', he told Americans in his first Fireside Chat after Pearl

* I wish to acknowledge a grant from the Research Sub-Committee, Faculty of Humanities, University of Ulster, which made it possible to work in the Franklin D. Roosevelt Library, Hyde Park, New York, and to thank the staff of the Library for their courtesy and assistance. The following abbreviations are used: FDRL – Franklin D. Roosevelt Library; *FRUS – Foreign Relations of the United States*. It is interesting to note that the most sensitive, and hence revealing, documents concerning China were declassified in early March 1972, days after Richard Nixon's visit to Peking. Hence, they do not appear in the relevant FRUS volumes.

Harbour.[2] But while his intentions towards Europe, and plans for the structure of international society, came to emerge in some detail in the course of the war, those for the future of Japan and the rest of East Asia can be identified less surely. Even so, an attempt to understand them helps explain many of the assumptions on which America's policies in the immediate postwar years came to be based.

Roosevelt did historians few favours. His administration was always somewhat haphazard. In 1941, a bureaucracy geared to an unambitious foreign policy and modest army had to be expanded to cope with the demands set by a world war and the country's emergence as the strongest power in history. This was done with flair but inevitably administrative corners were cut leaving gaps in the record which are now difficult to fill. The President himself did little to help. He was not in a position to leave memoirs but he was not a diarist nor under the pressure of war was he much of a correspondent even at the official level. His despatches, even those to close allies like Winston Churchill, were drafted for his approval and, although sometimes containing his amendments, they reveal little of the inner man. He was always secretive, frustrating close associates by his unwillingness to confide his true purpose. His preferred method of conducting business was the individual meeting where he could use his undoubted charm and powers of persuasion to considerable effect. But these did not lend themselves to minutes or records. The problem for historians is too obvious to need stating but one example should be given. Central to any understanding of Roosevelt's intentions towards East Asia is his relationship with the Chinese President Chiang Kai-shek. He met Chiang four times at the Cairo Conference in November 1943, presumably forming his impression of the man and his abilities, but no record was prepared nor minute kept of any of these meetings.[3] This is particularly frustrating, for one thing is sure: namely, that Roosevelt regarded foreign policy as his own preserve. His Secretary of State, Cordell Hull, and the Department of State might advise but ultimately they were the executors of the President's will. His purposes were not always easy to discern; some of his colleagues believed that his rather secretive methods of working verged on the devious. This was too harsh but he did have a tendency to postpone awkward decisions, even making contradictory promises in the hope of keeping two sides happy. By April 1945, he had given assurances over future intentions towards Palestine to the American Zionist leaders and to Ibn Saud of Saudi Arabia which he would have found it difficult to reconcile.[4] Even with these difficulties, some attempt should be made to reconstruct how Roosevelt and his administration saw the East Asia which might emerge from the war.

Roosevelt's thinking about the region took place in the context of an American public which had strong views about Japan and China. The contrasting tone of his messages to Congress on the outbreak of war in Asia and Europe reflected to an extent popular sentiment about the nature of America's struggle. The anti-German violence which had burst out in 1917 was absent in 1941; 'Hitler' and 'the Nazis' could conveniently cloud the fact that Americans were fighting a people who had contributed as much as any group to the development of their country. No so the Japanese. While popular lapel buttons predictably proclaimed 'To Hell with Hitler', those relating to Asia carried a crudely different message: 'Japan Wanted For Murder', 'We'll Pay Them Back For Their Sneak Attack', 'Let's Blast the Japs Clean Off the Map', or, more simply, 'Moider Dem Japs'. On recruiting posters the German soldier was invariably shown in shadow behind the familiar coal-scuttle helmet, whereas there was no reticence about the Japanese enemy, grinning sadistically in a grotesque caricature of supposed national characteristics. Enterprising patriots printed 'Jap Hunting Licences', encouraging citizens to 'hunt the Japanese Rat'; one sent to the President came with the hope that it would encourage him in his plan of 'exterminating the Japs'.[5] Motion pictures were little better. In May 1942, Universal released *Menace of the Rising Sun. Japan's Decade of Double Dealing*, a documentary chronicling how 'The Beast of the East' had played its 'filthy game of treachery' to repay 'kindness with ruthless murder'.[6] The real victims of this venom were, of course, the Japanese-Americans of the West Coast, whose expressions of loyalty in the days after Pearl Harbor did not save them from abuse, deportation and internment. Even the dying George M. Cohan, awarded the Congressional Medal of Honour for his services to the nation in the previous war, felt the need for a personal appeal to Roosevelt to retain the services of his Japanese-born servant.[7] Nothing remotely comparable happened to German- and Italian-Americans whose loyalty was taken for granted; indeed, in May 1942 the President went so far as to reassure the Governor of New York 'that no collective evacuation of German and Italian aliens is contemplated at this time'.[8] In short, despite the strategy of 'Hitler First' which had been agreed with the British, there was a racial edge to the war against the Japanese which was absent from that in Europe, even when the extent of Nazi brutality towards the Jews and others began to be revealed.

There was nothing new or particularly surprising about this, for racism was as American as apple pie. Even Roosevelt, patrician, educated and far more cosmopolitan than most of his countrymen, was not immune from it, as his ambiguous record on black civil rights shows. American attitudes towards East Asia had long combined the classic racial characteristics of paternalism and anxiety. Initial admiration for Japan's achievements in the Meiji period were replaced by apprehension over her growing industrial, military and naval power, and presumed expansionist intentions. This, combined with racial tensions on the Pacific coast, led to the complete exclusion of Japanese in 1924, an insult which was not forgotten in Japan. By the outbreak of the war, China was viewed very differently. Although in the nineteenth century her vulnerability to outside pressure had contrasted badly with the vigour of Japan, and her immigrants to California were as disliked as the Japanese, her popular reputation had undergone a considerable improvement. China could not help but benefit from becoming the target of Japan's aggressive foreign policy. She was helped, too, by the fact that China had long been an area of special interest to American missionaries and it was the son of two of them, Henry Luce of Time-Life, who saw to it his fellow-countrymen were aware of how the Chinese were resisting Japan under the leadership of their Nationalist President Chiang Kai-shek. Nothing more acutely symbolised for Americans the villainy of the Japanese contrasted with the suffering of the Chinese than the pictures of the Rape of Nanking.[9]

But if these negative and positive stereotypes of the Japanese and Chinese were typical of American attitudes in 1941, ten years later it was a very different story. By then, Japan was fast becoming rehabilitated as a democratic constitutional monarchy under the guidelines which had been set out by General MacArthur and was the compliant base for American military operations in Korea. China, however, had seen the overthrow of Chiang Kai-shek's regime by Mao Tse-tung's Communists in 1949, was to all intents in the opposing camp in the Cold War, and was engaged in fighting American forces in Korea. Small wonder, then, that the group of Foreign Service officers who had helped define American policy towards China in the war found themselves the target of Senator Joseph McCarthy, their careers ruined and reputations besmirched. This chapter attempts to probe the origins of this historic transformation of the status of Japan and China, and hence the structure of East Asia, in the thinking of Roosevelt and his associates.

Their inevitable preoccupation from December 1941 was military: first, how to contain Japan's dramatic advances in South-East Asia and the Pacific; and then how to penetrate her extensive defensive perimeter, held as it was by forces which hardly knew the meaning of surrender. As far as Roosevelt was concerned, victory over Japan was the clear, indeed unavoidable, priority. Even so, by 1943 both he and officials in the State

Department were already turning their thoughts to the country's postwar future. Their ability to do so was affected, at least in part, by their knowledge of Japan's failure to observe the terms of the Geneva Convention and their fruitless diplomatic campaign, through Swiss intermediaries, to try to reverse this. 'The hideous treatment of many American prisoners of war and civilian internees revealed a barbarism among the Japanese military which shocked the civilised world', Cordell Hull recalled.[10]

By the time Roosevelt came to consult Chiang at Cairo in November 1943 certain broad questions about Japan's future were forming. Although there is no American record of their meeting, a Chinese summary reveals that on 28 November the two men agreed that Japan would have to restore all the territories she had taken from China, including Taiwan, and cede reparations to the Chinese. Roosevelt also raised two fundamental questions which were to assume increasing importance in American thinking: the nature of the postwar military occupation of the country and the future of the monarchy.[11] Both were matters of substance which affected the war effort as much as the peace settlement. Anxious to counter Japan's claim that she was fighting Asia's war of liberation from the white man, the Americans wanted Asian troops to take part in the occupation; indeed, in this Chinese record, Roosevelt suggested that they assume the major role. Secondly, the fate of the Emperor touched directly the conduct of operations. 'We did not want', Hull said, 'to come out against the institution lest this give the Japanese militarists live coals to blow upon and bring up a flame of last-man resistance'.[12] Such were the broad outlines of the issues Hull's officials were analysing and which they presented in a major memorandum in May the following year at a time when Japan's defeat, though still some way off, was clearly inevitable.

Essentially, they thought of Japan's restoration in three stages. During the first phase, the occupying powers would ensure the disbandment of her armed forces and the dissolution of her empire. Japan herself was not to be partitioned but it was regarded as axiomatic that she should be shorn of her overseas acquisitions. This, of course, begged the still larger question of whether the liberation of these territories meant the return of the western empires in Asia. Roosevelt was consistently hostile to the idea that the predominantly American campaign against Japan was being waged for the benefit of British, French and Dutch imperialism but was caught in the dilemma that they were his allies.[13] These, of course, were precisely the issues which were to plague postwar Asia, most obviously in Indo-China. The second phase envisaged the reconstruction of Japan by the Civil Affairs officers of the occupying powers. Despite the professed desire to see other, especially Asian, countries take part in the occupation, the fact that matters relating to Japan's foreign policy were to be referred back to the State Department suggests the reality of American intentions. All the major policy-making elements in the constitution were to be abolished: the Privy Council, the Cabinet, the Diet, along with the ministries of War, Navy, Munitions, and Greater East Asia Affairs. The work of the remaining ministries, such as Home Affairs, Justice, Agriculture and Commerce, and Education, was to continue under the direction of the Civil Affairs officers. During this period, Japan was to be purged of its militarist and ultranationalist organisations while encouraging 'democratic thought'. The final stage was to be the restoration of a Japanese government.[14]

Given the determination of Japanese resistance in every theatre, the apparent assumption that this three-stage transformation of Japan would proceed peacefully might seem questionable, even quixotic. It rested, however, on two important elements: the continuing role of the Emperor, at least in the crucial early phase, and the interpretation of how the Japanese would react to the reality of defeat. The latter was investigated by John K. Emmerson, a State Department Japanese specialist, based upon his work with prisoners of war in China. 'At the moment of capture,' he reported in August 1944, 'the Japanese prisoner usually wishes to commit suicide. He is motivated not only by the instilled belief that capture is the ultimate disgrace of a Japanese soldier but also by the conviction that he will be killed or tortured. After a few days of medical care, good food and considerate treatment, his ideas begin to change. Thoughts of suicide leave him.' Here, he felt, was a clear pointer to the way in which the Japanese people as a whole would react to defeat and occupation. 'Once the inevitable is met, the desire for suicide may end. More easily than we expect, the fanatic faith may crumble and, in the spirit of "shikata ga nai" (it can't be helped), the people may look upon the Japan of the Great East Asia War even as the prisoner now looks upon his homeland. They may not obstruct the formation of a new government which offers them peace and rights never enjoyed before.' Essential to success would be to convince the Japanese that their constitution had been usurped, and defeat brought about, by the militarists. Emmerson also knew that the Emperor's role might be pivotal. In the initial phase, his authority would ensure the surrender of his armed forces; perhaps then, he speculated, he could be disposed of by his 'suicide or disappearance'.[15] His findings were interesting, for they were pointing a more compliant Japan than the ferocity of the Pacific fighting suggested.

As Emmerson's memorandum suggested, the tone of American policy was basically republican. Should the Japanese people wish to rid themselves of the monarchy, the Americans would do nothing to discourage them. What determined the fate of the Emperor, however, was the belief that he was an essential element in ensuring compliance, not just that his authority would be needed to ensure military surrender but that it would enable the bureaucracy to continue working. Convinced that they could only govern Japan with the assistance of Japanese administrators, the State Department suggested that the Emperor be retained as the established symbol of authority. The problem was how to do this while retaining the supreme authority of an Allied military government. It was a fine balancing act, for the Emperor had to be separated from his close connection with the military while retaining enough credibility to attract the continuing loyalty of administrators but not enough to sustain monarchism as such. A basic policy was set out whereby the Emperor was to be kept in seclusion and it made clear that his authority was subordinate to that of the occupation military government. His role was to be confined to whatever was necessary to ensure the compliance of the administration. In all their actions, the occupation authorities were to emphasise that the Emperor was a temporal ruler, avoiding any implication 'that he was of divine origin, that he was sacrosanct, and that he was indispensable'. In fact, if it emerged that retention of the Emperor was not aiding the civil administration, then he was to be dispensed with.[16]

Under Roosevelt, then, America's intentions towards postwar Japan became clear. But although he knew the broad outlines of what was being planned, there is no evidence of close personal involvement; rather, he seems to have been content to leave detailed planning to his officials in the State Department. No so China, for her fortunes increasingly called for his detailed interventions. Chinese affairs interested Roosevelt for a variety of reasons; it was, after all, the source of the Delano wealth and his mother had spent some time there as a young girl. What really engaged him, of course, was China's struggle against Japan and her perceived place in the postwar order. An effective Chinese war effort would keep substantial Japanese forces tied down and might lead to the opening of bomber bases. In American thinking about the structure of the postwar world, China was to replace Japan as the dominant power in the east, a bulwark of stability rather than expansion and aggression. For these reasons it was important that China be named one of the 'Big Four', with Chiang the co-equal of Roosevelt, Churchill and Stalin, at least in name. The course of American–Chinese relations in the succeeding years has been the subject of various analyses from very different viewpoints; what follows is an attempt to reconstruct what Roosevelt saw in relation to China and how this influenced his attitudes and policies towards his Asian ally.

If American purposes towards China were clear enough, their execution proved to be far from straightforward and in the course of their wartime relationship serious tensions were to emerge, not least within the American decision-making process itself, which had profound consequences after the war. Basic to this was the barely-concealed tension between Chiang's Kuomintang government in Chungking and its nominal ally against the Japanese, the Chinese Communist Party led by Mao Tse-tung from its bases in Yenan in north China. Although imperfectly grasped at first by the Americans, the Communist Eighth Route Army under Chu Teh was by far the most effective force fighting the Japanese. It became increasingly clear that China's postwar future would be determined by these two groups, which would either have to form a coalition or fight a civil war, and that the United States would need to define its policy towards them. Unlike the case of Japan, where Hull and his officials could work on policies largely unimpeded, China seemed to bring out the worst aspects of the Roosevelt administration. Although there was an impressive group of Foreign Service officers in China, notably the ambassador to Chungking, Clarence E. Gauss, and a group of able subordinates, notably John Paton Davies, John Carter Vincent, John Stewart Service and Owen Lattimore, they were only one element. China's war effort meant that the military were also closely concerned. In Washington, Admiral William D. Leahy and General George C. Marshall, as well as Treasury Secretary Henry Morgenthau and Harry L. Hopkins, were frequently involved in decisions over China. In China, two powerful figures competed for influence, Generals Joseph Stilwell and Claire Chennault. Chennault had caught the American public's imagination through his leadership of the American Volunteer Group of airmen, the 'Flying Tigers', in China before Pearl Harbor. He was an unabashed champion of air power and of Chiang Kai-shek, whose views he enthusiastically, if uncritically, promoted. Stilwell, commander of American forces in the China–Burma–India theatre and Chief-of-Staff to Chiang, loathed and despised his nominal chief – 'Peanut' as he dismissed him. An irascible, but wholly dedicated soldier, Stilwell felt that the Kuomintang was less than committed to the war against Japan.[17] Matters were further complicated by the fact that Chiang kept his own aides in Washington, T.V. Soong and H.H. Kung, who preferred to deal directly with Roosevelt, Morgenthau and Hopkins. Nor were they helped by Roosevelt persistently exercising his penchant for private diplomacy which had long stretched Hull's patience. In the end, the President's official and unofficial, civilian and military, advisers were giving him totally different advice about the direction policy should take, hardly a situation likely to produce either clarity or consistency.

In the early phase of the war, Roosevelt's clear priority was the nature and extent of the aid he could provide for his ally. There were difficulties almost from the start. In 1942, the United States was stretched enough to hold her own in the Pacific and prepare forces for the land war in Europe. In the circumstances it was inevitable that her ability to assist China fell far short of expectation, or at least demand. In June, Chiang presented the Americans with his 'minimum requirements' to keep his war effort going: three divisions for the Burma theatre, 500 aircraft continuously in service, and 5000 tons of supplies flown in monthly from India. None of this, especially the deployment of ground forces, was realistic, as Roosevelt had to tell him in a reply drafted by General Marshall.[18] Inevitably, Chiang felt that this was not enough. In February 1943, he returned to the offensive. Complaining of a 'negative approach', he now pitched his needs at 10 000 tons a month as against the 1700 tons the Americans were currently providing. Despite Marshall's objective that 'the dispatch of an additional 30 cargo planes to India-China, would be at the direct expense of our own forces, with little resulting benefit to China', Roosevelt felt the need to respond to the Chinese request, promising that 'as the facilities are improved, additional transport planes will be added to the line, with an ultimate goal of 10 000 tons'.[19]

At the same time as he was pressing Roosevelt for increased assistance, in July 1942 Chiang began his litany of complaints against Stilwell, beginning an enervating dispute which was to drag on for over two years, to the detriment of the Chinese war effort.[20] At the same time, the merits of Chennault, 'the one man of genius in the Far East', were extolled.[21] It was a dispute which was increasingly forced on Roosevelt's attention. In March 1943, he read a spirited defence of Stilwell, and devastating critique of Chiang's conduct of the war, by John P. Davies, the Foreign Service officer attached to the general's staff. The situation Stilwell had to deal with, he reported, was:

(1) a basic reluctance on the part of the Chinese Government to assume the offensive against Japan, (2) a Chinese inclination to rely upon the United States to defeat Japan, (3) a Chinese desire to conserve material rather than expend it, (4) attempts by Chinese political factions to use him, (5) the absence of central Chinese authority, whether individual or collective, with whom he can deal, (6) lack of organisation, political factionalism, incompetence, apathy and corruption in the Chinese army.

Faced with this, Stilwell, 'has not concealed from the Chinese what he thinks of their incompetence and corruption'. The one exception Davies was prepared to make in his gloomy analysis of the Chinese war effort was the Communist forces.[22] Roosevelt made no written comment on Davies's memorandum but it must have impressed him for he continued to receive his analyses. It certainly left him in no doubt about the military realities behind Chiang's demands for assistance.

As the Chinese war effort languished, hostilities between Stilwell and Chennault intensified. The air force commander was himself well aware of how desperate conditions in the country had become but was using this to argue for increased resources for his command.[23] Moreover, he had acquired an inside line to the White House through the presence at his headquarters of Eleanor Roosevelt's cousin, the journalist Joe Alsop, who pleaded his cause with Harry Hopkins.[24] By the middle of July 1943, Roosevelt, convinced 'that our whole business in China was an awful mess and ought to be straightened out at once', asked Hopkins to convene a conference with Marshall, Leahy and General Somervell. His frustration was clear and his inclination was to blame Stilwell: 'The President indicated his very strong dissatisfaction with the way our whole show is running in China. He stated that Stilwell obviously hated the Chinese and that his cablegrams are sarcastic about the Chinese and this feeling is undoubtedly known to the Chinese and the Generalissimo'. Marshall, who by this time had his own appreciation of the Chinese war effort, defended his subordinate, and pointed out that as Chennault had been for many years an employee of the Chinese government he was 'under the undue influence of the Generalissimo'. Nevertheless, the tone of the meeting showed Roosevelt and Hopkins as generally sympathetic to Chiang and Chennault.[25]

The key to this support for a regime which he knew to be corrupt and ineffectual was his belief that Chiang's recognition as one of the 'Big Four' was an essential element in his plans for the postwar stability of Asia. When Stalin questioned that status at Tehran in November 1943, Roosevelt replied that he wanted it 'not because he did not realise the weakness of China at present, but he was thinking farther into the future and that after all China was a nation of 400 million people, and it was better to have them as friends rather than as a potential source of trouble'.[26] In fact, on his way to Tehran Roosevelt had set the seal on that recognition by meeting Chiang and Churchill in Cairo. The Cairo conference provided an important opportunity for American, Chinese and British officers to plan their future operations against the Japanese but its real importance was political. As already indicated, the Americans kept no records of the key meetings Roosevelt had with Chiang but enough can be reconstructed to show that he went out of his way to flatter the Chinese leader by acknowledging him as one of the 'Big

Four', offering close postwar collaboration between their two countries and even holding out the prospect of a leading Chinese role in the occupation of Japan.[27] If China got rather less by way of tangible benefit, for a request for a $1 billion dollar loan was turned down. Chiang was well satisfied by what had happened, for he had acquired an important hold over Roosevelt which he was subsequently able to exploit with great skill.[28] By recognising Chiang's status in this way, Roosevelt had committed himself to sustaining his increasingly shaky authority.

Disgruntled American officials in China, frustrated by the reality of the Kuomintang regime, felt it necessary to enlighten the President and his advisers. On 2 December, while Roosevelt was at Tehran, the State Department prepared a memorandum for him summarising Ambassador Gauss's view that as the Chinese now believed that the United States and Britain were winning the war they could 'sit back, holding what they have against the Japanese, and concentrate their planning upon China's post-war political and economic problems'.[29] Davies was much more forthright. He had accompanied Stilwell to Cairo for consultations with Roosevelt and Hopkins. Alarmed by what had happened, he now tried to meet head on the basic assumption behind Roosevelt's policy; namely that the United States should try to sustain Chiang. 'The Generalissimo', he informed Hopkins on 31 December 1943, 'is probably the only Chinese who shares the popular American misconception that Chiang Kai-shek is China'. Instead, he argued that he was a man of 'limited intelligence' with a 'primitive power complex'. His party was no better: 'the Kuomintang, once an expression of genuine nationalist feeling, is now an uncertain equilibrium of decadent, competing factions, with neither dynamic principles nor a popular base'. Combined with the country's serious economic problems and the growing assertiveness of the 'so-called "Communists"', he questioned Chiang's ability to survive and hence whether 'we should avoid committing ourselves unalterably' to him. Instead, he advised that the United States could best realise its objective of securing a strong postwar China by encouraging a genuine coalition with the Communists. Not only was this a remarkably perceptive, indeed prescient, analysis of the true nature of Chiang and his regime but it was clearly advocating as positive American move towards his bitter rivals.[30]

Hopkins waited until early February before referring this to Roosevelt by which time he had received a second memorandum from Davies arguing even more cogently for a positive American move towards what he termed 'Communist China'. Pointing out that this had become 'the most cohesive, disciplined and aggressively anti-Japanese regime in China', he argued that it was imperative that the United States should establish contact, not least because of the possibility that it might become a separate state in north China, 'perhaps even a Russian satellite'. If this were to be prevented, it would be necessary for the Americans to establish contact with the Communist leaders 'while it is still welcome', and hence he advised the sending of a military and political mission to Yenan. Because of Chiang's certain hostility to any such initiative, Davies recommended direct presidential action. This was advice which was running counter to the Cairo strategy but Hopkins was impressed by the strength of his arguments and referred it to his chief as 'an excellent recommendation'. Somewhat surprisingly in view of his recent Cairo strategy, Roosevelt agreed and, after consultations with Marshall and Leahy, on 9 February he sent a message to Chiang asking his consent to an American mission to north China.[31]

Even more surprising was Chiang's apparent agreement. Then to the Americans' dismay it became clear that permission for a mission in north China did not include the Communist area, thus defeating its purpose. Just as significant was information reaching Marshall that Chiang's military were hoping to use American Lend-Lease equipment in operations against the Communists. Marshall was evidently furious but advised Roosevelt against forcing the issue of the Yenan mission as he was engaged in trying to persuade Chiang to take the offensive against a weakened Japanese force in Burma.[32] Although the issue was temporarily shelved, it seemed to indicate an important change in Roosevelt's attitude to events in China. He said as much in replying to a private letter from Marine Lieutenant-Colonel Evans Carlson, who had found fame as the leader of 'Carlson's Raiders' in the Pacific and was a friend of the President's son. More important, however, was the fact that Carlson knew China well and on 23 February 1944 he wrote to Roosevelt in the warmest terms about Mao, Chu and the Communist leadership. Roosevelt's reply indicated his growing awareness of the Communists: 'In regard to China, I think we are going through a transition period – especially the part relating to North China. I have done my best to keep some of the Chinese leaders from taking more positive action against the Eighth Route Army leaders, but it seems to go hard with the Generalissimo'.[33]

Roosevelt now decided to give Chiang a push. In early March, he suggested to his Vice-President, Henry Wallace, that he make a visit to Chungking, his principal purpose being to unite the Kuomintang and the Communists against the Japanese. It was not before time, for in the early summer the Japanese began their last great offensive, delivering serious blows to the government forces. By the time Wallace arrived in late June, Chiang had little choice but to allow the American mission to go to Yenan.[34]

The Americans arrived at Communist headquarters in late July and what they reported must have confirmed Chiang's worst fears. The most penetrating analyses were those of the young Foreign Service officer who accompanied the mission, John S. Service. Born in China of missionary parents, Service had as close a knowledge of the country as any American and, at Gauss's prompting, had kept in touch with Communist sources. Over the next nine months, his reports were to provide what should have been invaluable insights to affairs at Yenan, the depth and breadth of his analyses reinforcing the arguments of those who were advocating a positive policy towards Mao and his followers. 'One cannot help coming to feel that this movement is strong and successful, and that it has such drive behind it and has tied itself so closely to the people that it will not easily be killed', he reported six days after arriving in Yenan. Above all, he told his superiors: 'Morale is very high. The war seems close and real. There is no defeatism, but rather confidence. There is no war-weariness'. Hopkins judged his information to be of such interest that he passed his report to Roosevelt on 6 September.[35] This confirmation that the Communists were capable of standing up to the Japanese offensive stood in dramatic contrast to the Chiefs of Staffs' depressing Fourth of July message to the President that the 'Chinese ground forces in China, in their present state of discipline, training and equipment, and under their present leadership, are impotent'.[36]

What they proposed, as a matter of urgency, was that Roosevelt insist that Stilwell be given command of all Chinese forces. Two days later, the President telegraphed Chiang requesting that Stilwell be given full authority over all forces and operations in the China theatre, knowing perfectly well what a blow this would be to Chiang's prestige. Taken together with the Yenan mission, the Chinese leader's standing with the Americans seemed to have touched its nadir. But Chiang was nothing if not an astute political survivor and soon recovered his touch to mount a successful counter-offensive against both the detested Stilwell and the alarming new tone of American policy. Even at the moment of his triumph, Stilwell was being undermined. In reporting his mission to Roosevelt at the end of June, Wallace recommended that a senior American officer be sent to China who could prod Chiang into the necessary military and political reforms, including the formation of a united front. Stilwell, he felt, was too much *persona non grata* to do this.[37] His suggestion had a certain surface appeal but it held out the possibility of divide and rule in what was already a complex situation. Chiang clearly knew this. Even as he apparently agreed to Roosevelt's demand that Stilwell be given full authority, he suggested that a senior American be sent to Chungking.[38]

Roosevelt took the bait, for he did not really want to undermine Chiang. On 18 August, it was announced that Donald Nelson of the War Production Board, whom Roosevelt wanted out of Washington, and Major-General Patrick Hurley were to be sent to Chungking as the President's Personal Representatives. Hurley's qualification was his Republican politics; Roosevelt knew that one of Wilson's greatest failings had been his inability to sustain a bi-partisan approach after the last war. But he was a political general whose vanity and ambition were matched only by his arrogance and ignorance and his interventions in China proved disastrous. His instructions from Roosevelt were to work to keep China in the war and as part of this he had 'decided to sustain the leadership of Chiang Kai-shek'.[39]

This is not the place to examine the details of the so-called Hurley Mission but it was inevitable that the crisis would come about over the luckless Stilwell. As Chiang continued to stall on implementing Roosevelt's earlier request, on 16 September, still apparently convinced by his Joint Chiefs that the Chinese armies were facing disaster, the President repeated the demand that Stilwell be immediately placed 'in unrestricted command of all your forces'.[40] But Chiang now had an ally and he quickly moved in for the kill, his resolve strengthened, it would seem, by information from H. H. Kung in Washington that a move against Stilwell would not be resisted.[41] After intensive discussions with Hurley, on 9 October 1944 Chiang formally requested that Stilwell be relieved. In his supporting telegram, Hurley informed Roosevelt that there 'is no other Chinese known to me who possesses as many of the elements of leadership as Chiang Kai-shek. Chiang Kai-shek and Stilwell are fundamentally incompatible. Today you are confronted by a choice between Chiang Kai-shek and Stilwell'.[42] The choice was quickly made; within the week Stilwell was relieved by General Albert C. Wedemeyer. Why the choice was made is still unclear, but Chiang knew that he had become too essential to Roosevelt's Grand Coalition and Hurley presumably knew that as a leading Republican his wishes would not be flouted by the President so close to the presidential election. Their triumph was complete. Within days of Stilwell's departure, Clarence Gauss, with his thirty years' experience in the East, resigned as ambassador to be replaced by Patrick Hurley who had already asked for the job in August. Stilwell, on his return to the United States, was instructed not to discuss the situation in China.[43]

Roosevelt obviously felt that a corner had been turned, but his policy remained ambivalent to the end. Faced with the evidence he had seen from Davies and Service, what he seemed to have settled for was the hope of a revitalised Kuomintang regime which had come to terms with the reality of

Communist power. 'Things in Chungking look a little better', he optimistically told Colonel Carlson on 15 November, 'and I am hoping and praying for a real working out of the situation with the so-called Communists'. There is no doubt that by the beginning of 1945 he was once again both seriously concerned over the situation in China and impressed by the extent of opposition to Chiang's government.[44] This is, in effect what he told Stalin at Yalta in February when he reported on the progress Hurley and Wedemeyer were making in bringing the two sides together and indicated that the 'fault lay more with the Kuomintang and the Chungking Government than with the so-called Communists'.[45] But Chiang had no intention of going down this path and in Hurley he had a sympathetic ally. Moreover, with Gauss and Stilwell gone, Davies, Service and the other Foreign Service officers who were arguing for an opening towards the Communists were isolated and vulnerable.

Hurley conducted intensive negotiations between the two sides in the opening weeks of 1945 but made little progress, not least because of his scant grasp of the complex issues. On 19 February he left for consultations in Washington, having reached the basic conclusion that 'our Government was right in its decision to support the National Government of China and the leadership of Chiang Kai-shek'.[46] Service and the attaché in Chungking, George Atcheson, decided that the views of their chief had to be countered. On 28 February, they telegraphed Washington recommending that the United States should begin supplying and equipping the Communist forces. In this way, they argued, 'we could expect to secure the cooperation of all of China's forces in the war, to hold the Communists to our side rather than throw them into the arms of Russia (which is otherwise inevitable if Russia enters the war against Japan), to convince the Kmt of the undesirability of its apparent present plans for eventual civil war, and to bring about some unification which, even though not immediately complete, would provide the basis for peaceful future development toward full democracy'.[47] As a guide to future policy it was shrewd and not without vision and it was given to Roosevelt in preparation for his talks with Hurley. Once again, no record of these crucial discussions was kept, but it is clear that Hurley blamed his lack of progress on sabotage from Stilwell's officers and Foreign Service officers jealous at his appointment. On 27 March, he seemingly convinced the Joint Chiefs of Staff that the Communists could be suppressed with little trouble. For the time being at least, Roosevelt went along with his analysis. At a press conference on 2 April, notable for his ignorance of Chinese conditions, Hurley announced his triumph. The President had decided in his favour: there were to be no arms for the Chinese Communists on the grounds 'that we do recognise the National Government of China and not any armed war lords or armed political parties in China.'[48] This proved to be Roosevelt's final word on China, for just over a week later he died. Had he lived, he would certainly have used Japan's defeat to make major moves over China but it is pointless to guess what these might have been. Davies and Service were forced out of China and Hurley, the champion of a fatally weakened regime, was the new President's ambassador.

By the time of his death, Roosevelt had virtually won the war. His hopes of using his fourth term to win the peace could not be realised and how he would have faced the challenges of the postwar world can never be more than speculation, especially as he did not go out of his way to reveal his purposes. At Yalta, he helped set the European agenda for the next generation, but his legacy for East Asia is less certain. Yet the Japan which emerged in the late 1940s owed a great deal to the planning done by his administration and that was no small achievement given the virulent anti-Japanese racism which gripped the United States at that time. The vision of a Japan, economically restored and freed from those who had led her to war, taking an essential place in postwar East Asia was not an ignoble one. If pragmatism demanded that this be done under the aegis of the Emperor, then so be it – as long as it was clear that he was a mortal ruler, China was very different, for it was not a *tabula rasa* on which Roosevelt could write. Rightly concerned that the Allies should not be seen to be waging a white man's war, and certainly not one for the restoration of the old imperialisms, he sought to ensure Chiang an equal place with Churchill, Stalin and himself, even though he was well aware that China's war effort did not justify it. A contented China would stabilise postwar Asia just as a dis-satisfied Japan had destablised it. But once he had so elevated Chiang, he could not be seen to pull him down, a truth which the Chinese leader grasped. He was flexible. Once convinced by the analyses of his Foreign Service officers, he sanctioned an opening towards the Communists which seemed to promise that the United States would not over-commit herself to the Kuomintang. But he abandoned Stilwell and his last act was to back Hurley's anti-Communist stance. It is easy to castigate Hurley but it was Roosevelt who appointed and then backed him. This prepared the way for American support for the Kuomintang in the civil war which ended in Mao's triumph in the autumn of 1949. Just over a year later, Mao's troops were fighting the Americans in Korea. This was not the outcome Roosevelt had worked for. If he did not win the peace, the decisions he took and the policies he sanctioned towards Japan and China are an inescapable part of our understanding of how postwar East Asia emerged.

NOTES

1. The original is on display at the Roosevelt Library and Museum, New York. Samuel I, Rosenman (ed.), *The Public Papers and Addresses of Franklin D. Roosevelt* (New York, 1950), vol. 10, p. 552.
2. 'We Are Going to Win the War and We Are Going to Win the Peace That Follows', 9 December 1941, Rosenman (ed.) *Papers and Addresses*, pp. 522–31.
3. See, for example, Roosevelt–Chiang Meeting, 25 November 1943, *FRUS* The Conferences at Cairo and Tehran 1943 (Washington, 1961), pp. 349–50.
4. For discussion see the Introduction to T. G. Fraser, *The USA and the Middle East since World War 2* (London 1989).
5. See examples of 'Jap Hunting Licenses' in FDRL OF 197a Box 3.
6. See playbill 'Menace of the Rising Sun' in FDRL OF 197a Box 3.
7. Cohan to M. H. McIntyre, 27 August 1942, FDRL OF 197a Box 3.
8. Roosevelt to Herbert H. Lehman, 5 June 1942, FDRL OF 197a Box 3.
9. For a good discussion of this see Michael H. Hunt, *Ideology and U.S. Foreign Policy* (Yale, 1987), pp. 69–77; David Halberstam, *The Powers That Be* (New York, 1979), pp. 100–2.
10. *The Memoirs of Cordell Hull* (London, 1948), vol. 2, p. 1589.
11. Roosevelt–Chiang Dinner Meeting, 23 November 1943, *FRUS* Cairo and Tehran, pp. 322–5.
12. *Memoirs of Cordell Hull,* vol. 2, p. 1593.
13. See Christopher Thorne, *Allies of a Kind* (London, 1978).
14. *Memoirs of Cordell Hull,* vol. 2, pp. 1589–91.
15. 'A Policy Toward Japan', J. K. Emmerson, 18 August 1944, FDRL Hopkins Papers, Box 334.
16. *Memoirs of Cordell Hull,* vol. 2, pp. 1591–3.
17. See Theodore H. White (ed.), *The Stilwell Papers* (London, 1949); B. Tuchman, *Sand against The Wind: Stilwell and the American experience in China, 1911–45* (New York, 1970).
18. Marshall to Roosevelt, 2 October 1942, FDRL MR Box 10, President to Chiang Kai-shek, 1941–2.
19. Marshall to Roosevelt, 27 February 1943, and Roosevelt to Chiang, 9 March 1943, FDRL MR Box 10, President to Chiang Kai-shek, 1943.
20. Hopkins to Marshall, 9 July 1942, FDRL MR Box 10, President to Chiang Kai-shek, 1941–2.
21. Chiang to Roosevelt, 7 February 1943, FDRL MR Box 10, President to Chiang Kai-shek, 1943.
22. Grace Tully to Roosevelt, nd, enclosing memorandum by J. P. Davies, FDRL PSF Box 27, China 1943.
23. Chennault to Hopkins, 2 July 1943, FDRL Hopkins Papers, Box 331, Chinese Affairs 1943–4.
24. Alsop to Hopkins, 7 May 1943 and 2 July 1943, FDRL Hopkins Papers, Box 331, Chinese Affairs 1943–4.
25. Memorandum by Hopkins, 15 July 1943, FDRL Hopkins Papers, Box 331, Chinese Affairs 1943–4,
26. Roosevelt–Stalin Meeting, 29 November 1943, *FRUS* Cairo and Tehran, pp. 529–33.

27. The Cairo conference is covered in *FRUS* Cairo and Tehran.
28. Sol Adler to Dr White. 13 December 1943, FDRL Morgenthau 684.
29. Memorandum for the President, Department of State, 2 December 1943, FDRL PSF Box 27, China 1943.
30. Davies to Hopkins, 31 December 1943, FDRL Hopkins Papers, Box 334, 'Serious Trouble in China'.
31. Roosevelt to Leahy, 3 February 1943, FDRL MR Box 10, President to Chiang Kai-shek, 1944; Hopkins to Roosevelt, 7 February 1944, FDRL PSF Box 27, China, January–June 1944; Roosevelt to Chiang, 9 February 1944, FDRL MR Box 10, President to Chiang Kai-shek, 1944.
32. Marshall to Leahy, 28 February 1944 and Marshall to Roosevelt, 4 April 1944, FDRL MR Box 10, President to Chiang Kai-shek, 1944.
33. Carlson to Roosevelt, 23 February 1944 and Roosevelt to Carlson, 2 March 1944, FDRL PSF Box 27, China January – June 1944.
34. Wallace to Roosevelt, 28 June 1944, *FRUS*, 1944, vol. VI, China (Washington, 1967), pp. 234–5.
35. See the Introduction to J. W. Esherwick (ed.), *Lost Chance in China: The World War II Despatches of John S. Service* (New York, 1974); Memorandum of 28 July 1944, Hopkins to Roosevelt, 6 September 1944, FDRL PSF Box 27, China, July – December 1944.
36. Leahy to Roosevelt, 4 July 1944, FDRL MR Box 10, President to Chiang Kai-shek, 1944.
37. As reference 34.
38. Lyman P. Van Slyke (ed.), *The China White Paper* (Stanford, 1967), pp. 66–8.
39. Hurley to Roosevelt, 10 October 1944, *FRUS*, 1944, vol. VI, pp. 166–70.
40. Roosevelt to Chiang, 16 September 1944, FDRL MR Box 10, President to Chiang Kai-shek, 1944.
41. White (ed.), *Stilwell Papers*, pp. 310.
42. As reference 39.
43. White (ed.), *Stilwell Papers*, pp. 320–2.
44. Roosevelt to Carlson, 15 November 1944, FDRL PSF, China, January – December 1944; William D. Leahy, *I Was There* (London, 1950), p. 338.
45. See Fifth Plenary Meeting, 8 February 1945, *FRUS,* The Conferences at Malta and Yalta 1945 (Washington, 1955), p. 771.
46. Hurley to Secretary of State, *FRUS*, 1945, vol. VII, The Far East, China (Washington, 1969), p. 229.
47. Atcheson to Secretary of State, *FRUS*, 1945, vol. VII, pp. 242–6.
48. Leahy, *I Was There*, p. 395; Hurley Press Conference, 2 April 1945, *FRUS*, 1945, vol. VII, pp. 317–20.

8 A Particularly Vital Issue? Harry Truman and Japan, 1945–52

Roger Buckley

This is a brief essay in neglect. It asks whether President Truman's personal role in the conduct of US policies towards Japan deserves reconsideration after two generations of near silence. It is a topic that continues to evoke considerable heat at least in private among senior participants. Correspondence with presidential aides and General MacArthur's staff suggests that claims and counter-claims remain firmly held and might now be brought before the bar for possible adjudication against the available archival and secondary sources.[1]

Recent re-evaluation of the ending of the Pacific War and the subsequent occupation of Japan have greatly expanded the general focus of study but few commentators have stayed to examine the extent of Truman's involvement. Publications on the Truman presidency rarely tackle the question in these terms, preferring to see events either from a MacArthurian viewpoint centring on SCAP (Supreme Commander Allied Powers) GHQ in Tokyo or shifting the emphasis to Washington's bureaucratic machinery. In neither cases does the White House receive more than a modicum of attention.[2]

Coincidence or not, the entire history of Japan's surrender, occupation and belated peace settlements took place during the Truman years. That and the host of policy decisions enacted under his signature ought to be excuse enough to start excavating to discern the extent of presidential involvement. Three standard chronological divides will be employed in the hunt: first, the protracted and complicated process of ending the war and determining the Allied surrender terms; next the establishment of broad policy guidelines and general supervision of the occupation and lastly the equally messy business of 1950–51 that led eventually to the San Francisco terms. It will be suggested that President Truman's interest and participation was strongest during the first and third periods. His primary concern appears to have been in what broadly might be entitled the two very different grand strategies of ending war in 1945 and fashioning peace in 1951; both were vivid illustrations of American power and both sets of decisions were taken without overmuch consideration for the sensitivities of its allies.[3] Truman's handiwork with regard to Japan heralds the beginnings of an enormous advance by the United States in what some British authors still prefer to call the Far East. Any postwar history of United States foreign policy in the region must, at least from the perspective of the early 1990s, emphasise American unilateralism in regard to occupied Japan and the shift by 1951 to the creation of a tentative partnership with Tokyo. Successes in the establishment of this 'special relationship' invite the student to return to the years of its birth when talk of shared values and global partnerships were inconceivable.

Although much Western interest continues to focus on the roles of Truman and his advisers the decision to end the war was a Japanese one. Not even the overwhelming military and economic might of the United States could force the Japanese government to do as it wished. War termination was a battle fought out within establishment circles in Tokyo; it was of course, influenced by American (and Soviet) acts but the world's first atomic power could not get its way unless its strengths were seen as demonstrations of value to support those in the Japanese cabinet who wished to surrender. Continued atomic and conventional bombing coupled with the existing tight naval blockade would only have made the American government's objectives harder to realise, since the dangers of a possible Japanese breakdown in political and bureaucratic order would have left Truman's staff without a central authority to talk to.[4] Evidence from British records that the President on 14 August 1945 'remarked sadly that he now had no alternative but to order an atomic bomb to be dropped on Tokyo'[5] indicates how precarious the surrender process always was. The conclusion to what Japanese historians are now terming 'the Japanese–Anglo–American War'[6] was far from clear cut. The Japanese government took an inordinate amount of time over discussing the surrender question and the conditions that it finally elicited from the Truman administration over the future of the Imperial institution were bought dearly in additional Japanese blood.

While Harry Truman undeniably inherited political and technological programmes for use in defeating Japan his personal imprint is, as he never attempted to deny, also evident. Truman's bravado in public statements and in private correspondence during the long years of his retirement leaves one uneasy and is not the entire picture. The President, it has been argued above, was obliged to wait for Imperial Japan's decisions and in both earlier policy over the deployment of the atomic bomb and the question of how to respond to Japan's insistence on retaining its *kokutai* (national polity based on the Throne) Truman looked to others for advice. His own mind does not appear to have been as quickly or completely made up as his published works would suggest. We now know that John McCloy, for example, sensed that Truman may have had hopes of avoiding the use of the atomic bomb[7] and evidence published in the past decade shows the President displaying a conflicting variety of attitudes towards Japan. Truman could talk of severe punishment and revenge; he would also note in his diary that the bomb should only be used against 'a purely military' target.[8] Unfortunately, as Truman was only too well aware, saturation bombing had by 1945 been widely used in Europe and Asia without overmuch compunction; equally members of the Roosevelt cabinet in the spring of 1945 had already coined the new verb 'to morgenthau' (to punish severely) when considering how to treat the surrendered populations in Germany and Japan.[9]

'The primary task facing the nation today is to win the war in Japan – to win it completely and to win it as quickly as possible'[10]: these had been Truman's opening remarks of his address to Congress on 1 June 1945 but the speed and successes of the summer had been unimaginable three months earlier. Truman was at the centre of events over the ending of the war in the Pacific without perhaps possessing the decisiveness that he constantly wished to project. It is hard to dissent from the suggestion made specifically over the atomic bomb by Richard Haynes that 'it would have been difficult for Truman to have decided otherwise. He was new to command, overawed by the reputations of Stimson and Marshall, and untutored in international relations'.[11] To have not used the bomb would have been surprising since 'the system, circumstances, and his own predisposition led Truman to accept a military conclusion'. As Richard Haynes has pointed out, Truman noted, after 'discussing with his advisers the Japanese cities to be marked as targets, "I then agreed (emphasis added) to use of the atomic bomb" '.[12] Certainly the President had the final word but to have gone against the bulk of the advice he received would have required remarkable character. That Truman may have had mental reservations is perhaps suggested by his statement to cabinet members on 26 October 1945 when he told them that he did not know the number of atomic bombs that the US possessed.[13] Secretaries Forrestal and Wallace, speaking from very different ideological positions quickly said that the commander-in-chief ought to be fully acquainted with such vital information. Likewise Truman's letter to Dr Carl Compton of December 1946 is very much the conventional defence of his position. There was no need for Truman to argue that 'the Japanese were given fair warning and were offered the terms, which they finally accepted, well in advance of the dropping of the bomb. I imagine the bomb caused them to accept the terms'.[14]

Once Japan had surrendered Truman worked to ensure that the United States' claims to paramountcy over Japan were respected by its former Allies. For a few brief weeks the subject of Japan's occupation and Washington's concern for north-east Asia had a priority in the White House that would not be seen again until 1950. President Truman, in the immediate aftermath of the Potsdam conference and his doubts over Soviet behaviour in central Europe and the Far East,[15] was more concerned with asserting and maintaining American power over Japan than considering the details of how this power might be translated into policies towards Japan.

Truman's involvement in the regional picture followed from Japan's surrender and the need for policy decisions over American, British, Soviet and Chinese responsibilities in the aftermath of Japan's sudden capitulation. The ending of Imperial Japan's rule led to immense improvisation. Correspondence files, maps and directives had to be searched and programmes rewritten constantly. The Liaotung peninsula needed to be distinguished from the Shantung peninsula; the question of who got what in Manchuria, Korea and the Kuriles decided by balancing earlier Allied agreements against national interests. The future of a good percentage of the globe was at stake. Much was left deliberately unclear as the United States attempted, for example, to keep simultaneously in the good books of both Britain and China over the reoccupation or repossession of Hong Kong,[16] and the wish to take the Japanese surrender of the Kuriles was placed against past Yalta promises to the Soviet Union.

In the scramble Truman took a number of important decisions. He nominated Douglas MacArthur first as the United States' commander in Japan and then as the senior Allied figure responsible for the occupation. Despite the president's reservations over MacArthur's personality, (Truman's diary bristles with remarks on 'Mr Prima Donna'), he surely made the correct appointment. It need not be seen, however, as an inevitable one; John Emmerson after all was assigned as Admiral Nimitz's political adviser in 1945 on the assumption that the navy might be running Japan, and there were Democrats aplenty who cautioned Truman against creating a political rival in MacArthur.[17]

Truman's personal interventions concerned American–Soviet relations towards post-surrender Japan. The object, as Truman noted in his famous 'I'm tired [of] babying the Soviets' letter to Secretary James Byrnes was that 'we should maintain complete control of Japan and the Pacific',[18] while expecting Allied military cooperation in the burden-sharing involved and support for 'the occupation authority in Japan . . . organised on the principle of centralised administration, avoiding the division of the country into national zones of independent responsibility administered separately'.[19] Truman eventually gained his first goal, though only after excluding Moscow and most American Allies from any effective role in the occupation. Yet the issues of the international arrangements under which Japan was occupied until 1952 were hardly an immediate and automatic exercise in American power in an emerging bipolar world. The suggestion that the great powers had a preordained 'Yalta system' in their diplomatic pouches[20] or that the history of the Cold War in east Asia saw a clear-cut division into spheres of influence does not correspond to the manoeuvrings of the autumn of 1945.[21] For one thing it ignores the substantial objections of states such as Britain and Australia to American designs on and for Japan and neglects the occasions when the Soviet Union and Western powers were in agreement against the United States' bid to run the occupation entirely in its own way. Foreign Secretary Ernest Bevin, for example, initially thought of not attending the proposed Moscow foreign ministers' conference of December 1945 out of pique at James Byrnes' private diplomacy. Britain probably had higher expectations of sharing in the control of occupied Japan and therefore greater losses over the eventual creation of a weak Far Eastern Commission in Washington and an ineffective Allied Council for Japan than the Soviet Union. The international negotiations over how Japan should be run are less evidence of an early phase of the Cold War in Asia than a demonstration of American regionalism that had no truck with challengers from any quarter.

On securing a strong American stance against Soviet claims over occupied Japan Truman had very definite views. He and his administration could not accept that the Soviet Union's military contribution to the Pacific War entitled Moscow to any substantial role in the post-surrender arrangements. Probably, as Secretary Byrnes admitted in his memoirs, the American government had underestimated the extent of Stalin's disappointment at US proposals for control machinery that left General MacArthur in the driving seat.[22] The failure of a personal message from Truman to Stalin, for example, in late October 1945, to deal with the international arrangements for Japan led Stalin to remark to Ambassador Harriman that the Soviet Union was being treated 'as a piece of furniture'.[23] The Soviet leader had previously said 'the Soviet Union had become an American satellite in the Pacific. This was a role it could not accept. It was not being treated as an ally. The Soviet Union would not be a satellite of the United States in the Far East or elsewhere'.[24] Doubtless there were British diplomats who would have been happy (in private) to substitute their own country for Russia in Stalin's complaint list and mutter, too, of American unilateralism.

Truman's interest in securing the fruits of victory in the Pacific did not apparently extend to concern over personal involvement in how the occupation of Japan was conducted. The president, of course, was required to initial all major policy directives but his role beyond this was slight. Charles Kades, in dissenting from Clark Clifford's view that 'President Truman considered US occupation policy a particularly vital issue',[25] doubts that the US Initial Post-Surrender Policy for Japan had 'any input whatsoever by the White House'.[26] Kades, who until 25 August 1945 had worked in the war Department's Civil Affairs Division with General Hilldring and Assistant Secretary of War McCloy, is unaware of any presidential discussion on the preparation of early occupation policy.[27] Once the international arrangements for Japan had been broadly agreed to and it was apparent that MacArthur was very much in charge of affairs, Truman appears to have taken only a casual interest in the progress of the occupation. This could be justified on at least three grounds. Firstly, the President had immediate and continuous difficulties with regard to Soviet behaviour in Europe that inevitably claimed his attention; secondly the occupation appeared to be in capable hands and thirdly movement towards a peace settlement would be contingent on cooperative agreements among the wartime Allies that patently did not exist in the mid-1940s.[28]

Truman's known interventions over occupation policy are rare. He did have some differences with MacArthur but these should not be exaggerated. The first concerned the unfortunate statements from SCAP on the lowering of troop requirements for occupation duties at the moment when President Truman's administration was attempting to persuade a sceptical Congress of the necessity of slowing the rate of demobilisation. MacArthur's biographer has called this 'a Minor But Revealing Confrontation',[29] yet neither the troop question nor MacArthur's refusal to return to Washington to accept a hero's welcome can be said to have led to any swift alterations in who would run the occupation and what policy might be. No doubt it left Truman more wary of MacArthur but this was hardly a new revelation and the President was not about to deny the liabilities or popularity of SCAP. Truman clearly needed MacArthur if the occupation of Japan was to succeed. Nearly two years later in reply to correspondence from the US Political Adviser for Japan George Atcheson Jr over the future of Japan, Truman's response was merely the lame comment 'I sincerely hope that we can get matters successfully concluded in Japan and I am very sure that we will accomplish that'.[30]

The available evidence would suggest that aside from limited personal correspondence and occasional discussion of occupation issues in his cabinet[31] Truman maintained a 'hands off' approach for most of his presidency.

Truman's attitude, in the opinion of Clark Clifford, was that:

> The United States had fought a long and arduous war against Japanese
> aggression and militarism during World War II. President Truman sought
> to prevent a repetition of this ordeal by fostering a politically democratic
> and economically prosperous postwar Japan.
>
>   American occupation policy hinged on this objective. It aimed to
> disarm and demobilise Japan's armed forces, democratise its political
> process, codify individual civil liberties, and broaden land ownership.
> President Truman and his advisers believed these measures promised the
> best hope for lasting reconstruction.[32]

Clearly as long as MacArthur and his staff were engaged on implementing
these policies Japan was best left alone. The fact remains, however, that
both the White House and SCAP GHQ in the Dai-Ichi Building would
claim responsibility for the American successes during the occupation.
With some notable exceptions, land reform being an obvious example, the
Truman administration could feel that its directives formed the basis for
what was occurring in Japan, while SCAP staff continue to insist, at least
until 1949, that 'the policies in Japan were pretty much what MacArthur
desired'.[33] It may be that the prize can best be divided by noting that
MacArthur's reforms were largely in place before Washington, under its
concern for America's security in the Pacific as the Cold War in Asia
evolved in 1948, began to 're-discover' Japan. MacArthur, under loose
instructions which he interpreted as he judged fit, created the foundations of
a more liberal Japan, while the Truman administration concentrated after
1949 in devising schemes for integrating a hesitant Japan within American-
designed political and military regional orders.

   Truman's personal role is in evidence on the long road to the San
Francisco peace settlements. By the spring of 1949 the acting secretary of
state is reminding Secretary of Defense Louis Johnson that Truman had
approved National Security Council paper 'Recommendations with Respect
to US Policy Toward Japan' (NSC 13/2) and its revised version NSC 13/3
and that action is now required on a mass of issues relating to these recent
changes to occupation policy.[34] Yet not even presidential signatures would
easily shift some in Washington and Tokyo – MacArthur had neglected, for
example, to circulate the confidential version of NSC 13/2 to his own staff.
These measures called for SCAP GHQ to alter some economic policies
within Japan and to scrap what the CIA as late as September 1948 had
assumed in its security assessments would be the continuing reality that
'Japan will not be permitted to maintain a military establishment'.[35]

Evidence of the evolution of Truman's views on Japan is perhaps illustrated by the nature of presidential appointments with reference to the occupation. The change in attitude between Truman's blessing that Edwin Pauley conduct a reparations survey in the autumn of 1945 which Pauley at least saw as being based on the principle of 'severity combined with fairness' and the appointments of first Joseph Dodge and then John Foster Dulles is striking.[36] Dodge's austerity package for salvaging the Japanese economy and Truman's invitation to Dulles to devise as comprehensive a peace settlement as possible suggest that by late 1948 or the spring of 1949 the Japan question was once again a presidential concern. It also marks the beginning of the end for General MacArthur's viceregal sway over Japan as both the State and Army departments began to claw back responsibilities that had long been held by SCAP.[37] Yet any diminution of MacArthur's control was no easy matter and the State Department in December 1950 was still complaining that recommendations in NSC 13/3 and the earlier Kennan report of March 1948 had yet to be implemented.[38] No wonder President Truman avoided tackling MacArthur during the occupation and adopted the alternative approach of leaving him well alone in public, while complaining in private of his behaviour.[39]

In retrospect it is apparent that differences within the US bureaucracy were the greatest obstacle to what by 1950 was already a lengthy and frustrating period of consultations and set-backs. What mattered most, as the American diplomat Robert Fearey noted in his lengthy summary on the events leading to San Francisco, was 'the fact that the prime prerequisite of a treaty was an arrangement in or in connection with the treaty to ensure Japan's post-treaty security'.[40] The problem, as first Ernest Bevin and later President Truman[41] agreed, was not the prospect of anger from the Soviet Union or the People's Republic of China but dissension among American diplomats and generals.

Secretary of State Acheson, assisted by Dean Rusk, appears to have employed some general comments from Truman to revive the peace momentum and turn back the reservations of the Pentagon who, both before and again in the midst of the Korean War, had no wish to contemplate further restrictions on US bases within Japan. Truman's reference to the ability of the United States and Britain to press ahead with a treaty 'whether the USSR participated or not'[42] and the transfer of Dean Rusk to the post of assistant secretary for far eastern affairs in late March 1950 got the ball rolling. Rusk, who volunteered to move to his new job knowing full well that it was a demotion to a highly sensitive and potentially thankless task,[43] was able to use his friendship with Dulles to good advantage. The President gritted his teeth and in April Dulles joined the State Department to work on a peace settlement for Japan. The choice of a leading Republican was made less for Dulles' knowledge of Asia – he did not have any – than as a means of deflecting mounting criticism from the conservatives in Congress angry at the administration for the 'loss' of China.

By the autumn of 1950 the log-jam had been broken. Truman's signing of first authorisation to Dulles to get on with treaty negotiations in late July,[44] and then his approval of NSC 60/1 on 8 September, ensured that the peace process could be accelerated.[45] The convolutions of the next twelve months involved gaining a rough consensus in the American civil and military establishments and then working with other powers prepared to accept Japan back in an American-dominated Asian-Pacific system. It was in essence a repeat of the United States' strategy in the autumn of 1945. There was a similar reluctance to make substantial concessions to America's allies, a cold-shouldering of the Soviet Union and little hesitancy to instruct the Japanese government on what it had to do to regain its sovereignty. It is surely stretching the bounds of credibility to see the reception of the various signatories to the San Francisco settlements as 'effective witness to the genuinely collaborative nature of the treaty negotiations and of the final text'.[46] The victor nation was not about to accept major alterations to its design for Japan and Japan's place in the region. Dulles captured the scale and nature of American long-term policy best when he noted in the summer of 1950 that planned security arrangements 'gave the United States the right to maintain in Japan as much force as we wanted, anywhere we wanted, for as long as we wanted . . .'.[47] The realities of American strength were similarly spelt out when the United States described itself as 'the principal occupying Power' at the San Francisco peace conference.

The minutiae of the eventual text and the months of prior consultation were the work of Dulles and his staff. Truman's hand, however, should be recalled in starting the process in motion and approving the final treaty and the associated security arrangements. It was an accomplishment that needs to be placed in its context. The Truman administration by 1950 was under attack from Republican senators for its Far East policies and then by a wider public for the conduct of its limited war in Korea, yet work on the Japanese peace treaty continued. This could only succeed if those involved had instructions and support. Truman's approach is well caught in his letter to Dulles of January 1951 that both designated Dulles as special representative of the President, with ambassadorial ranking, and stated that 'our principal purpose in the proposed settlement is to secure the adherence of the Japanese nation to the free nations of the world and to assure that it will play its full part in resisting the further expansion of communist imperialism'.[48] Truman insisted that Dulles work 'to bring about a peace settlement with Japan without awaiting a favourable resolution of the military situation in Korea'. The President also hinted at his own reservations over Japan's future conduct. He told Dulles that 'Japan should increasingly acquire the ability to defend itself' and that a Pacific pact, comprising 'Australia, New Zealand, the Philippines, Japan, the United States, and perhaps Indonesia' ought to be established. Truman cautioned, however, that any such body 'would have the dual purpose of assuring combined action as between the members to resist aggression from without and also to resist attack by one of the members, e.g. Japan, if Japan should again become aggressive'. He continued; 'In connection with this latter point, the United States Government should agree to this course of action only as the other nations accept the general basis on which the United States is prepared to conclude a peace settlement with Japan'.[49] Translated into cruder terms Truman was prepared to accept that many Pacific nations (whose wariness was shared by elements of domestic public opinion inside the United States) would find his administration sympathetic to a Pacific pact. At the end of the day bilateral security arrangements replaced the original design but as the CIA predicted in April 1951, 'the present governments in these countries are reconciled to the necessity of Japanese defensive rearmament'.[50] They had little choice in the matter, of course, if they wished to retain Washington's support.

Once the San Francisco peace treaty had been concluded the Truman administration turned to one final challenge in Japan. Although the US–Japan security pact had been signed by Prime Minister Yoshida immediately after the peace treaty in September 1951, it was important that an administrative agreement on US military installations be initialled in 1952 to flesh out the broad policy outlines. It is no coincidence that President Truman selected Dean Rusk for this task, since the State Department official had influenced Truman over moving forward on the peace treaty in 1950. Indeed, Rusk's biographer has gone so far as to claim that the real architect of San Francisco was not Dulles but Rusk. Thomas Schoenbaum suggests, rather breathlessly, that 'Dulles was the up-front negotiator and performed admirably, but insiders at State knew that Rusk was calling most of the shots'.[51] Rusk's deferential correspondence with Truman must have come as something of a relief to a president beset on all sides by criticism and dismal public opinion polls.[52]

Days before the final administrative agreement meetings headed by Rusk and Foreign Minister Okazaki, Truman issued a lengthy memorandum to the National Security Council on 'interim policy with respect to

Japan'. In a 13-point paper Truman approved recommendations from his secretaries of State and Defense that looked forward to a fresh relationship with Tokyo. The report was both negative and positive. It began in cautious language by noting that the 'security of Japan is of such vital strategic importance to the United States position in the Far East that the United States cannot permit hostile forces to gain control of the territory of Japan',[53] and then reckoned with the prospects of a 'genuinely voluntary United States–Japanese partnership' that 'will add greatly to United States prestige and influence throughout Asia'.[54] In what would shortly prove to be an area of considerable disappointment for the next administration, Truman's memorandum spoke of intending to 'support the establishment of Japanese military forces consistent with the requirements of a sound economy and the needs of collective security in the Far East'.[55] Thus by the spring of 1952 the political and military foundations of American policies towards Japan that have survived far longer than the original architects could have possibly imagined were approximately in place.

President Truman's dealings with Japan in the years from the last months of the Pacific War to the first months of the post-treaty period form an important thread running through his years in office. It was a field in which Truman had no particular expertise; neither his extensive readings in history nor any of his earlier careers before attaining the White House had had the slightest Asian dimension.[56] Truman's mental map put Europe at the centre of international affairs. Yet even if east Asia received less attention thanks to its lower priority with Truman, the linked questions of the United States' supremacy over Japan both in war and peace could hardly be ignored. The President's involvement was at critical moments; the rest of the time he kept out of MacArthur's way and let him get on with the daunting task of running occupied Japan.

The evidence – much of it admittedly fragmentary – suggests that Truman's policies for Japan relied on key individuals, such as Acheson and Rusk, and certain institutions, particularly the State Department and the National Security Council. If the secret of deploying presidential power is the ability to delegate, then Truman's apparently casual approach to Japan was not unsuccessful. Truman acted under advice but within a clear framework that wished to ensure continued American dominance over and around both an occupied and newly-independent Japan. Truman would not have wished to claim the credit that is due to others, yet he deserves more than merely an honorary mention. In a characteristically unsent letter to the columnist Arthur Krock in September 1952, Truman posed the question 'were the Japanese Treaty and the Pacific Agreements blunders?',[57] to which this paper can give only one answer. Post-revisionism ought to be able to find a place for Truman inside MacArthur's pantheon.

NOTES

The following abbreviation has been used: HSTL – Harry S. Truman Library, Independence, Missouri. I am grateful for financial and scholarly assistance from the staff of the Truman Library in the preparation of this paper.

1. I am grateful for correspondence from Clark Clifford, President Truman's aide, and Charles Kades, Deputy Head of Government Section, SCAP GHQ. Mr Clifford's remarks on President Truman stand in strong contrast to those of Mr Kades. It must be stressed that interpretations of their remarks are my responsibility. Extracts from the correspondence appear later in this paper.
2. For a recent survey of the literature see John. W. Dower, 'Occupied Japan and the cold war in Asia', in Michael J. Lacey (ed.), *The Truman Presidency* (Cambridge, 1989), footnotes pp. 370–3. A more exhaustive treatment can be found in chapter 8, 'The Allied Occupation of Japan, 1945–1952' of Sadao Asada's edited bibliographical guide *Japan and the World, 1853–1952* (Columbia, 1989).
3. On British reservations see R. Buckley, *Occupation Diplomacy: Britain, the United States and Japan, 1945–1952* (Cambridge, 1982).
4. The issue is discussed at length in Leon V. Sigal's *Fighting to a Finish* (Ithaca,1988). See also Buckley, 'Waiting till Midnight: Japan's Reluctance to Surrender and its immediate post-war behaviour', *The Journal of Social Science, (ICU),* October 1980.
5. Balfour to Bevin, most immediate/top secret, 14 August 1945, Bevin private papers (FO 800), PRO. Confirmation that Truman met with Balfour can be found in Truman's appointments schedule, HSTL PSF Box 82.
6. See, for example, Shiozaki Hiroaki, 'The Round Table Movement and the Path to the Japanese–Anglo–American War', in a special number of *Kokusai seiji (International Relations)* entitled 'From the Sino–Japanese War to the Japanese–Anglo–American War', vol. 91, May 1989.
7. Statement entitled 'President Truman and the Atom Bomb', by James McCloy, forwarded with covering letter by McCloy to Clark M. Clifford, 17 September 1984. McCloy suggests that 'I have what I consider to be a convincing indication of the fact that President Truman sought and hoped to find a solution to the prompt and successful end to the war with Japan without the necessity of dropping any atomic bombs, though he was wholly prepared to accept the full and final responsibility in the end for having done so after the rejection of the Potsdam ultimatum', HSTL Clifford Papers. McCloy felt that opposition from James Byrnes ended the possibility of warning Japan of the bomb and preserving a modified Imperial structure after Japan had surrendered.

8.   On the contradictions displayed by Truman see Paul Boyer '"Some sort of peace": President Truman, the American people, and the atomic bomb', in Michael J. Lacey (ed.) *The Truman Presidency;* Buckley, *Occupation Diplomacy,* endnotes.

9.   See entry for 1 May 1945 in Walter Millis (ed.), *The Forrestal Diaries* (London, 1952), p. 67. Secretary Forrestal's reservations over a Carthaginian occupation of Japan were not out of any apparent sympathy for Japan but concerned 'our political objectives in the Far East'.

10. Quoted in 'The Road to Tokyo and Beyond', from the director of war mobilization and reconversion, 1 July 1945, HSTL PSF, Japan Box 182.

11. Richard F. Haynes, *The Awesome Power: Harry S. Truman as Commander-in-Chief* (Baton Rouge, 1973), p. 59.

12. Ibid., p. 60.

13. Cabinet meeting, 26 October 1945, HSTL, Matthew J. Connelly Papers.

14. Truman to Dr. Compton, 16 December 1946, HSTL, PSF, General File, Atomic Bomb. Compton was to defend Truman shortly in *The Atlantic Monthly,* December 1946.

15. See Marc S. Gallichio, *The Cold War Begins in Asia* (New York, 1988) for an examination of the Truman administration's Asian actions in 1945.

16. On the Japanese surrender in the region see Louis Allen, *The End of the War in Asia* (London, 1976); over Hong Kong see R. Buckley, 'From Reoccupation to EXPO: Hong Kong–Japanese relations, 1945–1970, *Journal of Social Science (ICU),* October 1989. Anti-colonialism may have been a lesser factor in Truman's behaviour than it was in the thinking of Roosevelt.

17. See Michael Schaller, *The American Occupation of Japan* (Oxford, 1985), p. 21. Presumably Truman feared that the immediate consequences of not appointing MacArthur outweighed any long-term difficulties.

18. Truman diary entry, 5 January 1946; whether this unsent letter was shown to Byrnes remains unclear. Robert H. Ferrell, *Off The Record* (Harmondworth, 1980), p. 80.

19. State-War-Navy Coordinating Committee memorandum for the President on 'national composition of forces to occupy Japan proper in the post-defeat period', approved by Truman, 18 August 1945, HSTL PSF. The relative ease with which the USA and Japan began the occupation soon reduced this Allied troop priority.

20. The phrase is Iriye Akira's. See Iriye, *The Cold War in Asia* (Englewood Cliffs, 1974).

21. On respect for spheres of influence see John Gaddis, *The Long Peace* (Oxford, 1989), p. 239. On British dissatisfaction see Buckley *Occupation Diplomacy,* pp. 48–55.

22. James F. Byrnes, *Speaking Frankly* (London, 1948), p. 216.

23. W. Averell Harriman and Elie Abel, *Special Envoy to Churchill and Stalin* (London, 1976), p. 514. The American interpreter present felt that Stalin had not forgiven the US refusal to allow a Soviet claim to Hokkaido.

24. Ibid.

25. Clark Clifford to author, 30 May 1990.

26. Charles Kades to author, 7 July 1990. In Kades's opinion when 'Roosevelt was President there was plenty of White House input'.

27. Secretary Byrnes clearly had hopes of pressing ahead with a far eastern settlement. For his draft of a Japanese peace conference see *Speaking Frankly,* pp. 223–4. See also Byrnes to Truman on 'Peace Treaty regarding Japan, 27 February 1946, HSTL PSF Box 182.

28. Only when it was apparent that international cooperation was improbable and major differences within the US bureaucracy were solved could peace become a reality. See R. Buckley, 'Joining the Club: The Japanese Question and Anglo–American Peace Diplomacy, 1950–1951', *Modern Asian Studies,* April 1985.

29. D. Clayton James, *The Years of MacArthur,* vol. III, *Triumph and Disaster 1945–1964* (Boston, 1985), p. 17.

30. Truman to George Atcheson Jr, 10 July 1947, HSTL PSF Japan, Box 182. Atcheson had noted in his letter on future US 'lasting control' over Japan that 'General MacArthur concurs in this letter'.

31. Truman apparently said nothing when conflicting views on the food situation in Japan by Secretary of War Patterson and Secretary of Agriculture Anderson were voiced in March 1946 nor with reference in 1951 to the Japanese peace treaty when Dean Acheson spoke. See HSTL, Matthew Connelly Papers.

32. Clifford to author, 30 May 1990.

33. Kades to author, 7 July 1990.

34. James Webb to Louis Johnson, 23 May 1949, Bureau of Far Eastern Affairs, NSC-Box 2, lot 56D225, RG 59, State Dept. Papers, National Archives, Washington.

35. President's copy, CIA report SR-38 on Japan, September 1948, HSTL PSF.

36. Dodge had worked for the president in assessing the economic position of Germany. Truman had misgivings over asking Dulles to help the administration.

37. It is doubtful, however, if Schaller's view that 'during 1949 and 1950, MacArthur hung on in Tokyo as something of a figurehead, although he and the administration sustained the fiction of his authority' is entirely the case. See Michael Schaller, *Douglas MacArthur* (New York, 1989), p. 157.

38. Interim measures for the Security of Japan, 26 December 1950, Johnson Papers, Box 1, lot file 54D278, RG 59, State Dept Papers, National Archives.

39. MacArthur, of course, could be equally frank on the president and the JCS. Reports from the British mission in Tokyo provide revealing insights into SCAP's opinions on Washington.

40. Feary 'Summary of negotiations leading up to the conclusion of the Treaty of Peace with Japan', 18 September 1951, in Thomas W. Burkman (ed.) *The Occupation of Japan: The International Context* (Norfolk, Va., 1984), p. 280.

41. The slowness of the Truman administration to comply with assurances that had been given to London on drafting a peace treaty was complicated by the explosive domestic political debates involving east Asia after 1949.

42. Schaller, *The American Occupation of Japan,* p. 246.

43. On Rusk see Thomas J. Schoenbaum, *Waging Peace and War* (New York, 1988), pp. 226–9.

44. Ronald W. Pruessen, *John Foster Dulles: The Road to Power* (New York, 1982), p. 457.

45. Dower, op. cit., footnote p. 398. Dower terms US policy from 1949 to 1951 the 'hard cold-war' approach.

46. Feary, op. cit., p. 295.
47. Pruessen, *Dulles,* p. 459.
48. Truman to Dulles, 10 January 1951, HSTL PSF.
49. Ibid.
50. CIA report, NIEE-19, 20 April 1951, HSTL PSF.
51. Schoenbaum, *Waging Peace and War,* p. 226. He suggests that this was 'one of his most notable accomplishments'. The same is often claimed for Dulles's career as well.
52. Rusk to Truman, 3 March 1952, HSTL Official File.
53. Memorandum by Truman to National Security Council, 21 February 1952, NSC 125, HSTL PSF.
54. Ibid.
55. Ibid.
56. I am grateful for discussions with Professor Ferrell on Truman's character and background.
57. See Truman to Krock (unsent), 11 September 1952, in Ferrell, *Off The Record,* p. 270.

9 Coming to Terms with Japan: New Zealand's Experience 1945–63
Ann Trotter

Commenting on the official visit of Japanese Prime Minister Ikeda to Wellington in October 1963, the *New Zealand Herald* editorial writer noted:

> In international affairs, trade even more than time seems to act as the great healer. Not so many years ago when the Americans were urging an early peace treaty with Japan, New Zealand regarded the whole pro-position with certain doubts and reservations. Today the prime minister of Japan can visit New Zealand as an honoured guest and can discuss with our own prime minister shared interests aspirations and objectives. Trade rather than diplomacy has prompted amity and understanding.[1]

This statement neatly summed up the basis for the changed situation in New Zealand–Japanese relations since 1945. Economics was then, and remains, the key to the relationship. By the 1960s New Zealanders had realised that it was necessary, in the uncertain world in which they found themselves, to come to terms with Japan. The need to trade, rather than grand strategy or a desire to put bitter wartime memories behind them, was the spur for New Zealanders in the development of this relationship. Claims were made from 1945 about the importance and significance of the 'Pacific neighbourhood' in which New Zealand and Japan find themselves, but New Zealanders on the whole did not feel 'neighbourly' in the sense of being concerned for, excessively curious about, or anxious to be better informed about Japan. Indeed one of the problems for those diplomats involved in the cultivation of the relationship, as this came to be seen as more important by govern-ments in the 1960s, was to find ties with Japan, other than commercial, which would seem in any way significant to the New Zealand public. Nevertheless by 1963 expanding trade and New Zealand's increasing need of Japan had created a relationship which was, if not not close, amicable.

It can be argued that the New Zealand–Japan relationship has been a key indicator of an increasingly independent New Zealand foreign policy since 1945 and contains within it milestones in the development of New Zealand's approach to diplomatic and commercial relations with other countries. It demonstrates some of the problems faced by a small state anxious to make its voice heard in international affairs and, with trade its driving force, illustrates the importance of economic factors in the policy considerations of small states.

Until relatively recent times New Zealanders have not had much understanding of, or interest in Asia. The outbreak of war in the Pacific and the expansion of that war into the islands of South-East Asia demonstrated to New Zealanders that the Pacific Ocean might be an all too convenient and dangerous link between their islands and a military power which had hitherto seemed a distant and strangely 'foreign' Asian country on the Pacific's rim. Japan's actions at Pearl Harbor and thereafter made New Zealanders aware of the realities associated with their country's geographical position in the south Pacific. A feeling of remoteness has been identified as part of the New Zealand psyche until at least the mid-twentieth century and at the same time, somewhat paradoxically, New Zealanders' 'Pacific consciousness' was exceedingly low. In 1941 most New Zealanders knew more about the Straits of Dover than the Straits of Malacca but the fall of Singapore and the sinking of the *Prince of Wales* and the *Repulse* in 1942 forced New Zealanders to recognise not only that the British navy could no longer be their shield but that their future was bound up with the security of the Pacific as a whole. New Zealand governments had believed hitherto that the major threat to their security would occur in Europe, that events important to New Zealand and the world did not occur in their region, and in this belief had sent the bulk of their fighting forces to the Middle East and Europe in 1914 and 1939. Now a major threat to future stability in the Pacific seemed to come from Japan. Consequently, once the fighting was over, seeing that checks were placed on any future tendency of the Japanese to militarism became a major preoccupation of New Zealand policy-makers, and New Zealand wanted to be involved in decisions relating to the occupation of Japan and the Japanese peace treaty.

The war in the Pacific had, however, been 'an American show' and the United States was likely to have the major say in matters relating to Japan. The Americans were unused to listening to the concerns of lesser nations, like New Zealand, outside their area of strategic interest. In order to claim to the Americans in particular, but also to the great powers in general, the right to have a 'voice' in matters relating to postwar Japan, New Zealand, which had made only a small military contribution to the Pacific War, claimed that right as Japan's 'Pacific neighbour'. In the past N‿w Zealand might have based its claim to be heard in an international forum on its status as one of the 'old white Dominions'. Now, and for the first time, there seemed to be advantages for New Zealand in identifying itself as a'Pacific' nation. It was a situation brought about by the war against Japan. The claim that, 'New Zealand is a Pacific nation', taken for granted by New Zealanders in the 1990s, makes its first serious appearance as a diplomatic tool in discussions about the future of Japan after 1945. It can be recognised, in retrospect at least, as a milestone in the history of New Zealand's postwar diplomacy and indeed in the history of the development of an identifiable New Zealand nationality.

Concern over Japan's military potential and the evident determination of the Americans to sign a 'soft' treaty with Japan brought New Zealand, with Australia, to fight for a security treaty with the United States. The Australia, New Zealand, United States Security Treaty (ANZUS) which, historically, is part of the Japanese peace treaty arrangements was the first security treaty New Zealand had made independently of the United Kingdom and in the face of the United Kingdom's patent disapproval. Although the claim that New Zealand's major contribution to any future conflict would still be in the Middle East continued to be made after 1951, this treaty, which implied a recognition that New Zealand's security could only be underwritten by the United States, was to result in a reorientation of New Zealand policy towards Asia and the Pacific. Moreover in the United States, New Zealand and Japan had an ally in common. As New Zealand diplomats recognised, this fact gave New Zealand a link with Japan of more significance, for the Japanese at least, than any 'Pacific' connection.

The reorientation of New Zealand's policy after 1945 and indeed after the signing of the ANZUS treaty in 1951 came about only slowly but one concrete step which was taken in the early years was the establishment of diplomatic relations with Japan. In 1952 New Zealand established a legation in Tokyo. This was New Zealand's first diplomatic post in Asia and first in a country which was neither a member of the Commonwealth nor a wartime ally.[2] As such this post can be said to have signalled the beginning of a more sophisticated approach to New Zealand's requirements for diplomatic representation abroad. New Zealand felt it needed representation in Tokyo in order to obtain information and intelligence about a country and an area of extreme diplomatic sensitivity at the time. Hitherto sentiment, 'kinship' and wartime comradeship had dictated the distribution of New Zealand's few diplomatic posts abroad. The establishment of a post in Tokyo solely for practical reasons of diplomatic convenience marked a new development. When he heard of the decision to establish a legation when

the peace treaty had been ratified and a fully independent Japanese government established, the head of the New Zealand mission to the Supreme
Commander Allied Powers (SCAP) headquarters wrote:

> It is heartening to have this indication that the cabinet realises the
> importance to our future of events in the Far East and South East Asia.
> It is time we grew up and accepted the fact that, if we are to have the
> privilege of a voice and a vote in international affairs, there is some
> responsibility on us to keep ourselves informed.[3]

Commercial considerations were not a significant factor in the decision to
establish a post in Tokyo in 1952 but by 1960 New Zealand was seeking
seriously to establish markets in Japan for New Zealand's primary products.
In the battle to do this the New Zealand government and New Zealand
traders were involved, and learned the cruel realities associated with trying
to establish a foothold in a country in which they had no leverage, where no
ties of sentiment or common culture applied; a country moreover with a
highly protected market and quality-conscious consumers. New Zealand
producers and exporters were accustomed to bulk selling rather than the
cultivation of a market. The difficult, but for New Zealand by the 1960s
essential, Japanese market taught New Zealand exporters and bureaucrats
some of the basic requirements of market cultivation and the economic
diplomacy which have been major determinants of New Zealand policy and
progress since the 1960s.

Of course so-called milestones can be recognised as a rule only in
retrospect. In 1945 New Zealanders knew very little about Japan despite the
fright they had received in 1941 and 1942 when New Zealand itself seemed
threatened by Japanese expansionism. But in 1945 the Japanese were disliked and feared as the ex-enemy and stories of wartime cruelty confirmed
New Zealanders' well-established and well-documented racist beliefs about
the perfidy of Asiatics. Although relatively few New Zealanders had direct
experience of the Japanese as the enemy at first hand, anti-Japanese feeling
in the country was strong and New Zealand was determined, with Australia,
to be involved in the arrangements for making peace with Japan and
establishing security in the Pacific region. With, and led by, Australia, New
Zealand claimed a right as a principal Pacific nation in the war against
Japan to be separately represented at the surrender and, as one of the only
two Western countries whose destinies would be entirely decided by what
went on in the Pacific, to be consulted in the peacemaking process.[4]

New Zealand and Australia were aware that on the question of peacemaking, their interests might be different from those of the United Kingdom

and that, given the United Kingdom's postwar preoccupations and its need for United States support, there was always the chance that New Zealand and Australia would be 'double crossed' in the peacemaking debate. This meant that, in the process of the making of a peace treaty with Japan, New Zealand had to learn to make its mark as an independent country with the United States, the most influential party involved. For this purpose it could do no harm to be seen to take part willingly in the various structures relating to the occupation and in doing so to stress, as acting prime minister Walter Nash did when announcing that New Zealand would be a member of the International Military Tribunal for the Far East (IMTFE), New Zealand's 'special interest in the settlement in Japan and in the maintenance of peace and security in the Pacific'.[5] Similarly New Zealand's participation in the Far Eastern Commission (FEC), an eleven-nation body sitting in Washington which New Zealand's acting prime minister described, optimistically, as 'the supreme organ for deciding policies governing Japan', was presented as a demonstration of New Zealand's willingness to take responsibility for deciding policy concerning Japan.[6] The FEC was welcomed as a vehicle through which New Zealand's voice could be heard and in which its views as a champion of international justice and security might carry weight.[7] New Zealand's voice, usually in the stentorian tones of Sir Carl Berendsen, New Zealand's Minister (later ambassador) in Washington, was heard well enough in the FEC but of course its views, like the views of all the non-American members, carried no weight in the formulation of occupation policies determined largely by General MacArthur, SCAP.

For New Zealand the elimination of Japan as a military power seemed to be the basic prerequisite to securing peace and the protection of the political independence of countries in the Pacific. It was assumed that in Japan plans for expansion would continue to be fostered by an influential 'rightist' nucleus within the population unless Japan was thoroughly demilitarised and radical changes wrought in Japanese social and economic institutions. New Zealand called for the military disarmament, industrial disarmament and 'mental disarmament' of Japan and the protection and encouragement of such 'moderate elements' as might still exist there. Given this agenda a heavier deployment of force and a long and more 'thorough' occupation of Japan than the Americans seemed, by 1946, to be envisaging, was thought to be necessary.[8] A commitment to a long occupation would be a heavy burden for New Zealand but was accepted as part of the price it might have to pay for its long-run physical security and in order to demonstrate its serious intention to accept its responsibilities, as a Pacific nation, for security in the Pacific. New Zealand's participation in the British Commonwealth Occupation Force (BCOF) in Japan was popular neither with parliament nor the public in New Zealand but was undertaken both because the principle of sharing responsibility was genuinely believed in and because this was a further opportunity for New Zealand to show its flag as a Pacific nation.[9]

It was not long before Wellington began to have doubts about the style and substance of MacArthur's occupation policies. The New Zealand Labour government, proud of its social democratic tradition and conscious of New Zealand's record as a world leader in social legislation had imagined that in the FEC New Zealand's views on the treatment of Japan would be listened to and that in the areas of labour legislation and social security, areas in which, as Sir Carl Berendsen put it, American thought did not lead the world, New Zealand might make a contribution.[10] It was soon evident that this was not to be. The FEC was clearly nothing but a 'talking shop', MacArthur took no advice from it and would brook no interference. To the New Zealanders at the FEC it seemed that under MacArthur the Japanese were doing altogether too well. They complained that, as a result of American food policy, Japan was being better fed than its victims. SCAP's decisions in 1946 and 1947 to allow Japanese whaling expeditions to the Antarctic to alleviate Japanese food shortages were protested unavailingly by New Zealand on the grounds of equity as well as possible threats to its security and environment. There was concern in New Zealand when the purges in Japan soon stopped and conservatives remained in controlling positions.[11]

While New Zealand found itself unable to influence aspects of the occupation in any way, it for long held hopes of having some influence on the nature of the peace treaty. New Zealand's consistent stance was that the peace treaty should contain controls on Japan. In 1947 New Zealand officials prepared for the Canberra Conference at which it was hoped a joint Commonwealth approach to the Japanese peace treaty could be worked out. It was suggested that 'rigorous' controls on Japan should be imposed and that trust in Japanese promises of good faith or peaceful intentions was likely to be misplaced. New Zealanders felt there had been an 'amazing softening' in the attitude of other countries towards Japan by that time and that it had become hard to counter the argument that its high production, which in New Zealand's view was likely to lead to Japanese economic and political domination, was necessary to the well-being of the Far East. Prime Minister Peter Fraser represented New Zealand at the Canberra conference. There, advised by 'Dick' (later Sir Guy) Powles, then First Secretary at the New Zealand Legation in Washington and one of the few New Zealanders who argued for a Japanese peace treaty which secured the rehabilitation of Japan and obtained and strengthened Japanese goodwill, he took a line on the treaty softer than that proposed by Wellington but still based on an assumption that guarantees against the resumption of Japanese aggression might be obtained.[12] No conclusions were reached at the conference.

By 1948 New Zealand officials were arguing that a peace treaty with Japan, which might be kinder to Japan than they wished, would have to be accompanied by something like a mutual defence pact between signatories guaranteeing each other against Japanese aggression. Prime Minister Fraser expressed New Zealand's concerns. The smaller nations of the Pacific still feared a recurrence of the 'Japanese menace': clearly Japan could not be 'kept under' but was the building of Japan's war potential to be allowed? What was being done to re-educate the Japanese people?[13] These issues became the more urgent as the United States reassessed its east Asian policy in the face of the deepening Cold War and communist victory in China. By the end of 1949 it had become clear that a non-punitive peace treaty providing for minimum post-treaty controls and designed to keep Japan within the western bloc was increasingly favoured. Such a treaty might be accompanied by a bilateral United States–Japan security arrangement which would deny Japan to a potential aggressor. But what of the security of nations in the south Pacific? The idea of a Pacific pact to accompany peace treaty arrangements began to be heard from a number of directions. From the New Zealand point of view any regional grouping which did not include the great powers and especially the United States was felt to be 'unreal'. The Americans, however, made it clear that the interest of the United States in the stability of the Pacific should be accepted by New Zealand and Australia as a sufficient guarantee of their security without the conclusion of any formal arrangement. New Zealand had to decide whether it would commit an 'act of faith' and go forward with the United States in the belief that the Americans would support New Zealand if it should be menaced from Japan, from the new communist government in China or the Soviet Union.

It was evident by 1950 that New Zealand and Australia were on their own, not only in relation to the Americans but also within the Commonwealth, in their demand for security guarantees in the peace treaty. The United Kingdom clearly would not risk crossing the United States and the Asian members of the Commonwealth were, according to Alister McIntosh, Secretary of External Affairs, 'all in favour of kissing and making friends and tossing hostages to fortune'.[14] In both New Zealand and Australia new conservative governments had now taken office. In New Zealand the

National government in so far as it had a foreign policy was orientated to 'the dear old empire' and against 'the Red Menace'. New Zealand officials continued to urge on the government that a guarantee against Japanese aggression must be obtained and argued that a remilitarised Japan was simply an invitation to such aggression. Wellington suggested that, although all the signs were that New Zealand would not get what it wanted, it must fight on, if necessary exaggerate its exposure to and fear of Japan and hope this might bring the United States, in its desire to obtain support from all its allies for a 'soft' treaty, to go some way towards the kind of security guarantee for which New Zealand looked.

The appointment in April 1950 of John Foster Dulles as a special consultant and the outbreak of war in Korea in June hastened action on the Japanese peace treaty. New Zealand, aware that in hoping to see security considerations built into the treaty it was out on a limb, tried to prepare itself for whatever proposals the Americans might put forward. The National government's minister of external affairs, Frederick Doidge, wrote to Berendsen in 1950: 'it has been fundamental to New Zealand's approach to the settlement with Japan that the potential menace of Japan to the security of the Pacific should not be ignored'. New Zealand, he said, recognised that the threat of a military revival in Japan was a long-term one; nevertheless, the security problem should be given full weight in the preparation of the final settlement.[15] Doidge reflected the view of McIntosh, the head of his department, and of many other New Zealanders who felt Japan was unlikely ever to become a trustworthy ally. To McIntosh it seemed Japan was engaged in the tricky acrobatic feat of getting as much out of the West as possible without destroying its chances of coming to terms with Asia where both Soviet and Chinese communist activity gave cause for concern.[16] But could or should New Zealand hold out against a soft treaty and possible Japanese rearmament? Doidge talked of a Pacific pact throughout 1950 but never stated clearly what exactly this meant for him.

It was in Australia that the Pacific pact idea was promoted most vigorously by Percy Spender, Minister for External Affairs, and Australia which led the discussions with Dulles in Canberra in February 1951. There a 'soft' Japanese peace treaty was accepted because in the ANZUS security treaty, drafted at that meeting, Australia and New Zealand gained American commitment to their security. The New Zealanders had hoped a Pacific security treaty might include the United Kingdom but in the end a tripartite treaty, to be signed at the same time as the Japanese peace treaty, was accepted as 'by far the best solution' to New Zealand's concern for security against future Japanese aggression and for stability in the Pacific.[17] Doidge declared that the peace treaty would 'liberate New Zealand from the nightmare of a resurgence of Japanese militarism'. The treaty, he said, was itself a 'peace of reconciliation'.[18] The treaty did not become a matter of party politics in New Zealand. Walter Nash, leader of the opposition, expressed its view in characteristic fashion: New Zealand, he said, could 'only adopt the Christian course and hope that the policy of trusting Japan would bring its reward'.[19]

This rather lofty line was also taken by Sir Carl Berendsen who signed the peace treaty in San Francisco on behalf of New Zealand. Acknowledging that New Zealand would have welcomed some reasonable limitation of Japanese armaments his tone was nevertheless magnanimous. New Zealanders, he said, wished the Japanese well, they had no desire to 'hold Japan in bondage nor reduce a proud energetic and capable people to a status of inferiority'. Geography had determined that Japan and New Zealand alike must live in the Pacific. If it was a risk to have left open the possibility of a rearmed Japan, Berendsen said, it was a risk that the people of New Zealand had taken 'with their eyes open' as an earnest of the intention of their small country to play its part as a good neighbour in the Pacific. He went on, 'The onus is on Japan to fulfil this trust as we hope and believe Japan will fulfil it'.[20]

Altogether up to this point New Zealand's public attitude towards Japan had been apparently high-minded. The Secretary of External Affairs had been able to note reassuringly in 1946 that New Zealand could perform a 'useful function' in matters relating to Japan because New Zealand's distinctive national interests there were not so powerful as to endanger its wider interest in international justice and security. New Zealand could 'champion' these causes.[21] Unlike the United Kingdom which was interested in commercial prospects in Japan, or Australia which was interested in demonstrating in Japan its willingness and capacity to lead the Commonwealth in the Pacific, New Zealand's only real interest was in security against possible Japanese aggression. As a result New Zealand was wont to see itself as having a more disinterested view and 'purer' diplomatic motives than some of its allies. Not surprisingly, to some observers since it has seemed that New Zealand's attitude was detached from harsh diplomatic realities.[22] A high moral tone is of course a not unknown stance of small nations without power or influence seeking to make their presence felt and possibly keep great powers honest, but in the case of the planning of the future of Japan New Zealand had had quickly to learn that this stance carried little weight. In fact, repeatedly expressed self-interested doubts and fears about the Japanese capacity to menace the Pacific world had proved a better diplomatic weapon, in the face of American desire for solidarity among its allies on the matter of the peace treaty, than had the 'championing of international interests'.

Now in 1952 with the signing of the peace treaty and of the ANZUS treaty the way was open for a new relationship between New Zealand and Japan. There was no sense of urgency about this and in spite of all the claims it is clear that Japan still was not trusted. The New Zealand Institute of International Affairs published a pamphlet in 1952 entitled *Must We Trust Japan?* The eight contributors to this publication clearly thought the answer to the question was no. Democracy in Japan was deemed to be fragile and New Zealanders were urged to consider their security first.[23] When in 1954 a military aid agreement which provided for the assumption by Japan of greater responsibility for her own defence was signed between Japan and the United States, New Zealand's minister for external affairs commented that New Zealand would have preferred that any rearmament of Japan be avoided and noted, 'The possible supply of armaments which are of a potentially aggressive character is a matter which cannot be overlooked'.[24] Clearly suspicion of Japan lingered on. On the other hand New Zealand supported Japan's applications from 1952 for entry to the United Nations and her admission to other international organisations like the IMF, ECAFE, FAO and the Colombo Plan. These were regarded by New Zealand as 'timely steps' in Japan's postwar progress towards the resumption of 'normal' diplomatic relations.

It was easier for New Zealand to welcome Japan back into international organisations where it might be supposed that good behaviour could be impressed upon her than to accept her back unreservedly into the international trading community. Commercial contracts between New Zealand and Japan were very limited during the occupation. The only significant trade between the two countries before the war had been in wool and this trade resumed in 1948. In that year the sterling area to which New Zealand belonged signed a trade agreement with Japan which provided for a considerable increase in Japan's trade with the area. It was, however, difficult in the early years, given the limited range of Japan's production and an exchange rate fixed in April 1949 which undervalued the yen, to find goods to the value of the wool purchased. In 1950 Japan, short of sterling, actually banned further purchases of New Zealand wool and Australian wool and wheat for a time, claiming that these countries had made insufficient effort to buy Japanese goods. In 1950 wool was the only one of New Zealand's major exports which was sold on the open market. Meat and dairy products were the subject of wartime bulk purchase arrangements with the United

Kingdom, New Zealand's major trading partner. Indeed it seemed in 1952 that Japan might need New Zealand rather more than New Zealand was likely to need Japan. In that year, R. G. Challis, chargé d'affairs at the New Zealand legation in Tokyo, in a press supplement promoting New Zealand to the Japanese, could claim confidently that New Zealand's trading pattern centred on the United Kingdom was strong in tradition, sound in economics, tested in adversity and unlikely to change.[25]

Quite apart from the restriction of its small size, the New Zealand market was not an easy or necessarily attractive one for Japan. New Zealand manufacturers, heavily protected by high tariffs and restrictive import licensing, and the agents of British manufacturers who had a tight hold on the New Zealand market for imported manufactured goods, were sensitive to what were regarded as Japan's past 'unfair' trading practices. New Zealand governments had to be aware of this powerful lobby just as they had to be sensitive to the protection of jobs in New Zealand. In 1952 the Secretary of the New Zealand Manufacturers Federation, warning against anything but the most cautious expansion of trade with Japan wrote, 'Our first duty is to keep New Zealand strong and prosperous.'[26] Comments like this sent a clear message to New Zealand's government.

In 1952 therefore, when Japan notified its wish to negotiate its accession to GATT, New Zealand was one of the countries which objected. But by 1954 it was clear that New Zealand, with Britain and Australia, was in a minority and that a majority of member countries were likely to favour Japanese accession. More ominous for New Zealand was the fact that in that same year the United Kingdom indicated that it wished to end the fifteen-year-old Bulk Purchase Agreements. As a result New Zealand could expect its meat and dairy produce to have to face stiff competition on the British market. The implications of these changes for New Zealand's economy as a whole were extremely serious. In the face of this threat the potential of the Japanese market for New Zealand's increasing production of its traditional exports and for its new export item, timber, could not be ignored whatever the fears of Japanese trading practice. The New Zealand government therefore indicated to its Japanese counterpart in 1954 that, while it could not support Japan's admission to GATT, it was prepared to discuss trade relations on a bilateral basis. Japan responded positively to this invitation.[27]

The scope of the proposed talks became a matter of contention between government departments in New Zealand. The Department of External Affairs which, as might be expected, had a global view, believed it might well be in New Zealand's interests to make unilateral concessions to Japan and pointed out that the development of New Zealand's exports to Japan must depend in part at least on willingness to accept Japanese imports. An increase in the trade was also likely, it was felt, to have the desirable political result of assisting Japan to become economically more stable and more closely tied, through these trading relationships, to the western powers.[28] But the Department of Industries and Commerce, responsible for the protection and development of domestic industry, argued against any rapid expansion of trade with Japan which, it was claimed, might both disrupt domestic industry and interrupt the flow of trade from countries regularly supplying the New Zealand market. There were 'factors', it was argued, applying to Japan which did not apply to other countries and made it necessary to retain the full panoply of import controls against Japanese exports.[29]

In spite of this department's unpromising attitude talks were held and an agreement reached and initialled by New Zealand and Japan in July 1954. It involved an expansion of import licences for Japan and tariff reductions on some items which might be imported from that country. The initialling of the agreement with its very limited concessions was accepted by the New Zealand press as necessary to keep Japan 'on the right side politically'. The outcry came from New Zealand's allies, Britain and the United States. The United Kingdom protested because the agreement implied some competition from Japan in a hitherto almost exclusively British market; the United States because the Americans wanted Japan in GATT with all GATT members granting Japan most-favoured-nation treatment.[30] This was heavy pressure from allies whose viewpoints, conflicting though they were, the New Zealand government felt it could not ignore. In these circumstances it was helpful to find in domestic political considerations an additional justification for not signing the treaty. Elections were to be held in New Zealand in November 1954 and some in the government feared that a treaty signed with Japan might become a sensitive political issue. Anti-Japanese sentiment was felt to be easily roused. As one newspaper put it in the mid-fifties, the 'average' New Zealander still did not regard the Japanese nation 'with the same degree of approval as he would extend to most other peoples'.[31] The New Zealand Labour Party, then in opposition, could be expected to exploit this 'lack of approval' and make 'selling out to Japan', to the detriment of the interests of New Zealand manufacturers and their employees, an election issue.[32] As a result of these pressures from without and within, the New Zealand government deferred signing the agreement and announced that it would be reviewed later in the year.

Predictably, this deferral was not good for New Zealand–Japanese relations. The Japanese made it clear that they were offended by the delay and by New Zealand's reluctance even to name a date when the signature might take place. By April 1955, however, when the safely-returned National government was finally prepared to complete negotiations Japan 'was no longer enthusiastic.[33] The far more important negotiations for Japanese entry to GATT were by then well advanced. In June Japan became a full member. New Zealand, with the United Kingdom and other members of the sterling bloc invoked Article 35 of the GATT Agreement which meant that, rather than giving Japan most-favoured-nation treatment which otherwise applied between GATT members, New Zealand continued to apply the general tariff. Since there was no bi-lateral trade arrangement between New Zealand and Japan technically neither could expect any special consideration in the market of the other. New Zealand, whose narrow range of exports was vulnerable to the trend to world-wide agricultural protectionism of which Japan was an exponent, was likely to suffer in this situation more than Japan.

In spite of the seemingly unpromising situation, trade between the two countries expanded in the mid-fifties and achieved a better balance as New Zealand importers increasingly turned to Japan for items like iron and steel. Efforts were made to promote goodwill between the two nations. The status of the New Zealand representative in Japan was raised to that of minister and the first visit of a New Zealand prime minister to Japan took place in 1956. Sidney Holland, a conservative prime minister not known for the breadth of his world view, returned from Japan declaring that country to be 'worthy' of New Zealand's friendship and stressing the importance of boosting trade with Japan.[34]

It had become clear that trade with Japan rather than security against Japan was the issue on which New Zealanders should concentrate. It was evident by 1957 that that key to New Zealand's established trading pattern, the system of Commonwealth preferences established at Ottawa in 1932, was crumbling. Adding to the uncertainties was a European Economic Community which might be expected to have adverse implications for New Zealand's markets in Community countries when it came into being on 1 January 1958. A trade treaty with Japan was therefore once again advocated by New Zealand officials and the government agreed that negotiations should begin. Now, however, New Zealand had to take its place in a queue since in 1957 Japan was also negotiating trade treaties with the United Kingdom and Australia. When negotiations finally began in July New Zealand officials were once again in an embarrassing position; the government 'dragged its feet'. This was again an election year in New Zealand and fears that the opposition might use a treaty to stimulate the assumed anti-Japanese feeling among the voting public again surfaced in government circles. Although a satisfactory agreement was reached between New Zealand and Japanese officials, the government decided it would not sign this until after the election which was to be held in November.[35]

To the embarrassment of all concerned the government then lost the election. This embarrassment was compounded by the fact that Japanese Prime Minister Kishi arrived for a two-day visit in the period between the changeover from the National to a Labour government. The result was that nothing of substance could be discussed or decided though Kishi had 'friendly talks' with the outgoing and incoming prime ministers. The Labour Party was committed to the protection of New Zealand industry and had been wont to raise the spectre of unfair Japanese competition in the past. At the state luncheon for Kishi, Walter Nash, the British-born incoming prime minister, referred to the need to protect New Zealand's living standards and, in his interview with Kishi, said that New Zealand was keen both to maintain its preferences with and to help the United Kingdom.[36] It seemed that the projected New Zealand–Japanese trade agreement would once again lapse although New Zealand officials in Tokyo pointed out that the balance of New Zealand–Japanese trade was in the former's favour and that New Zealand was in danger of losing markets in Japan to competitors who had formal agreements with her. New Zealanders, they argued, obsessed with the danger of a 'flood' of Japanese goods, tended to forget that the Japanese had a right to be at least equally concerned with the dangers of a 'flood' of comparatively cheap products from her trading partner.[37]

To the relief of these officials, spurred on by the threats to New Zealand's markets in Britain and Europe, the Labour government reopened negotiations and in September 1958 a New Zealand–Japanese trade treaty, which was substantially the same as that initialled in 1954, finally was signed. Each country extended to the other unconditional most-favoured-nation treatment in regard to customs duties, import licensing and the control and allocation of foreign exchange. In addition Japan undertook specific commitments with regard to access to the Japanese market of New Zealand beef, wool, tallow, hides and dairy produce while accepting certain 'safeguard' clauses for New Zealand domestic industry. New Zealand agreed to discuss within three years the possibility of entering a full GATT relationship with Japan.[38] The Department of External Affairs in fact thought New Zealand might have shown good will by withdrawing Article 35 during negotiations but in the end the more cautious counsels prevailed.

The regularisation of New Zealand–Japanese trade relationships had come not before time and when truly alarming cracks were beginning to appear in New Zealand's trading system. Not only was the Ottawa system of preferences creaking under modifications made in 1957 but the first suggestions that Britain might seek entry to the Common Market were beginning to be heard. In these circumstances New Zealand's economic relationship with Japan was likely to become increasingly important to New Zealand and in addition since both countries feared the protectionism which might now be exercised by the European Community it was felt in New Zealand that there might be a new bond between the two which could be exploited.

In February 1959 Prime Minister Nash, not originally an enthusiast for Japan, made an official visit to that country. Now he expressed hopes for the expansion of trade between New Zealand and Japan, which he declared to be 'a Pacific neighbour of great and ever-increasing importance to the free world'.[39] The trade balance was still heavily in New Zealand's favour. This put New Zealand, which maintained tariff preferences in the United Kingdom's favour, at a disadvantage in discussions about trade expansion with the Japanese. Japan could point to this discrimination as a factor inhibiting the expansion of two-way trade. Though nothing concrete came out of the Nash visit which was in any case primarily a goodwill exercise, two-way trade increased by a remarkable 25 per cent in 1959 in spite of severe import restrictions imposed by the Labour government in 1958 in response to New Zealand's balance of payments problems. The trade treaty had evidently stimulated their trade and it was clear that the Japanese had made every effort to meet New Zealand sensitivities regarding certain items. From an economic point of view officials agreed there was now little reason for New Zealand to continue to invoke Article 35 of the GATT treaty but the government remained deaf to Japanese requests in 1959, 1960 and 1961 for its removal.[40] The issue had become a political one and neither the Labour government, nor the National government which succeeded it in November 1960, was willing to risk the possibility of an anti-Japanese backlash in New Zealand or criticism from its main, if increasingly difficult, trading partner, the United Kingdom, which still invoked Article 35.

Nevertheless, the increasing economic importance of the Japanese market and Japanese goodwill to New Zealand could not be denied and became critical to that country after July 1961 when the British prime minister announced that Britain would seek entry to the European Community. New Zealand had to look for ways to off-set the losses in markets which might be expected from British entry and the growth and development of an enlarged Community. It was true that the value of New Zealand's trade with Japan had been increasingly rapidly and in dairy products alone increased by 500 per cent in the five years to the end of 1962, but this rate of increase, even if it could be sustained, was not enough to absorb the surplus New

Zealand was likely to have to sell. New Zealand had been selling meat to Japan since 1957 but mutton and lamb were products with which the Japanese were unfamiliar and the New Zealanders were taking time to learn how best to promote and market them in a form acceptable to the Japanese.

For New Zealand exporters, familiar almost exclusively with the British market, Japan was a difficult and exceedingly complex market. Moreover it had to be understood that agricultural policy was a sensitive political issue there. The effect of these things, especially since New Zealand's trade with Japan was primarily in agricultural products, was to make New Zealand traders in Japan rather more demanding of New Zealand diplomats there by way of assistance through the bureaucratic maze. Economics as a driving force in diplomacy was nowhere more apparent than in Japan. It may be argued that, from the time Britain signalled its intention to apply for entry to the European Community, the focus of New Zealand's diplomatic efforts everywhere changed and what might be called economic diplomacy became the norm. Japan, where New Zealand seemed to have no significant ties other than economic ones, was the extreme case of this phenomenon.

In February 1962 John Marshall, deputy prime minister, minister for overseas trade and New Zealand's chief negotiator with the United Kingdom and the European Community, went to Tokyo. As a result of his discussions there it was agreed that New Zealand should no longer apply the provisions of Article 35 of the GATT treaty to Japan; that the New Zealand–Japan Trade Agreement of 1958 should be renewed and its terms enlarged; and that negotiations for reductions in tariffs should begin at an early date. Marshall made it clear that the New Zealand government was trying to remove trade barriers and create trading opportunities for Japan.

Britain's application to join the European Community came to nothing in 1963, giving New Zealand a temporary reprieve, but it was clear by then that it could not afford not to cultivate new markets and to try to diversify its range of exports. Both New Zealand and Japan were fearful of the implications of an enlarged European Community. This to some degree provided a new sympathetic link, welcomed by New Zealand, and had the effect of stimulating New Zealand–Japan trade. Japanese Prime Minister Ikeda speaking in Wellington in October 1963 commented that the European Community's negotiations with Britain had taught both Japan and New Zealand a sharp lesson. He added, 'I would assume that in the mundane pursuit of markets you have learned not to put all your eggs in one basket any more, whether the basket is made in Britain or elsewhere'.[41]

Retaining sufficiently capacious baskets in Britain and Europe was to be the main task of New Zealand diplomacy in the next decade. Parallel with this effort ran the effort to enlarge the Japanese basket for New Zealand's exports. It was no easy task. The New Zealand market took less than one per cent of Japan's exports and inevitably New Zealand was peripheral to Japan. In their efforts to interest Japan and the home public in the relationship, New Zealand officials were not helped by the fact that New Zealand's political links with Japan were hard to promote. Shared membership of a 'Pacific neighbourhood', a shared ally in the United States and a shared concern about the future role in world trade of an enlarged European Community, were not seen by the 'average' New Zealander to constitute a bond or reason for some kind of 'special relationship' with Japan. They understood trade figures better. If, as the *New Zealand Herald* claimed in 1963, trade had promoted amity and understanding between New Zealand and Japan it is probably true that this amity and understanding was not very deep on either side. But foundations had been laid: time and circumstance had brought New Zealand to terms with Japan.

NOTES

1. *New Zealand Herald* (Auckland), 7 October 1963.
2. Before 1952 New Zealand had diplomatic posts in London, Canberra, Ottawa, Washington and, from 1944–50, Moscow.
3. Challis Report, 15 December 1951, EA 62/14/1 Pt. 2.
4. See Robin Kay (ed.), *Documents on New Zealand External Relations Volume II* (Wellington, 1982), nos. 50, 77, 80, 87. (Hereafter *NZER II*).
5. *NZER II*, no. 650.
6. *NZER II*, no. 580.
7. *NZER II*, no. 204.
8. *NZER II*, no. 136; Robin Kay (ed.), *Documents on New Zealand External Relations Volume III* (Wellington, 1985), no. 58. (Hereafter *NZER III*).
9. *NZER II*, nos. 542, 580.
10. *NZER II*, no. 177.
11. *NZER II*, nos. 196, 223, 295; *NZER III*, no. 58.
12. *NZER II*, no. 25; 'General Attitude to Japanese Peace Settlement', Comment by G.R.P., 2 June 1947, MFA 102/9/38; interviews with Sir Guy Powles, 1985, 1986.
13. *NZER III*, no. 94.
14. McIntosh to Berendsen, 1 February 1950, McIntosh correspondence (held at NZ Ministry of External Relations and Trade.
15. *NZER III*, no. 143.
16. McIntosh to Challis (Tokyo), 7 December 1950, EA 102/9/4.
17. *NZER III*, nos. 218, 224, 225.

18. *NZ Parliamentary Debates* (hereafter *NZPD*), vol. 294, 1951, pp. 318–29; *NZER III,* no. 392.

19. United Kingdom High Commissioner to Commonwealth Relations Office, 'Japanese Peace Treaty', 6 April 1951, FO 371/92539.

20. *NZER III,* no. 434.

21. *NZER II,* no. 204.

22. See Gordon Daniels, 'New Zealand and Occupied Japan', in Ian Nish (ed.), *The British Commonwealth and the Occupation of Japan* (London, 1983), p. 35.

23. *Must We Trust Japan?* (Wellington, 1952), pp. 6–21.

24. *External Affairs Review* (hereafter *EAR*), vol. IV, no. 3, 10 March 1954, p. 6.

25. *Japan News,* 26 January 1952.

26. A. R. Dellow in *Must We Trust Japan?,* p. 11.

27. External Affairs to Chargé d'Affaires, Tokyo, 2 February 1954, EA 58/12/2 Pt. 6; Chargé d'Affaires, Tokyo, to External Affairs, 3 March 1954, EA 58/12/2 Pt 6.

28. Memorandum for Comptroller of Customs and Secretary Industries and Commerce, 9 March 1954, EA 58/12/2 Pt 6.

29. Secretary Industries and Commerce to Secretary Board of Trade. 1 April 1954, EA 58/12/2 Pt 6.

30. Shanahan to Challis, 23 July 1954, EA 58/12/2 Pt. 7; US Embassy to External Affairs, 14 July 1954, EA 104/4/8/37 Pt. 3.

31. *Gisborne Herald,* 6 August 1956.

32. See speech, Labour candidate Heretaunga, *Evening Post* (Wellington), 21 November 1954.

33. Chargé d'Affaires, Tokyo, to External Affairs, 5 May 1955, 19 August 1955, EA 40/12/1 Pt 2.

34. Dominion (Wellington), 4 August 1956; *NZPD,* vol. 309, 1956, pp. 892–4.

35. Sir John Marshall, *Memoirs,* vol. I, (Auckland, 1983), p. 282.

36. Note of discussion Mr. Kishi and Mr. Nash, 2 December 1957, EA 40/12/1 Pt 8.

37. J. S. Scott, Tokyo, to Secretary Industries and Commerce, 29 April 1958, EA 40/12/2 Pt 1; J. S. Reid, Tokyo, to George Laking, 10 June 1958, EA 40/12/1 Pt 1.

38. *EAR,* vol. VII, no. 9, September 1958, pp. 12–13.

39. *EAR,* vol. IX, no. 1, January 1959, p. 13.

40. Note for file, 9 December 1959, EA 40/12/1 Pt 9.

41. *Nelson Evening Mail,* 8 October 1963.

10 Challenge and Readjustment: Anglo-American Exchanges over East Asia, 1949–53*
Peter Lowe

The period extending between the summers of 1949 and 1953 was one of astonishing tergiversations in the history of East Asia and the development of British and American policies in the region. In China the communists triumphed in the civil war and then intervened decisively in the Korean war to emphasise the might of the new China in preventing the Unified Command of the United Nations from liquidating North Korea. In Japan the allied occupation ended as a consequence of the signing of a peace treaty at San Francisco under which Japan shortly resumed exercise of sovereignty, if with continued American protection. In Korea a bloody conflict raged marking the escalation of the Cold War into a limited 'hot' war. East Asia moved to the centre of the world stage with real indicators of the importance attached to the region. For Britain and the United States these events illuminated the rapid transformation in their relationship accomplished by longer-term trends.

During 1948 it became clear that the Kuomintang government had lost the Chinese civil war. George Marshall, the American secretary of state, told a Kuomintang representative in October that there could be no question of American military intervention in China: corruption was so rampant as to inhibit gravely the fight against communism.[1] Esler Dening, one of the most influential officials in the British Foreign Office, wrote at the end of December 1948 that a stable American policy in East Asia was required urgently. Dening criticised the failure of the United States to react positively:

*I wish to acknowledge my warm thanks to the Nuffield Foundation for generously awarding me a grant through the Social Sciences Small Grants Scheme which made possible the research for this paper. Transcripts/translations of Crown copyright records in the Public Record Office, Kew, appear by permission of the Controller of H.M. Stationery Office.

We feel that unless there is a *concerted* Far Eastern policy soon the future can only develop to our common detriment. American policy failed in China because they failed to appreciate Chinese intransigence; it has virtually failed in Korea because they failed to appreciate Korean intransigence and it is my personal view that it will eventually fail in Japan because they fail to appreciate Japanese intransigence.[2]

The principal question in 1949 was how long it would take the Chinese communists to complete their advance and to form a government representing most of the mainland except for certain scattered border areas and also various islands off the coast. American policy was conditioned by the hatred of communism which had grown swiftly in 1947–8 and by the Republican party's use of China as a means of castigating the Truman administration.[3] President Truman was adamantly opposed to acceptance of the Chinese communists although his new secretary of state, Dean Acheson, was prepared to contemplate recognition ultimately.

American attitudes towards recognition of governments denoted moral approval as a significant element whereas British policy was dependent upon whether a government possessed convincing control of a country. Britain's reaction to Mao Tse-tung's victory comprised a mixture of wanting to protect commercial interests, keep in step with India, and come to terms with the inevitable. Ernest Bevin, the foreign secretary, believed in June 1949 that the communists were keen to open contacts with the British government and he wished to foster opportunities for trade.[4] Acheson wished to slow down a British move towards recognition. In a discussion with Bevin in mid-September 1949 Acheson emphasised that the United States would insist upon China's full acceptance of international commitments before considering recognition – 'Bevin said the British were not in a hurry to recognise but they have big commercial interests in and trade with China and were not in the same position as we were relatively or absolutely'.[5] Bevin added that 'by being too obdurate we will drive the Chinese into Russian hands, but that by playing a careful role we can weaken Russia's grip'.[6] Acheson agreed that care was necessary but doubted whether recognition would be a major factor in diminishing Russian influence over China. Bevin also indicated British anxiety regarding Hong Kong. In December the Labour cabinet determined to grant recognition. In a personal message to Acheson Bevin stated on 16 December that recognition would be extended at the beginning of the new year: he had waited as long as he could but would delay no longer. British interests in Hong Kong and in South-East Asia were affected and officials in these areas advocated recognition. The cabinet was influenced by the aim of separating China from the Soviet Union and accepting realities. Britain did not approve of Chinese communism but must deal with it diplomatically.[7]

Thus British and American paths diverged significantly. Although Britain was fighting a communist insurrection in Malaya and was worried at developments in French Indo-China, it was held that the escalation in the Cold War could be prevented through speaking to Mao's government. American reactions were critical: the right wing of the Republican party reacted vitriolically, and the private papers of Senator Robert A. Taft contain numerous letters from indignant citizens condemning British perfidy.[8] Matters were complicated by developing arguments over the fate of Taiwan: Truman and Acheson were weary of the Kuomintang as was made abundantly clear by the publication of the China White Paper in August 1949, and the American joint chiefs of staff and General MacArthur in Tokyo were alarmed at possible repercussions of the capture of Taiwan by the communists. Acheson told the British ambassador, Sir Oliver Franks, in December 1949 that Taiwan would probably be in communist hands by the end of 1950. Acheson dismissed fears that the loss of Taiwan would constitute a serious threat to American interests,[9] but MacArthur's opinion was very different. He informed the British liaison representative in Tokyo, Alvary Gascoigne, on 16 December that:

> he would, if he were the United States Government, make a unilateral declaration to the effect that the United States would not permit Formosa to be used either as a springboard for Chiang Kai-shek to attack Red China or as a goal of Red ambitions. He felt that this would stop Mao from making any efforts to seize the island.[10]

Interestingly this anticipated precisely the line adopted by Truman in his statement of 27 June 1950 following the outbreak of the Korean war. MacArthur appeared to be contemplating Taiwan being placed under a UN mandate. Truman added that Taiwan was the first line of defence in the Pacific: he favoured a solely American declaration, appreciating that Britain could be embarrassed because of its attitude towards Peking.[11] During the first five months of 1950 American policy concerning Taiwan hardened noticeably. The joint chiefs of staff argued that the island must be denied to the communists; Acheson, whose position had been weakened through the acrid domestic debate in 1949–50, acquiesced in the new tough stance. He told Franks early in June 1950 that Mao's forces would not be permitted to capture Taiwan.[12] Thus the occasion of the start of the Korean war was used in order to implement the new policy. Anglo–American differences over Taiwan were significant and the Labour government deprecated Truman's decision to link the discrete issues of Korea and Taiwan in his statement of 27 June. British anxiety diminished subsequently except for the speculation resulting from MacArthur's controversial visit to Taiwan at the end of July. However, the consequences of China's intervention in Korea in October–November 1950 increased British alarm. This was conveyed by Clement Attlee during his talks with Truman in December when the prime minister urged what he deemed to be a realistic policy of compromise on America's part which should include the admission of the Peking government to the UN and a solution to the Taiwan problem. It was not surprising that he encountered a hostile reaction. The savagery of the struggle in Korea in 1951 led the British to develop understanding for American policy towards Taiwan: it was accepted that nothing could be done for some years until the Korean conflict ended and a new era eventually dawned in Sino–American relations.

The Attlee cabinet hoped at the beginning of 1950 that recognition would quickly engender an improved relationship with China. They seriously underestimated the difficulties, in particular the isolationism prevailing within the communist government and their determination not to compromise too readily with British imperialism. This was accentuated by the dispute over the detention and escape of the frigate, HMS *Amethyst,* in the spring and summer of 1949.[13] Bevin met representatives of the China Association on 16 March 1950 and confessed to 'some doubts' concerning the decision to recognise Peking,[14] and Anthony Eden echoed Bevin's feelings when he returned to the Foreign Office in October 1951. Problems caused by communist policy were accentuated by a Kuomintang blockade of certain ports, and British firms in Shanghai experienced intensifying difficulty as the screw was inexorably tightened with a combination of subtlety and brutality. Many headaches faced the Foreign Office as Sino-British relations slowly deteriorated.

Commercial aspirations were further undermined by the American wish to impose rigorous economic sanctions on China as punishment for the humiliations inflicted on UN forces in Korea in 1950–1. In the UN General Assembly the British government was most reluctant to join in a formal condemnation of China for aggression but was persuaded to support the motion proposed by the United States on 1 February 1951. Considerable friction ensued and persisted for a prolonged period as American pressure for total British compliance was exerted in enforcing UN measures against China. Various complications resulted from the position of Hong Kong: for geopolitical and economic reasons Hong Kong's situation caused increasing tension. The peculiar problems inherent in Hong Kong were emphasised in a telegram sent to Washington on 1 March 1951 – participation in drastic economic measures could result in extensive unemployment with concomitant difficulties:

> Does the United States Government fully appreciate what the Chinese occupation of Hong Kong would . . . mean to them? It would provide the Chinese People's Government with a first-class naval base with repair facilities at a vantage point in South China. It would expose the flank of Indo-China and might even constitute a threat to the Philippines especially by air if Russia also became involved. Quite apart from that, the capture of Hong Kong would be of tremendous Communist propaganda value and would have very serious effects on the ability of ourselves and other nations to maintain our position against Communism in South-East Asia generally.
>
> These aspects of the matter are causing us the most serious concern. There is even a possibility that if China were tempted or provoked into attacking Hong Kong this might lead to a general war.[15]

Exports from Hong Kong to China increased from an annual rate of £76 million in 1950 to £136 million in March 1951; this figure included large quantities of rubber and rubber goods going to the mainland via Hong Kong until it was decided to end rubber exports.[16] Other exports included chemicals, pharmaceuticals, dyestuffs, and iron and steel. The Far Eastern (Official) Committee coordinated the response of government departments; it was recognised that Britain must apply a firmer policy than before and that this should meet some of the American objections:

> We should invite the U.S. Administration to put an end to the long period of bickering on this subject by recognising publicly the value of these measures and the validity of our reasons (which have much in common with those of Japan) for going no further in present circumstances.[17]

A full statement explaining British policy should be communicated to the Additional Measures Committee of the UN. Therefore, British policy as determined in June 1951 included export licence control and embargoes on various commodities given in a 'prohibited' list, the latter incorporating all aircraft defence equipment and munitions, atomic energy materials and equipment, all ships and all petroleum products, rubber and other goods which might assist China's military and strategic strength. The Foreign Office maintained that British obligations under the UN resolution of 18 May had been met and it was not feasible to move beyond this.[18]

Anglo–American exchanges over China demonstrated the differing perspectives of the two countries. The United States severed its connections with the mainland in 1949: the rift was exacerbated through actions for which the United States and China were each responsible. The depth of the American commitment in Korea lent passion and zeal to the determination in Washington to apply as much pressure as possible to the Chinese economy. Britain still believed, if with diminishing confidence, in maintaining contact with Peking in the hope that it might assist trade and lessen the perils of further escalation in Korea, but the effects of the Korean war doomed any prospect for reaching an understanding with the Peking government for a lengthy period to come.

Let us turn now to Japan. The allied occupation placed the United States in a position of dominance, for the other allied states played only a minor role in deciding how Japan was to be treated. The chief American aims were to purge Japan of militarism and establish there a stable democracy with the retention of a reformed monarchy, and to ensure that Japan remained squarely within the western sphere of interest.[19] General MacArthur directed the occupation in an avuncular way; in the main he was benign but could be ruthless when the occasion demanded.[20] Britain somewhat resented being relegated to the periphery of the occupation: ministers and officials criticised the United States for prolonging the occupation and for not trying to conclude an early peace treaty. The British view of MacArthur's contribution in Japan was mostly positive: he was deemed to have discharged a demanding task capably and with panache, although his arrogance and egocentric manner were seen as tedious.[21] The onset of the Cold War increased the importance of Japan and accentuated the necessity for a reasonably generous peace settlement. While entirely agreeing that Japan should be retained within the western sphere if possible, British representatives were less inclined towards magnanimity. Sombre recollections of wartime defeats and atrocities were vivid and were reinforced by the vociferous opinions of former prisoners of war (POWs) and their organisations. British officials were cynical regarding the extent of the Japanese conversion to democracy and feared that Japan could prove dangerous again within a decade or so of the end of the occupation.

Sir George Sansom, the distinguished Japanologist and retired diplomat, visited Tokyo in January 1951 and met MacArthur. The general took a balanced view of his work in Japan amidst his current Korean preoccupations; he felt that the occupation should end soon and believed that the basis for stability had been laid effectively, with no likelihood of the Japanese reverting to militarism.[22] MacArthur's term as 'shogun' closed abruptly in

April 1951 with his dismissal by Truman for insubordination in Korea, his final months in Tokyo having in any case been overshadowed by a rival Republican, John Foster Dulles. MacArthur resented the appointment of Dulles to handle the negotiations leading to a Japanese peace treaty, believing that he (MacArthur) should preside over a peace conference as the leading authority on contemporary Japan. Dulles was a subtle operator, as his delicate balancing act in serving the Democratic administration of Truman and remaining central to the foreign policy deliberations of the Republican party underlined. He threw himself into the strenuous challenge of securing a peace treaty with immense energy and enthusiasm. He held passionately that the spirit of liberalism must prevail: he had witnessed retribution at the Paris peace conference in 1919 and argued that the only way of reconciling the Japanese to American leadership upon regaining sovereignty was to propose a fair, reasonably generous treaty.

Britain favoured a treaty of a less liberal character. At the beginning of 1951 the British desired the retention of Japanese gold deposits, the insertion of a war guilt clause into a peace treaty, and the imposition of restrictions on Japanese shipbuilding. British textile and pottery firms conveyed their apprehension at threatened Japanese competition emphatically though it was doubtful whether such straightforward commercial concern could be met in a peace treaty; but since shipbuilding embraced strategic matters it might be possible to pursue this within a treaty. The cabinet was not noticeably sympathetic towards Japan; Labour ministers were influenced by fears of future unemployment resulting from Japanese competition, by memories of the Pacific war, and by the agitation of former POWs. Ernest Bevin was a dying man and contributed little to the exchanges over a peace treaty. He was worried at the strains in the Anglo–American relationship caused by the Korean war and did not wish to see these extended into other spheres. Bevin resigned early in March and died a month later, succeeded by Herbert Morrison who was ambitious to become Labour leader and correspondingly was driven on by the need to have a positive effect on the issues he handled.[23] The chief critic of Japan within the cabinet was the chancellor of the exchequer, Hugh Gaitskell, who was as ambitious as Morrison to obtain the leadership of the party after Attlee.[24] Gaitskell argued that Japan had escaped leniently from responsibility for starting the Pacific war and he saw no reason why Japan should be treated with additional kindness.

The attitudes of individual ministers were revealed in June 1951 when Dulles visited London for crucial discussions on the shape of a treaty. Dulles worked with great patience to surmount the obstacles created by the vested interests of the parties concerned: he was critical of the British role, in the spring and summer of 1951, maintaining that Britain was unduly carping and querulous. His exchanges with ministers showed clearly the contrasting views of the two sides together with the realisation on the British side that there were limits to how far their objections could be pressed. Gaitskell was probably the member of the cabinet most sympathetic to the United States after Bevin's death. Politically he was firmly committed to the right wing of the Labour party and his post as chancellor of the exchequer reinforced appreciation of how vital American support was for Britain financially. However, Gaitskell advanced his opinions robustly when he met Dulles on 6 June. He reminded Dulles of the vocal anti-Japanese lobby in Britain, drawing its tenacity from the atrocities perpetrated during the Pacific war: people in Britain would deplore unduly moderate treatment for Japan.[25] Dulles emphasised the powerful American economic support for the occupation of Japan. Despite the temptation to do so the Truman administration refrained from using Japanese gold deposits because these would be required by the Japanese government when the occupation ended. If it came to a decision on carving up Japanese gold among the allies, then the United States would submit a claim for priority based on the sums spent in Japan. Dulles rejected Gaitskell's analogy with the treatment of Germany because this ignored the huge loss of colonial territories suffered by Japan which would be confirmed in a peace treaty. Gaitskell responded that a distinction should be drawn between the losses incurred by a state as a result of defeat and the gains made by the victors. He regarded the difference in approach regarding reparations expected from Germany and Japan as striking. Gaitskell agreed that it was a political issue: he would prefer the United States to keep all of the Japanese gold, thus denying it to a sovereign Japanese administration.[26]

On 8 June Dulles saw Sir Hartley Shawcross, the president of the Board of Trade. Shawcross explained his concern over the question of the Congo Basin treaties. This seemingly obscure matter concerned the apprehension of the textile industry over future competition. Shawcross indicated that Britain did not want to exclude Japan entirely from the African market, for example in west Africa where Britain possessed the power so to act. But fears were real of a large influx of cheap Japanese textiles. Shawcross emphasised anxiety in the light of the British balance of payments: the pressure caused by rearmament meant that textile exports were envisaged as increasing by 40 per cent over the previous year so as to cover the fallback in other exports. Dulles replied that it should be feasible to follow the decision reached regarding Italy: it had been agreed that Italy should remain a signatory to the Saint-Germain convention but on a modified basis. The same approach could be applied to Japan; under the Potsdam agreement Japan forfeited its colonial possessions but was promised access to raw materials and ultimate involvement in world trade relations. Shawcross dismissed Dulles's comparison with Italy because the latter had held colonies in Africa and did not experience the inferior labour standards of Japan.[27] He reiterated the perturbation within the Lancashire textile industry.

During his visit Dulles met Morrison and the minister of state at the Foreign Office, Kenneth Younger, on several occasions. On 4 June Morrison summarised British views concerning rearmament. He referred to the strength of feeling arising from wartime atrocities; members of the cabinet felt that current American proposals for a treaty afforded excessive scope for future Japanese rearmament. Differences between the United States and Britain over China's role in a peace treaty must be resolved: Britain was not willing to work with Chiang Kai-shek.[28] Dulles skilfully expounded his commitment to achieving a liberal treaty. He observed that in America hatred of Japan subsided swiftly at the end of the Pacific war, implying the contrast with Britain. As regards China it might be possible for each of the rival Chinese governments to sign a treaty for that part of China it occupied.[29] At a subsequent meeting on 5 June Younger supported a Canadian suggestion that neither the communist nor the Kuomintang administration should sign and that a treaty should include arrangements for Chinese accession at a later date – 'There was some disadvantage in committing the Japanese to a Treaty signed by the Chinese Nationalist Government with possible prejudice to their future relations with the mainland of China'.[30] Dulles stressed his wish for a solution permitting maximum adherence to a treaty by those countries concerned. He played a trump card in stating the fundamental importance of devising a treaty which would be ratified by the American Senate. Dulles somewhat exaggerated this point for his own reasons (and benefit) but the history of the Senate's reaction to treaties submitted to it indicated caution. He reflected on possible solutions to the Chinese conundrum which included not requiring a Chinese signature, securing a series of bilateral peace treaties rather than a multilateral agreement, or permitted governments other than the principals to adhere to a multilateral agreement before or following ratification.[31] He wanted to defend the position of the Kuomintang government which the United States recognised. Younger expressed scepticism as to what would be accomplished by Kuomintang signature.

On 6 June Morrison underlined anxiety regarding rearmament and cited parliamentary questions that day referring to POWs and the compensation they might receive in disposing of Japanese assets. Morrison wished to see an assurance given by the Japanese government repudiating aggression in future.[32] Dulles candidly remarked that the only way to be certain of averting a future military threat from Japan was to extend the occupation and that he was endeavouring to produce a settlement acceptable to Japan under which American armed forces would remain on Japanese soil with Japanese support. Morrison wanted compensation for POWs to be forwarded through the Red Cross instead of being advanced by the state. He deemed Dulles's proposal undesirable.[33] Morrison explained the strength of British feeling regarding shipping capacity which was perceived as difficult for strategic and economic reasons. After further discussions Dulles returned to Washington on 14 June.

The Foreign Office summarised the principal decisions reached as comprising agreement that neither Chinese government would be invited to sign a treaty with provision for Japan to negotiate a bilateral treaty subsequently on terms similar to the peace treaty itself; on gold the British government reluctantly concurred that Japan should not be compelled to surrender it; a formal Japanese liability to pay reparations would be included; Japanese assets in neutral and former enemy states would be transferred to the Red Cross, to be used for assisting former POWs; Dulles accepted the British case over the Congo Basin treaties; the only aspect upon which divergence remained centred on shipping, where Britain preferred a more restrictive approach.[34] The Foreign Office regarded the outcome of Dulles's visit as essentially satisfactory with concessions having been made by both sides.

The climax to the lengthy exchanges occurred in San Francisco at the beginning of September 1951 with the formal gathering of the nations to mark the official conclusion of the Pacific War. The Americans were more astute and forward-looking than the British in deciding the most fitting course to pursue. The chief credit for the successful record in Japan belonged to those ill-assorted Republicans, MacArthur and Dulles. Although each erred on occasion, they were right on the central issues involving the future of Japan. Japan should be generously treated and assimilated within the western sphere in East Asia. The British looked backwards rather than forward and would have favoured a more restrictive policy. The San Francisco conference was a triumph for American policy-making: the Truman administration's handling of Japan was far more impressive than its dealings with China or Korea. Dean Acheson chaired the peace conference ably and easily suppressed a half-hearted Soviet attempt to cause difficulty.[35] Herbert Morrison arrived in San Francisco for the concluding ceremonies and enjoyed amicable discussions with Acheson, Dulles, and Yoshida Shigeru. The feature which turned sour involved the Chinese dimension: contrary to assurances given during his talks in London, Dulles induced Yoshida to conclude a treaty with Chiang Kai-shek's regime, thus foreclosing any possibility of a deal being struck with Peking. This annoyed Conservative and Labour politicians; Eden and Morrison were at one in denouncing Dulles's action.[36] They should not have been surprised: Dulles wanted to guarantee ratification by the Senate and to advance his own claim to be secretary of state in the next administration.

The Korean war marked the centrepoint of Anglo–American endeavours, arguments, and consultations regarding the fate of East Asia. The course of the conflict demonstrated the steady decline in the British contribution to allied policy-making. While formally the UN was committed in Korea, it was overwhelmingly an American military operation. British and Commonwealth assistance was welcomed warmly when the war began but the prolonged, disillusioning experience in Korea led the Americans to regard the British in a patronising manner. Anglo–American relations during the war were frequently strained, tense, and full of mutual recrimination.[37] Truman decided that American intervention was imperative because the North Korean action in advancing south of the 38th Parallel was Soviet-controlled or inspired; in accordance with the document NSC 68, approved by Truman in April 1950, any threat to the 'free world' must be strongly rebuffed. The Attlee government agreed and placed emphasis, for the benefit of the Labour rank and file and British public opinion, upon sustaining the principles contained in the UN Charter. However, Attlee and his colleagues had no wish to see American resources diverted to East Asia at the expense of Europe. The fear that America might overreact was present in London throughout the war. Pierson Dixon, a leading official in the Foreign Office, minuted on 1 July that the United States might be tempted to deploy the atomic weapon. Dixon saw a token British military contribution to Korean operations as affording the justification for insisting on full consultation, particularly concerning contemplated use of atomic weapons.[38] Bevin was recovering from an operation in a nursing home but kept in touch with developments. British policy-makers thought that the Soviet Union was most probably deeply involved in North Korean aggression yet wished to keep open diplomatic channels to Moscow in the first half of July so as to avoid exacerbating matters. Acheson agreed without enthusiasm to the British ambassador talking to Andrei Gromyko, the Soviet foreign minister. Bevin sent a message to Acheson on 7 July commenting on the issues implicit in Korea and Taiwan. As he saw it the weakness of the American position was that while world opinion mostly supported American action in Korea, this did not apply to Taiwan:

> In general I think that the United States Government would be wise in their public statements to concentrate on the Korean issue and play down the other parts of the President's statement of 27th. June, otherwise there may be a risk of a breach in the international solidarity happily achieved over Korea.[39]

Acheson responded with vigour and directness. The menace of communism must be resisted and repulsed and he felt that little would be achieved by pressing the Soviet Union to assist.[40] In an additional personal message for Bevin Acheson emphasised the strength of his feelings:

> I think you might well remind Bevin orally of grave doubts he himself expressed to me in private conversations in London as to wisdom of Britain's own China policy and ask him frankly what possible practical advantages he sees in trying to get Communist China into S[ecurity] C[ouncil] and return to SC of USSR in present situation.[41]

Kenneth Younger, the minister of state, commented that the Americans needed to bear in mind the importance of not driving the Soviet Union out of the UN and that their policy over Taiwan was very dangerous. The Americans inevitably responded with deep emotion and he repeated Dixon's earlier observation that a commitment of British ground forces in Korea could increase British influence over American decision-making.[42] The United States was most anxious to see British troops joining their naval colleagues in assisting UN operations so that the dual arguments for British military intervention blended in the course of July. The hopes of Younger and Dixon that Britain could influence American strategy proved unduly sanguine in the months and years to come.

British troops were committed with the unenthusiastic acquiescence of the chiefs of staff late in July.[43] UN and South Korean forces were pinned down in the south-east of the peninsula but the North Korean offensive failed in its chief aim of administering a knock-out blow. Given the degree of commitment within the UN, it was a question of time before the tide was reversed. This occurred in the middle of September following MacArthur's boldly executed, if predictable, landing at Inchon. The Korean struggle underwent another in the frequent tergiversations which marked its first year. The Unified Command moved swiftly from a defensive to an offensive strategy intended to accomplish what Kim Il Sung's forces had sought to do previously – liquidate the opposition within Korea through ensuring total dominance. Attlee, Bevin and their cabinet colleagues were caught up in the excessive, misplaced optimism surrounding the rapid advance northwards of UN forces in October 1950: Britain sponsored the resolution in the UN General Assembly on 7 October authorising the continued sweep northwards beyond the 38th Parallel upon which MacArthur had already embarked. Thus the danger of provoking Chinese intervention was underestimated: the British chiefs of staff were more prescient than politicians or civil servants or their opposite numbers (the joint chiefs) in Washington and warned of the peril.[44] The cabinet belatedly awoke to the problem and urged the merits of creating a buffer zone in the north, so as to reduce the contingency of a clash with the Chinese occurring.[45] The meretricious appeal of 'rollback', together with the immense prestige enjoyed by MacArthur, dissuaded Truman and Acheson from slowing the march to the Yalu river.

Chinese forces first intervened late in October and then acted with maximum efficacy a month later. The whole character of the war changed ominously. The danger of a third world war developing from the Korean conflict loomed large and produced a hastily arranged summit meeting between Attlee and Truman. Attlee held that the situation was so grave as to necessitate taking stock comprehensively. He told Truman on 4 December that the Chinese communists were influenced by fear accentuated by their exclusion from the UN. They felt strongly about Taiwan and, to a lesser degree, about Hong Kong. Chinese aims in Korea itself were unclear: would China demand that Kim Il Sung should dominate all of Korea?[46] Korea had to be viewed in the light of global responsibilities and the priority lay in Europe. Acheson commented that Attlee had raised questions with profound implications: giving too much to China would simply encourage communist appetites. Truman categorically described the Chinese as 'satellites of Russia' and they must be treated on the same basis as the Soviets.[47] At the second meeting, on 5 December, Truman confirmed that American troops would remain in Korea: there would be no evacuation of the peninsula. Attlee spoke of the desirability of attempting to drive a wedge between the Soviet Union and China.[48] At dinner on that evening Acheson stated that there was a feeling in Washington that Britain could do more to assist in Korea. Attlee referred to one of the most delicate features, the conduct of General MacArthur: it was considered in Europe that MacArthur was playing too big a part in the implementation of policy.[49] Generals Marshall and Bradley defended MacArthur, although Acheson expressed doubt as to who could control MacArthur according to the British record of the talks.[50] The Attlee–Truman talks led to a temporary improvement in Anglo–American relations and assurances came from Truman to the effect that the use of the atomic weapon would not be contemplated unless the situation became far more serious. However, the war in Korea was so fluid as to stimulate wide-ranging speculation concerning American motives in December 1950 and January 1951.

The rapidity of MacArthur's retreat down the Korean peninsula suggested that UN evacuation of Korea was possible notwithstanding Truman's assurances. The Labour government wished to see negotiations with China encouraged as the best method of achieving a compromise while retaining UN forces in Korea; the Truman administration did not wish to negotiate with China but recognised the strength of feeling of its allies. Acheson gambled on the Chinese emissaries in New York proving too obdurate and the gamble was vindicated: the possibility of achieving a solution to Korean and other far eastern problems foundered on Chinese obstinacy. American leaders, stung by the severity of Korean setbacks, determined to secure condemnation of China in the UN General Assembly, and this led to acrimonious exchanges between the British and American governments in January 1951.

Bevin's grave ill-health sharply reduced his impact: he did not want to jeopardise Anglo–American cooperation and was reluctant to carry criticism too far. His minister of state, Younger, had become extremely critical and advocated a tougher approach even if this led to Britain failing to support the United States in a key vote in the General Assembly. The cabinet was divided and dissatisfaction with American policy grew; at one stage it appeared that Younger's indignation would carry the majority of the cabinet into a decision not to support the Americans in a vote on Chinese aggression.[51] Hugh Gaitskell was appalled at the political and economic consequences of pursuing this line and was instrumental in convincing Attlee to change policy so as to reach an accommodation with Washington.[52] The cabinet duly modified its previous decision; Acheson revealed a more conciliatory attitude in amending the wording of the American motion. Britain voted in favour when the General Assembly voted on 1 February 1951 and the most dangerous phase in Anglo–American relations during the war was over, though numerous difficulties remained, especially those surrounding the enforcement of economic sanctions against China and the behaviour of MacArthur. The latter problem was solved through Truman's dismissal of MacArthur in April 1951: British and American leaders agreed that MacArthur's cavalier actions must be terminated.

In the summer of 1951 the Korean war reached a crucial point where a military victory was perceived as impossible by each side. The Soviet

Union took the lead in promoting armistice talks which opened in July 1951.[53] Neither side was prepared to make large enough concessions to obtain a settlement: rather each waited for the other's resolve to falter, amidst singularly tedious propaganda exchanges. The talks proceeded for exactly two years before an armistice was eventually signed at the end of July 1953. The general election in October 1951 had resulted in the replacement of the Labour administration by a Conservative government headed by Churchill and Anthony Eden returned to the Foreign Office. At first Churchill and Eden suspected that American weariness could engender lack of caution with rash concessions being made. Churchill feared that the Chinese and North Koreans might rebuild their strength in preparation for a renewed offensive. Despite bitter verbal onslaughts during the deliberations at Panmunjom, progress was made gradually in reducing the areas of fundamental disagreement. The outstanding intractable problem revolved around the disposal of POWs. Truman decided, with Churchill's full approval, that it would be wrong to compel POWs to return against their wishes to the states for which they had fought. The issue was rendered still more complex in 1952 by the revelations of the inept administration of POW camps and of pressures exerted in varying ways on individuals to declare for or against repatriation.[54] The determination to sustain the principle of voluntary repatriation prolonged the talks appreciably.

In the summer and autumn of 1952 Britain became more critical again of American policy over Korea. This was in part prompted by protests from the relatives of British and Commonwealth POWs, by pressure from India for an initiative in the UN General Assembly, and by controversy over the running of the POW camps. Eden's relations with Acheson were poor and they were involved in acrid conversations in New York in October and November 1952 arising from the Indian endeavour to secure a solution to the POW deadlock.[55] In November 1952 twenty years of Democratic tenure of the White House ended with General Eisenhower's sweeping victory over Governor Adlai Stevenson. Churchill and Eden greatly respected Truman; Eisenhower was equally admired. Their wartime comradeship led the prime minister and foreign secretary to believe Anglo–American consultation might become closer and more effective, and Eisenhower did show much personal goodwill when he assumed office, yet the familiar problems continued. Churchill and Eden did not enthuse at the appointment of Dulles as secretary of state. The turning-point in British views towards Korea in 1953 was stimulated by the repercussions of Stalin's death in March. Churchill had become more alarmed at the danger of global war and believed that it was imperative to secure *rapprochement* with the new

Soviet leaders, and urged this course upon a sceptical Eisenhower. Korea was important as an annoying obstacle and Churchill argued with growing passion that the Korean war must be ended.[56] He felt that Eisenhower and Dulles were insufficiently resolute in their dealings with the obstreperous South Korean president, Syngman Rhee. Rhee was as obstinate as ever in urging Korean unification and did not relish the end of the war on a basis which would confirm the previous division into two states. Rhee was a shrewd operator and knew that he was a vital element: he preferred to prevent an armistice being signed if possible. For this reason he released POWs held in South Korea in June. This caused furious protests from Churchill: the prime minister suffered a stroke in the second half of June but ire at Rhee continued to dominate his minutes in early July.[57]

Eisenhower and Dulles were as exasperated as Churchill but they bore the chief responsibility in confronting the slippery Rhee. If provoked far enough Eisenhower was prepared to remove Rhee through implementing a coup but it was a risky strategy. It was more sensible to induce Rhee to cooperate with offers of economic aid and a mutual security treaty backed up by the threat of much tougher action if required. Rhee understood how far he could go and appreciated that he had reached this point in July. He sullenly agreed to take no further action to sabotage a settlement but refused to endorse an armistice. British leaders nudged their American counterparts towards the armistice agreement signed at Panmunjom on 27 July but the ending of the war at this time was mainly a vindication of the tactics pursued by Eisenhower and Dulles in June to July 1953.[58]

The termination of the Korean war closed four years of Anglo–American exchanges regarding the fate of East Asia. The readjustments necessitated by the communist triumph in China, by the impending conclusion to the occupation of Japan, and by the military challenge thrown down by Kim Il Sung in Korea had been met in a variety of ways. The most constructive aspect comprised the peace treaty with Japan: here the bulk of the credit belonged to the United States which was more far-sighted than Britain. If British politicians and officials had been left to resolve Japanese issues it may safely be stated that a less liberal treaty would have emerged. Britain's lead in recognising the Chinese communist government was constructive and was undoubtedly correct despite the inability to make progress owing to the negative attitude adopted by Mao and his colleagues. The bitter American detestation of the Chinese communists was unwise in its consequences for Sino–American relations and was more immediately difficult because of developments in Korea in 1950. Although the Attlee cabinet seriously underestimated Chinese capabilities in the autumn of 1950, the chiefs of staff understood how challenging the Chinese might prove to be; the British awoke to the perils sooner than the Americans but they could not stop the UN from blundering into a war of a highly dangerous character. The principal British achievement in the Korean context lay in restraining the Americans from actions which could have exacerbated matters excessively. The United States and Britain were instrumental in preventing a North Korean takeover of the south but the Korean conflict was such a muddled one for all concerned that it appears fair to conclude that no one gained from it at the time.

Anglo–American exchanges over East Asia between 1949 and 1953 confirmed the decline in British power. The Japanese were dominated by the Americans and the British became less relevant; the Chinese ignored the British and refused to grant full diplomatic relations; the South Korean government regarded the British as tedious advocates of pure democracy, unsuited to its exposed position. Europe was the priority for the British and American governments but events in Korea meant that for the next twenty years the United States would be occupied in the unrewarding task of containing the perceived threat from 'Red' China.

NOTES

1. Memorandum by Marshall, 25 October 1948, *FRUS, 1948*, vol. VII, pp. 183–4.
2. Letter from Dening to Graves, 29 December 1948, FO 371/69550/18545/G.
3. For assessments of developments concerning China see Tang Tsou, *America's Failure in China, 1941–1950* (Chicago, 1963), Suzanne Pepper, 'The KMT–CCP conflict, 1945–1949', in J. K. Fairbank and A. Feuerwerker (eds), *The Cambridge History of China*, vol. XIII, part 2 (Cambridge, 1986), pp. 723–88, and N. B. Tucker, *Patterns in the Dust: Chinese–American Relations and the Recognition Controversy 1949–1950* (New York, 1983).
4. FO minutes, 10 June 1949, FO 371/75812/8543.
5. Memorandum by Acheson, 13 September 1949, *FRUS, 1949*, vol. IX, p. 82.
6. Ibid., p. 83.
7. FO to Washington, 16 December 1949, FO 371/75828/19057.
8. Numerous examples are to be found in the correspondence contained in the Robert A. Taft Sr Papers, Manuscript Division, Library of Congress, Washington.
9. Washington to FO, 8 December 1949, FO 371/75805/18448.
10. Tokyo to FO, 16 December 1949, FO 371/75805/18891.
11. Ibid.
12. See letter from Franks to Dening, 7 June 1950, FO 371/83320/9.

13. *HMS Amethyst* was caught up in the final stages of the Chinese civil war and was forcibly detained by Chinese communist troops on the Yangtze in April 1949. As negotiations made little progress, *Amethyst's* commander made a daring and successful escape. The episode was given considerable publicity in the British press and the intrepid ships's company was enthusiastically greeted on the vessel's return to Britain. In essence the affair belonged to the dying era of imperialism in China but it caused appreciable interest in Britain, the Commonwealth, and in the United States, as much, if not more, because of the impact of the Cold War upon popular thinking in the west.

14. Record of Bevin's meeting with representatives of the China Association, 16 March 1950, FO 371/183344/30.

15. FO to Washington, 1 March 1951, FO 371/92276/111.

16. Memorandum, 'Control of United Kingdom Exports to China', 23 May 1951, FO 371/922279/111.

17. Ibid.

18. FO to Washington, 14 June 1951, FO 371/92281/228.

19. For accounts of the occupation see K. Kawai, *Japan's American Interlude* (Chicago, 1960), J. W. Dower, *Empire and Aftermath: Yoshida Shigeru and the Japanese Experience, 1878–1954* (London, 1979), and Michael Schaller, *The American Occupation of Japan: the Origins of the Cold War in Asia* (Oxford, 1985).

20. For two valuable, contrasting studies of MacArthur see D. Clayton James, *The Years of MacArthur*, vol. III, *Triumph and Disaster, 1945–1964* (Boston, 1985) and Michael Schaller, *Douglas MacArthur* (New York, 1989).

21. For a discussion of British perceptions of MacArthur see Peter Lowe, 'British Attitudes to General MacArthur and Japan, 1948–50' in Gordon Daniels (ed.), *Europe Interprets Japan* (Tenterden, 1984), pp. 117–26.

22. Record of interview between Sansom and MacArthur, 22 January 1951, enclosed in letter from Gascoigne to R. H. Scott, 22 January 1951, FO 371/92521/3.

23. For biographies of Bevin and Morrison see Alan Bullock, *The Life and Times of Ernest Bevin*, vol. III, *Foreign Secretary, 1945–51* (London, 1983) and B. Donoughue and G. W. Jones, *Herbert Morrison: Portrait of a Politician* (London, 1973).

24. For examples of cabinet discussions see cabinet minutes, 22 January 1951, CM5(51)3; 25 January 1951, CM8(51)1; 26 January 1951, CM9(51); 29 January 1951, CM10(51)3; 1 February 1951, CM11(51)7, Cab 128/19.

25. Treasury memorandum by A. J. Phelps, 6 June 1951, FO 371/92557/564A.

26. Ibid.

27. Record of meeting held in the House of Commons, 8 June 1951, FO 371/92554/516.

28. Record of meeting between Morrison and Dulles, 4 June 1951, FO 371/92553/498.

29. Ibid.

30. Record of meeting held in the House of Commons, 5 June 1951, FO 371/92554/513.

31. Ibid.

32. Record of meeting held in the Foreign Office, 6 June 1951, FO 371/92554/515.

33. Ibid.

34. FO to Washington, (two telegrams), 15 June 1951, FO 371/92555/539.

35. San Francisco to FO, 12 September 1951, FO 371/92616/5 and FO 371/92614/5.

36. See the somewhat acrid exchange of minutes by R. H. Scott, 17 November; W. Strang, 19 November, and A. Eden, 19 November; with FO to Paris (for Acheson), 19 November 1951, FO 371/92605/23.

37. For discussion of Anglo–American exchanges see Peter Lowe, 'The Frustrations of Alliance: Britain, the United States, and the Korean War, 1950–1', and Michael Dockrill, 'The Foreign Office, Anglo–American Relations, and the Korean Truce Negotiations, July 1951–July 1953', in James Cotton and Ian Neary (eds), *The Korean War in History* (Manchester,1989), pp. 80–119. For valuable general studies of the war see Rosemary Foot, *The Wrong War* (London, 1985) and Callum MacDonald, *Korea: the War before Vietnam* (London, 1986).

38. Minute by Dixon, 1 July 1950, FO 371/84091/208G.

39. Message from Bevin to Franks, 7 July, handed to Acheson, 8 July 1950, *FRUS, 1950*, vol. VII, pp. 330.

40. Acheson to embassy in London, 10 July 1950, ibid., pp. 347–51.

41. Ibid., pp. 351–52.

42. Memorandum by Younger, 11 July 1950, FO 371/84191/215G.

43. For a lucid analysis of the British military role in Korea see Anthony Farrar-Hockley, *The British Part in the Korean War*, vol. I, *A Distant Obligation* (London, 1990).

44. For warnings by the chiefs of staff of the dangers of existing policy see chiefs of staff minutes, COS(50)160, confidential annexe, 3 October 1950, Defe 4/36; COS(50)175(7), 6 November 1950; COS(50)176(1), 7 November 1950; COS(50)178(1), Defe 4/37; confidential annexe, COS(50)182(1), 20 November 1950, Defe 4/37. See also Peter Lowe, 'An Ally and a Recalcitrant General: Great Britain, Douglas MacArthur and the Korean War, 1950–1', *English Historical Review*, vol. CV, no. 416, July 1990, pp. 624–53.

45. See P. N. Farrar, 'A Pause for Peace Negotiations: the British Buffer Zone Plan of November 1950', in Cotton and Neary (eds), *The Korean War in History*, pp. 66–79.

46. Minutes of first meeting between Truman and Attlee, 4 December 1950, *FRUS, 1950*, vol. VII, p. 1365.

47. Ibid., p. 1368.

48. Minutes of second meeting, 5 December 1950, ibid., pp. 1395–8.

49. Memorandum by Battle, 6 December 1950, ibid., pp. 1430–1.

50. See Prem. 8/1200 for the British record of Attlee's visit.

51. See cabinet minutes, 25 January 1951, CM8(51)1; 26 January 1951, CM9(51); 29 January 1951, CM10(51)3, Cab. 128/19. See also note by Hugh Dalton, 2 February 1951, Dalton diary, vol. 39, British Library of Political and Economic Science, London School of Economics.

52. Cabinet minutes, 26 January 1951, Cab. 128/19.

53. For discussion of the armistice talks see B. J. Bernstein, 'The struggle over the Korean armistice: prisoners of repatriation', in Bruce Cumings (ed.), *Child of Conflict* (London, 1983), pp. 261–307; Michael Dockrill, 'The Foreign Office, Anglo–American Relations and the Korean Truce Negotiations',

in Cotton and Neary (eds), *The Korean War in History*, pp. 100–19; and Peter Lowe, 'The Settlement of the Korean War', in J. W. Young (ed.), *The Foreign Policy of Churchill's Peacetime Administration, 1951–1955* (Leicester, 1988), pp. 207–31.

54.   See Callum MacDonald, 'Heroes behind Barbed Wire – the United States, Britain, and the POW issue in the Korean War', in Cotton and Neary (eds), *The Korean War in History*, pp. 135–50.

55.   See Roger Bullen, 'Great Britain, the United States, and the Indian Armistice Resolution on the Korean War, November 1952', in Ian Nish (ed.), *Aspects of Anglo–Korean Negotiations* (London, 1984), pp. 27–44.

56.   See minute by John Addis, 4 May 1953, FO 371/105489/212 and message from Churchill to Molotov, 20 June 1953, Prem. 11/406.

57.   Ibid.

58.   See Lowe, 'The Settlement of the Korean War', in Young (ed.), *The Foreign Policy of Churchill's Peacetime Administration*, pp. 227–8.

11 Britain and Japan: A Personal View of Postwar Economic Relations
Sir Hugh Cortazzi

Economic relations between Britain and Japan since the end of the Second World War in 1945 have frequently been acrimonious. There has been a significant imbalance in trade for most of the last twenty years. British suspicions and fears of Japanese competition have been deep-seated and the Japanese market has been regarded as a particularly difficult one for British exporters. Japanese exports to Britain were at first confined to traditional items such as tinned mandarin oranges and salmon, cheap toys, pottery ornament and textiles. As Japanese industry expanded and improved Japanese exports to Britain grew in sophistication and quality. Japanese electronic goods, motor cycles, cars, ships and robots found a ready market in Britain but Japanese exporters were forced to agree to 'Voluntary Export Restraints' (VRAs) as British manufacturers could not compete. The emphasis in the 1980s changed from Britain being regarded primarily as a market for Japanese exports to Britain as a location for Japanese investment. The city of London was recognised by the Japanese as the major European financial centre and attracted a growing number of Japanese financial institutions. Suspicions have gradually been reduced and co-operation has begun to replace confrontation in Britain's economic relations with Japan, but until the imbalance in trade of more than three to one has been reduced to much smaller proportions trade friction will not disappear.

Many books could be written about various aspects of Britain's postwar economic relations with Japan. A study of British attitudes towards trade with Japan in the first fifteen years after the Second World War would shed light on the anachronistic attitudes prevailing in British industry after the war and its lack of understanding of Japan. The negotiations leading up to the conclusion in November 1962 of the Anglo–Japanese Treaty of Commerce and Navigation with its protocols and exchanges of notes would make a fascinating subject for a doctoral thesis. The efforts, successes and failures of British companies to increase British exports to Japan would make another book. Much more could also be written on subjects such as licensing and investment by British companies in the Japanese market including the problems of mergers and acquisitions. A full review of Japanese export and marketing strategy in the British market and the changing pattern of Japanese exports could help us to understand better our own failures. A detailed assessment of the negotiation and operation of VRAs would make it clear how much the interests of British consumers have been damaged by these anti-competitive arrangements. Such a study could also show how much, or more probably how little, advantage has been taken by the British industries involved of the protection offered by VRAs to make themselves more competitive. Much has been written about Japanese investment in Britain and about the Japanese in the city of London, but there is scope for more in-depth studies of particular aspects.

In this essay I have tried to record briefly my own involvement with aspects of our economic relations with Japan in the postwar era. It is based on memory and is in no sense a scholarly account or objective assessment of any aspect. I hope, however, that it may provide some hints for historians about the way in which diplomatic officials were involved in Britain's economic and trade relations with Japan in the last 40 or so years.

My first stay in Japan of just over a year was in 1946–7 when I was a member of the British Commonwealth Occupation Forces. Japanese industry was in ruins and the Japanese economy reduced to little more than subsistence agriculture. Inflation was rampant and the only Japanese who flourished were black-market traders and racketeers. The only direct involvement I had with the economy was to supervise the packing of some machinery which had survived American air raids and was supposed to be sent to territories in South-East Asia which had been occupied by Japanese forces. I do not know whether this was ever sent or used. During the occupation some British merchants returned to Japan, but foreign exchange was limited and profitable business hard to find. When I graduated from London University in 1949, having studied Japanese at the School of Oriental and African Studies (SOAS), I joined the Foreign Service. I had considered the possibility of working in commerce but British firms operating in Japan at that time were not interested in young men with a knowledge of Japan and the Japanese language. My second tour in Japan was from October 1951 to February 1954. I arrived as a Third Secretary in the United Kingdom Liaison Mission (UKLM) to the Supreme Commander Allied Powers (SCAP). My task was to help in preparations for the entry into force of the San Francisco Peace Treaty in April 1952.

The British had tried and failed to have restrictive commercial clauses included in the treaty. My only direct experience of the background to this effort came from a visit I made to Manchester and Stoke-on-Trent before I went out to Japan in 1951. The British textile and pottery industries were very suspicious of Japanese competition and sought protection. Questions in parliament underlined these suspicions.

In 1951 British opinion was generally hostile towards Japan. The mal-treatment of British prisoners of war and the shock of the British defeat at Singapore in 1942 had not been forgotten. Japan was seen as a producer of cheap and shoddy consumer goods manufactured with sweated labour.

The Labour government which had been in power from 1945 to October 1951 had wanted to do what they could to promote an independent and strong union movement. They hoped that the new Japanese unions could demand equality of wages with western workers. They had accordingly attached great importance to the post of Labour Attaché in the British mission to SCAP. This post was filled by an experienced official from the Ministry of Labour, and the post was retained for many years under sub-sequent administrations. As the Labour Attaché had no knowledge of Japanese or previous experience of Japan if fell to members of the chancery like myself to support him.

Most of my work in 1952 and 1953 was of a political and administrative nature. But I was involved briefly with one issue of an economic nature. Article 15 of the Peace Treaty dealt with claims in respect of the property of allied nationals in Japan. A section in the British Embassy spent some years sorting out these claims and arranging with the Japanese authorities for their settlement. In order to fulfil its obligations under the Treaty the Japanese Diet passed an Allied Powers Property Compensation Law. This law was drafted in legalistic Japanese and provided Japanese officials with opportunities to delay and frustrate claims. An unofficial English 'trans-lation' of the law produced by Japanese officials was incomprehensible gobbledegook and I spent one long week-end retranslating the law into English for the sake of our claims section.

After I returned to London in 1954 I was posted for a few months as Japan desk officer in the Far Eastern Department of the Foreign Office. Much of my time was taken up with discussions with the International Red Cross on the disposal of Japanese assets in neutral countries which, under Article 16 of the Peace Treaty, were to be used for the benefit of former prisoners of war. The sums eventually distributed to ex-prisoners of war were pitifully small.

There was not much work of a directly commercial or economic nature. Article 13 of the Peace Treaty provided that the Japanese would enter into negotiations with any of the allied powers so desiring for the conclusion of new treaties of commerce and navigation. The British Government, recognising that in such negotiations the Japanese would insist on most-favoured-nation (MFN) treatment, were in no hurry to start negotiations. But the Board of Trade had started a desultory study of their desiderata and I had some talks with Board of Trade officials on this subject. The safeguards which they proposed to seek from the Japanese were unrealistic. Board of Trade officials were, however, only reflecting opinion in Britain at that time. British hostility had been made plain to Yoshida Shigeru, the Japanese Prime Minister, who visited London in October 1954. When he spoke to a group of MPs at the Houses of Parliament on 26 October he was given a fairly rough ride and accusations of copying and cheating by Japanese manufacturers were made. Fortunately when he came to dinner with Sir Winston Churchill, then prime minister, on 27 October (I was present as interpreter) the atmosphere was altogether more amicable. (Yoshida Shigeru gave his account of these two occasions in his memoirs – see pages 117–18 of *The Yoshida Memoirs,* translated by Kenichi Yoshida, Boston 1962).

When Japan acceded to the General Agreement on Tariffs and Trade (GATT) in 1955 Britain and 13 other member states invoked Article 35 of the GATT which allowed them to withhold MFN treatment from new members acceding to the Treaty. Inevitably the removal of this discrimination became the first objective of the Japanese in negotiations for a new treaty. Agreement was eventually reached and a new Treaty of Commerce and Navigation was signed on 14 November 1962 and came into force after ratification on 4 May 1963. I had returned to Japan as First Secretary in the Chancery in 1961 (I stayed until 1965 becoming Head of Chancery in 1963). My only direct involvement with the Treaty at this time was over the Japanese wording. The English and Japanese texts were declared to be 'equally authentic' although the negotiations had been conducted entirely in English. We had to be satisfied that the Japanese version accurately reflected the English wording. F. J. Daniels, Professor of Japanese at SOAS in the University of London, was consulted and made various comments and suggestions. My task was to discuss and agree amendments with the Japanese official concerned. Unfortunately he resented even the slightest implication of criticism of the Japanese wording and the discussions were difficult. In the end the Japanese wording was generally accepted.

The two protocols and the two exchanges of notes attached to the Treaty became of great importance to me during my next assignment in Japan as Commercial and Economic Counsellor in the British Embassy between 1966 and 1970 and a brief account must be given of these protocols. The first of these was the so-called Safeguards Protocol. This provided that if goods were being imported 'in such increased quantities and under such conditions as to cause or threaten serious injury to producers' in the importing country the two governments would enter into consultations designed to find a solution. If a solution could not be found within thirty days the government of the importing country could take unilateral action 'to prevent or remedy the injury' but the other government was then empowered to take counteraction 'substantially equivalent in scope and duration'. The British authorities were often tempted to use this protocol against Japanese imports. In fact they have never done so. I consistently argued that use of this article would cause more damage to British exports to Japan than any respite which might be gained for British manufacturers by its use; instead Japanese exporters were 'persuaded' to use VRAs.

The second protocol provided that import restrictions 'continuously enforced by either Contracting Party with regard to any specific product' could be maintained despite the MFN provisions in the Treaty. This meant that existing British and Japanese quota restrictions could continue.

In one of the exchanges of notes the Japanese undertook to exercise 'voluntary export control' on some 12 different categories of textile products as well as on radio and television apparatus, domestic pottery and ceramic toys. A second exchange of notes provided that the British could continue to restrict imports from Japan of cigarette lighters, cutlery, sewing machines, fishing tackle, binoculars, toys and games as well as domestic pottery.

Japan had joined the International Monetary Fund (IMF) in 1952, but it was not until 1964 that it assumed the status under Article 8 of the Fund which required the removal of all foreign exchange restrictions. In 1964 Japan also joined the Organization for European Cooperation and Development (OECD) which required the removal of other restrictions on invisible transactions and capital movements as well as progress on trade liberalisation. Despite adherence to these agreements Japan continued to maintain various high tariffs and quotas on goods of particular interest to Britain. In 1966 whisky and wool cloth were subject to Japanese import quota restrictions.

I was appointed Commercial and Economic Counsellor in the British Embassy in 1966 at a time when the Diplomatic Service had begun to recognise the growing importance of commercial work. The Japanese market was then a relatively small and difficult one for Britain but its potential was beginning to be perceived. Japanese recovery had been demonstrated by the holding of the Olympic Games in Tokyo in 1964, by the development of the *Shinkansen* (called by some foreigners the 'bullet train') and by the income-doubling plans of Prime Minister Ikeda Hayato (1899–1965, Prime Minister 1960–64).

The work of the Commercial and Economic Department of the embassy grew rapidly in these years and suitable staff both British and Japanese had to be found. The work fell broadly into two main categories. The economic section headed by John Whitehead, then a First Secretary (Sir John Whitehead became Ambassador to Japan in 1986), dealt with official relations with Japanese governmental organisations and involved such matters as negotiating quota and tariff reductions, discussions over patents, designs and trade marks, helping British firms with particular problems involving Japanese official organisations and economic reporting. The trade promotion section headed by Alan Harvey, First Secretary, covered the provision of services and advice to individual British firms and exporters, the seeking out of specific opportunities for British products and services and the organisation of trade missions, trade fairs and store promotions.

The British sought increased access to the Japanese market while the Japanese wanted the removal of the remaining British restrictions which they saw as discriminatory. This involved annual negotiations on quotas and other barriers. The main British officials involved in the Department of Trade were able and helpful. Although I had not had previous experience as a commercial officer we got on well. The Embassy could refer to the Foreign and Commonwealth Office if they thought Department of Trade instructions were inappropriate but I never found any real difficulty in working to the Department of Trade. We were at one in finding Japanese negotiators obstinate and tiresome. They would insist on going over the same ground time and again and would only make concessions at the last minute and in order to avoid a total breakdown. They seemed to take delight in forcing the talks to continue until late at night and would even ring up after midnight to try some new formula which usually represented a step back. They did not seem to realise that these tactics were in the end counterproductive. Even the most patient negotiator was tried so much that he was tempted to vow that he would not renew negotiations with such tiresome people. Gradually we got the Japanese to increase the quotas for whisky, wool textiles and other products of interest to British exporters while the British agreed to increased opportunities for Japanese products covered by the exchanges of notes attached to the Treaty. The Japanese were at this stage primarily concerned to get increased quotas for textile items and netting, but they also sought increases for pottery and toys.

Negotiations on air traffic rights with the Japanese Ministry of Transportation under the Civil Aviation Agreement were even more tiresome. Britain had not yet espoused deregulation and liberalisation and both sides were determined to drive a hard bargain on behalf of their carriers. The talks were often acrimonious. Unfortunately British Airways had been slow in the early 1960s to come onto the Polar route and this had given an advantage to Japan Air Lines.

There were many other problems of an official character. Fishing tackle was covered in the second exchange of notes but this did not cover fishing reels. A British manufacturer of reels had set himself up in Plymouth, a development area with a high level of unemployment. He found his livelihood threatened by Japanese exports and brought pressure to bear on the government to take action to save him from bankruptcy. This involved seemingly endless discussions with officials in the Ministry of Trade and Industry (MITI) and the relevant Japanese trade association. Eventually we managed to persuade the Japanese to agree to a VRA to allow the British manufacturer to continue in business temporarily at least.

British manufacturers still complained about Japanese copying of designs. Some of these complaints were justified and required action with the Japanese authorities. Sometimes Japanese importers of British products tried to pull an unfair advantage. The Japanese importer of Twinings tea, for instance, registered Earl Grey, a well known blend of China and Indian tea, as a trade mark.

The Japanese customs and the Ministry of Health and Welfare could be particularly difficult. One winter had been very cold and in a consignment of Scotch whisky some bottles had gathered a small quantity of sediment. The Japanese authorities banned the whole shipment.

Some Japanese tariffs, for example on chocolate, sugar confectionery and biscuits, were very high. We did all we could to persuade the Ministry of Agriculture that Japan did not need such high tariffs which discriminated against British products.

Accusations were made from time to time that Japanese manufacturers were dumping products – such as pocket handkerchiefs and thermometers – in the British market. Such allegations had to be investigated but they were deeply resented by the Japanese manufacturers concerned and by MITI and it was very difficult to get accurate price information. Sometimes Japanese manufacturers preferred to increase voluntarily the prices at which they were selling their products in Britain rather than face the stigma of having to pay anti-dumping duties.

The Embassy did not at that time include a Treasury or Bank of England representative. So it fell to us to conduct discussions on financial and banking issues with the Ministry of Finance (MOF) and it fell to me to take senior British official visitors to call on the first of the MOF's Vice Ministers for International Affairs, Kashiwagi Yusuke, now Chairman of the

Bank of Tokyo. British clearing banks were only just beginning to open offices in Japan and there were then few signs of Japanese financial liberalisation.

Much of my time had to be spent in helping individual British exporters. It was encouraging when an exporter who had really done his homework came in to seek advice. But some did not know what they were looking for and had not begun to understand how to do business in Japan. The Board of Trade had always had booklets for the various markets of 'Hints to Exporters', but these did not seem to me to be adequate for the complex Japanese market. So we organised our own collection of papers including papers on 'How to do business in Japan' and advice on import procedures, patents, licensing, etc.

The British Chamber of Commerce in Tokyo in the second half of the 1960s was small and its main members were the trading companies such as Dodwells, Cornes and Jardine Mathesons. The major British banks who belonged to the Chamber were the Hongkong and Shanghai and the Chartered. Only a few companies such as Rolls-Royce had their own permanent representatives in Japan. As Commercial Counsellor I was an honorary member of the Chamber and its executive committee. Indeed the Embassy provided much of the information which the Chamber distributed to its members at this time. We tried hard to persuade other British companies to open offices in Tokyo with only limited success. One company which did so in those days was English Electric but this was closed when the company was taken over by GEC. The directors of the company resented the difficulties which GEC had encountered over the first Japanese nuclear power station at Tokai Mura (a Calder Hall type reactor). The design and construction of this had been complicated by the need to make it earthquake-proof and there were initially a number of problems in getting the reactor to work efficiently.

One visitor whom I entertained as Commercial Counsellor was Lord Stokes, then head of British Leyland. I urged him to have a representative on the ground in Japan to keep in touch with the Japanese motor manufacturing scene. He did not think this necessary. Had not Nissan had to import models from Britain after the war? He saw little prospect of selling more than a few cars each year in the protected Japanese market and was content to leave the existing limited distribution arrangements as they were.

Some British exporters in those days were indeed content to leave the running to their agents. As a result we had to spend much time chasing up agents and trying to improve the dialogue between them and their principals.

At that time the Department of Trade had both a Fairs and Promotions Branch and an Export Services Division to whom we looked for help with and subsidies for trade missions, fairs and store promotions. They provided the back-up to the British National Export Council (BNEC), the forerunner of the British Overseas Trade Board (BOTB). Japan came within the orbit of the Asia Committee which was then headed by Michael Montagu, Chairman of Valor. He was eventually succeeded by Edmond de Rothschild.

Rarely a week passed in the autumn and spring without a trade mission. The numbers increased dramatically in 1968 and 1969 as we were then preparing for a major promotion of British goods in Tokyo in the autumn of 1969 which was one of a series of 'British Weeks' (see below). The missions which were organised by Chambers of Commerce in Britain and by industry associations consisted of exporters who got a subsidy to come out to Japan if they came in a group. Some members of Chamber of Commerce missions were well prepared and caused us no difficulty. Some others had done little preparation and a few were clearly free riders. Each member had to be given help with market information, programme arrangements and contacts. The mission also had to be briefed, and we did our best to educate the missions about Japan. Some preferred to keep their prejudices intact. I recall that after I had spoken to a Scottish Council Mission one member complained that I had not told them about strikes and other troubles in Japan! Some of the best Chamber of Commerce missions came from the London and Birmingham Chambers, but on the whole I preferred the specialist missions organised by trade associations such as the Scientific Instrument Manufacturers Association (SIMA) as they tended to be more professional and were easier to brief.

Gradually more Japanese trade fairs admitted foreign participants and we did our best to organise so-called 'joint venture' participations by relevant British manufacturers who could get financial help from the Department of Trade to enable them to participate in a British corner. We did our best to ensure that there was adequate follow-up. Some firms did this as a matter of routine and knew how to benefit from their participation in trade fairs. The reaction of other firms was frankly disappointing.

Until the second half of the 1960s Japanese imports of consumer goods had been limited both because of general foreign exchange problems and because of the lack of demand due to relatively low incomes. By 1966, however, incomes had risen and there was a noticeable demand for foreign luxury goods. In 1966 the Mitsukoshi Department Store in Nihonbashi, Tokyo, put on a French promotion with a Napoleon exhibition. I immediately asked them to follow this up with a British promotion in 1967. I suggested Wellington as a theme but they preferred Nelson. The promotion and the accompanying exhibition were a great success and ever since the

Mitsukoshi have put on British store promotions every other year in the autumn.

The Mitsukoshi's example was followed by other stores and provided the incentive to organise the 'British Week' in 1969. The Department of Trade appointed a small staff led by Ben Thorne as First Secretary to galvanise all the stores in Tokyo to put on a simultaneous show. We also took over the Science Museum for an exhibition of British scientific instruments and medical equipment. The Budokan hall nearby was turned into an exhibition of Britain and London buses were brought out to Tokyo to attract the crowds. Her Royal Highness The Princess Margaret came to open the exhibitions and visit all the stores. The late Prince William of Gloucester was at that time working in the commercial department and was made responsible for the organisation of the Princess's programme. The Lord Mayor of London also came out for the week. British Week involved an immense amount of work, but it was successful in attracting new buying by Japanese stores and did a good deal for Britain's reputation as a supplier of high-quality consumer goods.

Britain achieved in 1969 a broad balance of trade at around 100 million pound sterling each way. The invisible balance was much in our favour. The pattern of Japanese exports was changing. Instead of tinned salmon and mandarin oranges, textiles, pottery and toys the Japanese began to expand their exports of more sophisticated items. The Japanese electronic and machinery industries were growing fast, and the ship-building and steel industries were particularly successful. Many British shipowners ordered ships from Japan and British shipbuilders sent to Japan a mission including a trade union representative to see how the Japanese managed to produce ships· so cheaply and efficiently. British Steel also sent a mission to learn about Japanese methods of steel production. Some British exporters began to wake up to the opportunities in the Japanese market, but there was only limited recognition at this time of the threat which the Japanese drive to increase their exports of sophisticated consumer goods would pose to foreign manufacturers in the next decade. There was also as yet little understanding in Britain of the nature of the new Japan. Japanese tariff and non-tariff barriers had begun to come down, but in 1970 the Japanese market was as yet nowhere near as liberal and open as European and North American markets. It was rightly regarded as a difficult market.

The basis for the trade friction of the 1970s and 1980s had been laid but in 1970 it was by no means clear that Japan would achieve a permanent balance of trade surplus. The Japanese argued with some justification that they had no natural resources and were becoming almost totally dependent on foreign supplies of energy. They accordingly had to export more than they imported. They could also point to the backward state of much of their infrastructure and the quite appalling pollution which poisoned the air of most Japanese cities in 1970 and made many Japanese rivers into noisome waste canals.

I spent 1971 at the Royal College of Defence Studies in London and my only involvement with Japanese economic questions was during the Showa Emperor's visit to London when I had to interpret at the Lord Mayor's banquet between Edward Heath, the British prime minister, and Fukuda Takeo, then the Japanese foreign minister. The conversation was mostly about the current Japanese dispute with the USA about Japanese textile exports.

Trade relations with Japan figured as one subject for discussion with the Americans during my next posting as Minister (Commercial) in the British Embassy in Washington (1972–5). The American authorities were beginning to become concerned about the threat to US industries from Japan, but it was not yet the hot issue it was soon to be. The American Embassy in Tokyo was still much more preoccupied with political issues and did not generally assign State Department Japanese language officers to the Commercial Department.

When I returned to London in the autumn of 1975 as Deputy Under Secretary of State in the Foreign and Commonwealth Office my portfolio of responsibilities was a wide one covering not only Asia and the Pacific, but also Latin America and the Caribbean. Relations with Japan were, however, becoming troublesome. The Japanese had come out of the two oil shocks rather better than most other developed countries. They had brought inflation fairly quickly under control and worked hard both to diversify their sources of energy and to institute energy saving measures. Japanese exporters redoubled their efforts and competed against one another to dominate foreign markets. The Japanese were accused of indulging in 'concentrated and torrential' (*shuchu gou-teki*) exporting. Whether this accusation was fair or not a number of industries were overwhelmed including the British motor cycle industry.

The British television and audio industry felt threatened and, with government backing, the British Electrical Appliance Manufacturers Association (BEAMA), led by Lord Thorneycroft, entered into an arrangement with the Electrical Industry Association of Japan (EIAJ) for a VRA which was reviewed annually before being renewed. Sony and Matsushita among other Japanese companies established factories in South Wales to manufacture TV sets in Britain. Hitachi sought to establish a plant in the north east but as a result of trade union opposition which the Labour government were unwilling to overrule the investment was not made. Instead Hitachi were persuaded to enter into a joint venture with GEC at Hirwaun in south Wales. At about the same time a similar joint venture was established at Plymouth by Toshiba with Rank. Both joint ventures encountered difficulties and were ended by mutual consent. Hitachi and Toshiba then took over the respective facilities. They went ahead alone and were successful.

The British motor car industry was unable to compete with imports of Japanese cars and pressed the government to take action to prevent them from being overwhelmed. The Department of Trade supported the Society of Motor Manufacturers and Traders (SMMT) and after some difficult discussions with MITI a VRA was agreed with the Japanese Automobile Manufacturers Association (JAMA) under which the Japanese would not take more than 10.8 per cent of the British car market in any one year. As the market varied from year to year it was difficult for the Japanese to match this target and there were occasional overruns. These led to accusations that the Japanese were cheating. The problems were regarded as of such importance that the Permanent Secretary in the Department of Trade, Sir Leo Pliatsky, was personally involved on a number of occasions. I recall one evening when at about 8 pm I was telephoned in my office by Sir Leo about a telegram which he was then discussing with senior officials of his department instructing Sir Michael Wilford, then British ambassador to Japan, to urge the Japanese authorities to persuade JAMA to be more 'reasonable'. The arrangement which was reviewed annually was supposed to be temporary but has continued to the time of writing.

Despite these VRAs and others which were negotiated from time to time covering numerically controlled machine tools, hydraulic equipment and other types of sophisticated machinery British imports from Japan continued to grow during the 1970s while British exports failed to increase as quickly despite unprecedented government efforts to promote exports to Japan. Following a visit by Edward Heath, then prime minister, an Exports to Japan Unit (EJU) was established in the Department of Trade under a senior member of the British Diplomatic Service (the first head of the unit was Peter Wakefield (later Sir Peter)). A British Marketing Centre was also opened in Tokyo with Ben Thorne, who had headed the British Week Office in Tokyo in 1968/9, as its first director. A great deal had been done to galvanise British exporters to target the Japanese market. But the task was not complete and in 1980 the imbalance had become increasingly serious. There was a strong feeling in the British government and in industry that the Japanese were not trading fairly. Ministers repeated the complaint that 'the playing field was not a level one'.

By 1980 financial services had become increasingly important and many British financial institutions were seeking to establish branches in Tokyo while Japanese banks and security houses were expanding their operations in the City of London. The Bank of England had put one of their officials in the British Embassy as financial counsellor from the early 1970s.

When I was appointed as British Ambassador to Japan in October 1980 my first priority had to be economic relations. Before going out to Japan I talked to many British businessmen in industry and the city to gauge the position and also did a tour of Japanese investments in Britain. I concluded that in addition to action in support of British exports to Japan the promotion of inward investment would have to be a major task.

A British ambassador inevitably has a mass of representational duties to perform and much of his time has to be devoted to looking after visitors from the United Kingdom including ministers, members of parliament and senior officials. But business visitors were of equal importance in this posting. Introductions to Japanese companies could be affected by the ambassador and his staff which might lead to business being done. The ambassador could also help directly by attending and giving speeches at ceremonial openings of British promotions and by seeking to publicise British industrial and commercial achievements. But the top priority had to be to try to ensure that British businessmen understood the facts about the Japanese market and how to do business in Japan. It was also important that while being realistic about British prospects the ambassador must do all he could to arouse interest in and enthusiasm for the Japanese market.

It was encouraging to talk with companies such as Rolls-Royce which had a long experience of Japan but who could benefit from the help and advice which we could give in relations with the Japanese government. We were always delighted when companies explained to us particular problems, often of a highly technical nature, where we could intervene and help. But it was depressing when senior people came in who had not a clue about their role and who seemed only to want to record that their programme had included a call on the British Ambassador. I recall one particularly frustrating meeting. The representative in Tokyo of one of the biggest British clearing banks wanted to bring in his Vice-Chairman. I had to rearrange my schedule to accommodate him and assumed that he had some specific request to make. Not a bit of it! In front of his representative he simply asked 'tell me about Japan'.

While I was Ambassador in Japan we decided with regret that as there were now many more Japanese specialist trade fairs in which British firms could participate the British Marketing Centre was no longer necessary and should be closed down, but this did not mean any lessening of our export promotion efforts. We redoubled our efforts to persuade Japanese department stores to put on British promotions not only in Tokyo and Ōsaka but in provincial centres where there was a growing demand for British consumer goods. We did not neglect capital goods. For example we did everything possible to persuade Japanese airlines to purchase the BAe 146, a very quiet jet capable of taking off and landing on short runways. I used every speech opportunity I could find to promote the aircraft, alas without success.

The main task of the Defence Attaché and the service attachés was to promote sales of defence equipment. As Ambassador I did my best to back up these efforts. Some successes were achieved, for example over the FH70 howitzer.

In the early 1980s Japanese companies partly in response to protectionist pressures abroad but also because of rising costs in Japan were becoming increasingly interested in investing in production facilities in Europe. The British reputation as a country with high inflation and frequent strikes was not a good one in the 1970s but with the advent of Margaret Thatcher's administration the British image changed dramatically. British ministers made particular efforts to attract investments from Japan. Seminars were held and missions organised to ensure that Japanese companies were aware of what could be done for them in the British regions. The Invest in Britain Bureau in the Department of Trade and Industry took the lead while the regional development agencies competed against one another to provide incentives, with the Secretaries of State for Scotland and Wales in the vanguard. I was concerned that the competition between the regions might lead us to expend more resources than necessary in these efforts and might confuse Japanese companies or lead them to play one region off against another. I represented these dangers strongly to London. An effort was made to improve coordination but political realities ensured that the central role of the Department of Trade and Industry was never fully recognised.

The most important inward investment issue in my time as Ambassador was that of the Nissan motor company. Soon after I arrived in Japan I managed to work out a formula with Ishihara Takashi, then President of Nissan, confirming their positive interest in making a large-scale investment in Britain for the manufacture of motor cars for the European market. The final decision to go ahead came as I was about to leave Japan. There were differing views in London about how much we should provide as incentives to Nissan. Within Nissan the chairman Kawamata was at best lukewarm towards the project and Shoji, the head of the Nissan union, was firmly against the proposed investment. Negotiations with Nissan were tortuous and long drawn out. Kawamata was eventually won over by Margaret

Thatcher. (I used to say that Kawamata only believed in talking to two people – God and Mrs Thatcher!). I believed throughout that the benefits of a Nissan investment to Britain would be significant. Apart from the numbers who would be directly employed by Nissan many jobs would be created or retained in component suppliers. The effects on management practices and labour relations would be beneficial, but above all it seemed to me that the British motor industry if it was to improve its efficiency needed the competitive spur which a Nissan investment would give.

There was a continuing problem over the position of British Leyland (BL) (later Austin-Rover and then Rover) in relation to Japan. I believed that the cooperation established with Honda was vital for the future of BL. Indeed I should have liked to see the two companies getting much closer together at an early stage, but there were too many mutual suspicions to be overcome for this to be achieved quickly. I felt that a Honda take-over or at least a major shareholding in BL should be the objective but the political objections to a Japanese take-over were such that the first objective was never realisable.

Although some British industrialists such as Lord Weinstock and some British trade union leaders continued to oppose an expansion of Japanese investment in the United Kingdom British opinion became increasingly favourable towards Japanese investment as the benefits to Britain became more obvious. The British government made it clear that they would fight to ensure that exports to Europe from Japanese factories in Britain were treated as British products. This and the relative absence of strident anti-Japanese sentiments in parliament helped to make the Japanese prefer a British location to, for example a French one. The interest shown in Japanese factories from the highest levels also helped. The Prince of Wales had opened the Sony factory in South Wales, the Queen opened the NEC factory in Scotland and Margaret Thatcher the Nissan factory in Sunderland. The scene was thus set for a considerable further expansion of Japanese investment in Britain.

One element in Japan's postwar industrial success had been Japanese imports of foreign technology. It seemed to me in 1980 that the time had come for a reverse flow. We had much to learn from Japan. The Embassy had a Science and Technology Counsellor and First Secretary from the Department of Trade and Industry (DTI). The Counsellors while I was Ambassador were Dr Graham Marshall and Dr Clive Bradley. They did much to promote scientific and technical cooperation although the flow of technology continued to be more towards Japan than from Japan. One important collaboration in the field of computers was established with DTI help (under the leadership of Kenneth Baker as Minister for Communication Technology) between ICL, which later became part of STC, and Fujitsu. The Embassy had a role to play in the development of this cooperation.

Unfortunately there continued to be a number of British complaints about Japanese exports threatening British industries. So from time to time I had to put the case to MITI for Japanese export restraint. I would have been happier in making these representations if I had felt sure that once agreed they really would be of strictly limited duration.

There were other issues on which we had to make representations to the Japanese authorities. These involved many Japanese ministries. The Ministry of Transportation were involved over Japanese regulations which continued to discriminate against foreign cars as well as with civil aviation and shipping issues. The Ministry of Health and Welfare were the responsible organisation for rules about drugs and other health matters which frequently seemed to cause difficulties for foreign manufacturers. The Ministry of Posts and Telecommunications were the responsible ministry when the interests of British Telecom and Cable and Wireless were involved. Japanese officials in such ministries in the early 1980s still seemed to have a blinkered vision. They fought hard to retain their own bureaucratic powers and to protect the narrow interests of the Japanese industries under their control.

The Ministry of Finance, MITI and the Ministry of Foreign Affairs were generally able to take a somewhat wider view but our task was complicated by the jealousies and rivalries especially between the Ministry of Foreign Affairs and MITI but also between bureaux in the MOF. Financial services were increasingly important but had not reached the same level of urgency as they were to assume in the latter part of the 1980s. British banks which had been in Japan for some years were inclined to accept the small share of profitable business which the authorities allowed them to have and were loath to press for more. The merchant banks and the merchant banking subsidiaries of the clearing banks were more aggressive. Because of the line drawn in Japan between banking and securities business British merchant banking subsidiaries of the clearing banks had difficulty in obtaining licences to operate in securities business until the Japanese created a way round by agreeing to grant branch licences to subsidiaries which were only 50 per cent owned by clearing banks. The problems of branch status for merchant banks and stock exchange membership had not yet become prominent issues. The British insurance companies were also divided about what they wanted from the Japanese and accordingly it was not possible to press hard for concessions in the insurance area.

When I left Japan in 1984 on reaching retirement age it seemed to me that the fundamental premise in our economic relations with Japan must be to do all we could to make Britain more competitive. I noted that during my years in the diplomatic service the decline in British competitivity had undermined our diplomatic efforts. I thought that unless we got our economic and trade relations with Japan right all our efforts to improve political, defence and cultural cooperation would be prejudiced. In 1984 the trade imbalance of 4 to 1 in Japan's favour was continuing to grow and had to be reduced.

I noted that Japan was a difficult market especially for the small and medium-scale enterprise. I urged that we should put the emphasis on helping companies which had really done their homework. We should continue our efforts to persuade the large British companies to emulate companies such as ICI, Unilever and Glaxo which had made successful inroads into the Japanese market through licensing deals and major investments. We needed more British businessmen with a good knowledge of Japan and the Japanese language.

I noted that VRAs then covered nearly half of Japanese exports to Britain. I urged that we should take a long hard look at all the existing restraint arrangements to see how far they were really needed and how they could best be used to promote competitivity, efficiency and industrial cooperation. I recommend that if companies failed to make themselves more competitive within a specific time the British government should not bail them out by taking protectionist measures.

I referred to the argument put forward by some British Trade Unionists and businessmen that the Japanese because of their social system were unbeatable. I declared that this thesis was nonsense and damaging to long-term British interests. I pointed out that it was equal nonsense to say that more than a small percentage of British unemployment was directly attributable to Japanese competition.

I proposed that in relation to inward investment the resources available for promotion should be concentrated on industrial sectors where we could identify real benefits to Britain's industrial competitiveness. I also repeated that greater coordination was required between the regions.

I was conscious of the need for more internal demand in Japan and for a rise in the value of the yen. (Both were to come soon after I left Japan). But I noted that our exports to Japan were not particularly price-sensitive and that Japanese exporters could absorb relatively easily a rise in the value of the yen.

In general it seemed to me that we must work with the European Commission to agree on a common European policy towards Japan, but we could not expect that this would lead to an early improvement in the trade balance.

I concluded that the thrust of our policy should be to seek to persuade the Japanese to live up to their responsibilities as a powerful member of the countries which meet regularly at the summit and to internationalise their approach to our mutual problems. The Japanese wanted to be liked and in our dealings with them we needed to pay attention to form as well as substance. If we were to be effective in our diplomacy with Japan we had to be firm, consistent, sensitive and patient.

Since my retirement from the Diplomatic Service in 1984 my involvement with economic relations with Japan has inevitably been much less direct than it was . But I have continued to do what I can to help with the promotion of British exports to Japan and of Japanese investment in Britain. I have taken every opportunity to urge further liberalisation and deregulation in Japan. I have tried to help with the expansion of Japanese studies in Britain.

In the second half of the 1980s much progress was made. On the British side the 'Opportunity Japan' campaign launched by Lord Young as Secretary of State for Trade and Industry with the aim of doubling British exports to Japan in three years has alerted further sectors of British industry to the Japanese market and there have been significant increases in British exports. Much attention has been focused on the Japanese financial market and opportunities for British institutions. These have increased and the dialogue between the Ministry of Finance in Japan and the British Treasury, the Bank of England and the Department of Trade and Industry has been developed. Attention has been given to the need to produce more British people competent in the Japanese language for business purposes. But the imbalance in trade remains significant. There are still complaints about aspects of the Japanese market both for visible and invisible exports. British abilities in the Japanese language and British knowledge of Japan are still inadequate.

In Japan internal demand has been expanded. Major efforts have been made to expand imports of manufactured goods and to dismantle tariff and non-tariff barriers. The yen has greatly strengthened. Administrative reform has led to significant deregulation. But more needs to be done. Protective quotas and tariffs shield Japanese agriculture from foreign competition. The Ministry of Finance retains its grip on the financial sector and deregulation is implemented slowly. Distribution remains complex and overregulated. The system discriminates against the newcomer, Japanese as well as foreign. Foreign investment in Japan is limited not only by cost but by the difficulties of making mergers and acquisitions.

Japanese productive investment in Britain has continued to expand. This has brought significant benefits in the form of increased employment opportunities and of improvements in management methods. It has also forced British firms to become more competitive. Some Japanese companies have begun to develop R&D in Britain and to put down deeper roots. But more efforts are needed by Japanese companies to internationalise and localise their operations.

The Writings of Ian Nish

BOOKS

Anglo-Japanese Alliance, 1894–1907 (London, 1966).
The Story of Japan (London, 1968).
Alliance in Decline (London, 1972).
Japanese Foreign Policy, 1869–1942: Kasumigaseki to Miyakezaka (London, 1977).
The Origins of the Russo–Japanese War (London, 1985).
China, Japan and Nineteenth-Century Britain (with D. Steeds; Dublin, 1977).

Edited

Anglo–Japanese Alienation 1919–1952 (Cambridge, 1982).
Contemporary European Writing on Japan (Ashford, 1988).
British Documents on Foreign Affairs: Reports and Papers from the Foreign Office Confidential Print Pt. 1, Series E, vols 1–10, Japan 1860–1914 (University Publications of America, 1989).
European Studies on Japan (with C. Dunn; Tenterden, 1979).

ARTICLES

'Japan's Indecision during the Boxer Disturbances', *Journal of Asian Studies,* vol. 20, 1961, pp. 449–61.
'British Mercantile Co-operation in the India–China Trade', *Journal of South-East Asian History,* vol. 3, no. 2, pp. 74–91. September 1962.
'Dr. G. E. Morrison and the Portsmouth Conference', *Journal of Royal Australian Historical Society,* vol. 48, pp. 426–35, March 1963.
'Dr. G. E. Morrison and Japan', *Journal of the Oriental Society of Australia,* vol. II, no. 1, 1963.
'Australia and the Anglo–Japanese alliance, 1901–1911', *Australian Journal of Politics and History,* vol. LX, no. 2, November 1963.
'Japan Reverses the Unequal Treaties: The Anglo–Japanese Commercial Treaty of 1894', *Papers of Hong Kong International Conference on Asian History,* no. 20, September 1964.
'Korea, Focus of Russo-Japanese Diplomacy, 1898–1903', *Asian Studies,* vol. IV, no. 1, April 1966.
'Japan and the Ending of the Anglo–Japanese Alliance', in K. Bourne and D. C. Watt (eds), *Studies in International History. Essays Presented to W. N. Medlicott* (Longmans Green, 1967).

'Is Japan a Great Power?' in G. W. Keaton and G. Schwarzenberger (eds) *The Year Book of World Affairs,* Butterworth 1967.

'The Royal Navy and the Taking of Weihaiwei, 1895–1905' *The Mariner's Mirror,* vol. 54, no. 1, 1967.

'Britain and the Ending of the Anglo–Japanese Alliance', *Bulletin of the Japan Society of London,* vol. 53, 1967.

'Dr. Morrison and China's Entry into the World War, 1915–17', in R. M. Hatton and M. S. Anderson (eds), *Studies in Diplomatic History: Essays in Memory of David Bayne Horne,* Longman, 1970.

'Japan Goes to War', *History of the First World War,* December 1969.

'Japan and the 21 Demands', *History of the First World War,* June 1970.

'Admiral Jerram and the German Pacific Fleet 1913–15', *The Mariner's Mirror,* vol. 56, no. 4, 1970.

'George Watson', in H. L. Waugh (ed.), *George Watson's College,* George Watson's College, 1971.

'Japan and China – the Case of Wei-Hai-Wei, 1894–1906', *Fukwoka UNESCO Report,* no. 8, 1973.

'Japan Among the Powers' in *The Year Book of World Affairs* 28, pp. 90–104 (1974).

'British Trade with China in the Nineteenth Century' in *China and the Red Barbarians,* National Maritime Museum Monographs, no. 8, 1973.

'Japan's Policies Towards Britain', in J. W. Morley (ed.), *Japan's Foreign Policy, 1858–1941* New York: Columbia University Press, 1974, pp. 134–236.

'The Reemergence of Japan', in F. S. Northedge (ed.), *The Foreign Policies of the Powers,* pp. 296–319 (Faber, 1974).

'Economic Bases of Japan's Foreign Relations', *Rivista Internazionale di Science Economicle e Commerciali,* no. 4, pp. 353–368, 1975.

'Japan Reverses the Unequal Treaties: the Anglo–Japanese Commercial Treaty of 1894', *Journal of Oriental Studies,* vol. XIII, no. 2, 1975.

'Queen Elizabeth and Japan', *Contemporary Review,* vol. 227, no. 1317, October 1975, pp. 183–7.

'Japan and the Outbreak of War in 1941', in A. Sked and C. Cook (eds). *Crisis and Controversy. Essays in Honour of A. J. P. Taylor.* Macmillan, 1976.

'Japan's Electoral Prospects', *World Today,* November 1976.

'China and Japan, 1905–16', (with E. W. Edwards) in F. H. Hinsley (ed.), *British Foreign Policy under Sir Edward Grey,* Cambridge University Press, 1977.

'Japan's War History Series: List and Commentary', *Proceedings of the British Association for Japanese Studies,* vol. II, 1977.

'Diplomats in Japan', *Journal of the Institute of World Affairs,* vol. 26, 1978.

'Themes in Japan's Foreign Relations', *World Today,* May 1978.

'Themas in Japan's buitenlandse betrekkingen', *Internationale Spectator,* XXXII, no. 5 (May 1978) pp. 313–18.

'A Japanese Diplomat looks at Europe 1920–39' in I. H. Nish and C. Dunn (eds), *European Studies on Japan.* London: Norbury 1979.

'Nihongaku to Chagokugaku' (Japanese studies and Chinese studies), in *Kokusai Koryu,* no. 18, 1978.

'The Korean War', *English Historical Review,* vol. 93, 1978.

'Mr Yoshida at the London Embassy, 1936–8 Bulletin of the *Japan Society of London,* no. 87 (1978) pp. 3–7.

'Japan's Search for Security: the Last Hundred Years', *Perspectives on Japan*. vol. 2, 1979, pp. 13–16.

'Japan and the Singapore Base', Bulletin of the *Japan Society of London*, no. 92 (November 1980) pp. 11–13.

'Japan's Security Preoccupations', *The World Today*, November 1980.

'Japan's zorgen overzign veiligheid', *Internationale Spectator*, November 1980.

'Regaining Confidence: Japan After the Loss of Empire', *Journal of Contemporary History*, vol. 15, 1980.

'Japan in Britain's View of the International System, 1919–37' in I. H. Nish (ed.), *Anglo–Japanese Alienation, 1919–1952: Papers of the Anglo–Japanese Conference on the History of the Second World War*, Cambridge University Press, 1982.

'Japan – The Foreign Ministry' in Zara Steiner (ed.), *The Times Survey of Foreign Ministries of the World*, Time Books, 1982.

'Anglo–Japanese Relations', *Contemporary Review*, vol. 239, no. 1390, November 1981, pp. 231–6.

'The Three-Power Intervention of 1895', in A.R. Davis and A.D. Stefanowska (eds), *Austrina*, Oriental Society of Australia, 1982.

'Yoshida Shigeru: His Life and Times', *Hosei Occasional Papers*, 1983.

'Naval Thinking and the Anglo–Japanese Alliance, 1900–4', *Hogaku Kenkyu*, vol. 56, no. III, 1983.

'Japan's Second South-East Asia', Contemporary Review, vol. 243, no. 1411, August 1983, pp. 79–82.

The Greater East Asian Coprosperity Sphere' in K. Neilson (ed.), *Coalition Warfare*, St. Laurent Press, 1984.

'Japanese Intelligence and the Approach of the Russo-Japanese War' in D. N. Dilks and C. Andrews (eds), *The Missing Dimension*, Macmillan, 1984.

'Aston-Gwatkin to Nihon' in A. Iriye and T. Aruga (eds), *Senkanki no Nihon Guiko*, University of Tokyo Press, 1984.

'Ito Hirobumi in St. Petersburg, 1901' in Gordon Daniels (ed), *Europe Interprets Japan*, London: Norbury, 1984.

'British Perceptions of Occupied Japan: A Comment' T. W. Burkman (ed.), *The Occupation of Japan: The International Context*, MacArthur Foundation, Norfolk, Virginia, 1984.

'British Foreign Secretaries and Japan, 1892–1905' in B. J. C. McKercher and D. J. Moss (eds), *Shadow and Substance in British Foreign Policy, 1895–1939*, University of Alberta Press, 1984.

'Some Thoughts on Japanese Expansion' in W. J. Mommsen and J. Osterhammel (eds), *Imperialism and After: Continuities and Discontinuities*, Allen & Unwin, 1986.

'Jousting with Authority: The Tokyo Embassy of Sir Francis Lindley, 1931–4, *Proceedings of the Japan Society of London*, no. 105, (December 1986) pp. 9–19.

'Anglo–Japanese Alliance 1902–23', *Perspectives on Japan*, vol. 7 (1987) pp. 11–15.

INTERNATIONAL STUDIES
Discussion Paper Series: Edited

Index